New Economics and Its History

New Economics and Its History

Annual Supplement to Volume 29
History of Political Economy

Edited by John B. Davis

Duke University Press
Durham and London 1997

Printed in the United States of America
on acid-free paper ∞
ISBN 0-8223-2037-1
This is the 1997 annual supplement to
History of Political Economy, ISSN 0018-2702.

Contents

Introduction

John B. Davis

The history of economic thought is generally associated with study of the thinking of individuals who are no longer living. The unwritten rule seems to be that as long as one remains at least eligible for the Nobel prize in economics, one's work is not to be examined by historians of thought. Partly this is no doubt due to the wealth of thinking produced by past individuals whose work deserves and has received historians' attention. But in principle there does not appear to be any good reason why historians of economics should not also examine more recent, ongoing economics with the same care and insight they bring to past work. Indeed, a good case can be made for saying that historians' perspectives and modes of analysis would bring considerable illumination to recent economics. Much of contemporary economics seems to replicate past arguments and theories now largely forgotten, and what are sometimes regarded as new breakthroughs often amount to little more than new formalizations of old ideas. Since the vast majority of contemporary economists show little awareness of the history of their field, when they turn to current history as they regularly and perhaps increasingly now do in the form of survey articles, it seems almost inevitably to generate whig history—and not very good whig history at that. Why should historians of economics give up this field of investigation to an unprofessional and inadequate form of historical analysis? And might not the history of past ideas be sharpened if done in conjunction with attention to the history of recent economics?

In fact, historians of thought trained in the last ten years have begun to make contemporary economics their primary subject of investigation, recent evidence of which is Robert Leonard's 1996 History of Economics Society Best Paper award for his study of the origins of game theory appearing in the *Journal of Economic Literature*. Further, there is a strong if slim tradition in the field led by more senior scholars—for example, Geoffrey Harcourt and Roy Weintraub—that has always emphasized the recent history of economics. The "New Economics and Its Writing" conference held at Duke University in March 1996 was meant to build on these foundations. Initially, the idea of the conference was to take very recently written economics as its subject. To promote this focus, a session was held at the History of Economics Society June 1995 meetings at Notre Dame. Here a panel of individuals, who were signed up for the Duke conference, presented a variety of perspectives on recent economics and then engaged a large audience in an active discussion over what was involved in writing the history of recent economics. A valuable insight that emerged from this session was that it was not realistic to separate the study of recent economics from attention to new historiographic methods for producing histories of economics, where these new methods, it was also argued, were appropriate not just to the writing of recent economics but to the writing of past economics as well.

Writing the history of recent economics, it was initially suggested, raises a set of historiographic issues not typically encountered in the writing of past economics, where the principal resource for investigation has generally been simply past economists' published and unpublished writings. First, in the case of recent economics, typically a far greater variety and volume of resources are available, some of which—such as records of committee meetings, participation in hearings, or oral history reflections—place an individual's written work in context, and some of which—such as university curricula or government and foundation practices in funding research—concern the social-institutional framework in which economists' ideas develop. Second, the historian of recent ideas often finds that interaction with living individuals sensitive to the historian's project may influence the way in which those ideas can be researched. Not only do individual economists often attempt to put their ideas in the best possible light, but also practical problems associated with the assembly and access to recent archives create formidable barriers to investigation.

These, as it were, objective and subjective aspects of writing the recent history of economics make the marshaling of evidence a more complex affair than making trips to the library, and also inevitably position the historian within a set of social relations that ought not and ultimately cannot be elided from the written history that emerges. Yet, as was also argued at Notre Dame, if more sophisticated documentation and an increased self-awareness on the part of the historian make for good histories of recent economics, surely histories of past economics can be improved by attention to similar sorts of considerations. Indeed, as demonstrated by James Henderson in his 1996 History of Economics Society presidential address, which charted the beginnings of professional economics societies in nineteenth-century Britain, the resources for writing the history of past economics are more diverse and abundant than is generally recognized. Moreover, our interest in issues such as the early development of professional economics societies is not clearly separable from our related current interest in the nature of economics as a profession and of the place of historians in it. Thus, the writing of recent economics is arguably a model for new insights into writing the history of economics per se.

Perhaps not surprisingly, then, the 1996 Duke conference included a heterogenous collection of papers, the unity of which was worked out to a large extent in free discussion on the part of the participants. And, as befit the historiographic methodological themes raised earlier at Notre Dame, much of the discussion concerned methods by which history should be written. This ended up involving what I have roughly delineated as four often overlapping themes of interpretation:

1. the recent incursion of noneconomics methods of thinking into economics;
2. the emergence of subdisciplines or fields within the whole of economics;
3. social-contextual perspectives on how economists reason;
4. the dynamics of development of ideas and theories in economics.

Brief remarks on each of these themes and a rough classification of the papers that most reflect them follow. Note that many of the papers touched on all of these themes—and, indeed, on other themes I have not identified here in the interest of emphasizing these.

The Incursion of Noneconomics Methods into Economics

More familiar is the proposition that neoclassical economics is an imperialistic discipline imposing its concepts and methods on other fields, especially the notion of agents as being axiomatically, instrumentally reasonable and of static equilibrium as a self-contained characterization of social states of affairs. But unappreciated by many is recent economists' heavy reliance upon and willing import of operations research and game theory techniques, engineering methods, systems theory, and artificial intelligence and computer science strategies that have set out much of the modern agenda of mathematical economics. From this vantage point, economics as a discipline is more of a way station in the passage of mathematical physical science through economics—the entry point of least resistance—and on into social science as a whole.

Philip Mirowski labels this battery of ideas "cyborg science," following Andrew Pickering's 1995 discussion of sciences built on an ontology of machine-humans. Cyborg sciences describe the living, social world in inanimate terms. Many of the major theoretical innovations in economics in the postwar period—game theory, rational expectations, complexity, and bounded rationality—draw from noneconomics, cyborg-science roots of a generation earlier. Esther-Mirjam Sent begins by noting the twentieth-century rise of big science dictated less by academic pursuits than by industrial and military concerns. Engineering science prospered in this environment, and economists consequently soon found techniques for rigorous use of mathematics at hand, which only required the addition of an economics vocabulary. The phases in this development of engineering methods in economics are as follows: import of calculus of variations methods used in analyzing aerospace systems, hydrodynamics, and thermodynamics; application of optimal control techniques used for designing mechanical, electrical, electromechanical, electronic, and other systems; adoption of optimal prediction and filtering techniques used in communications engineering and signal prediction; and use of quadratic objective functions, linear transformation functions, and Gaussian noise analysis from feedback-control systems in electrical, communications, and control engineering. Marcel Boumans looks at the choices involved in seeing the economy as a complex system and designing sufficiently comprehensive economic models for its understanding. One strategy is to construct a mathematical system without empirical content, for which, in principle, a rigorous and complete solution is possible. Taking Robert

Lucas as a proponent, this strategy involves artificial intelligence and simulation methods that pass what are termed the Turing-Adelmans test.

Fields and Subdisciplines

Economics is popularly associated with high theory and abstract propositions. Yet far more economics is produced each year in applied fields and the various subdisciplines of economics. Little has been done to analyze this part of economics—or, relatedly, to describe the variety of practical ways in which economics actually gets used by noneconomists with the assistance of economists. At the same time, the impact of high-profile, high-theory economics is almost certainly not nearly as great as theorists like to imagine, because theory must be applied to circumstances to have practical effects. One might thus say that, to understand economics, one needs to understand the uses to which it is put. But the matter is more complicated than this since the application of ideas to the world requires their adaptation to concrete contexts, as well as a modeling of those contexts as settings in which economic relationships operate. It is in the study of fields and subdisciplines that these issues are worked out, and we have an opportunity to understand how ideas take on specific senses and concrete form.

Todd Lowry and Steven Medema investigate the subdiscipline of law and economics from perspectives distinct from those usually taken by the field's enthusiasts. Lowry adopts a historical perspective on the common methodological heritage of contemporary law and economics—particularly regarding the concept of rationality and process—recognizing that law and political economy have existed as parallel disciplines for over two thousand years. Understanding the contemporary subdiscipline involves moving behind its current attempt to translate all production and exchange processes into rational efficiency terms. It also involves understanding the dichotomy in legal thought between the real property tradition and the commercial law contract tradition. Medema addresses the issue of economics, imperialism, and law by returning to Ronald Coase's assertion nearly twenty years ago that utility theory had little to offer outside economics, and that economists tend to be ill-informed about the subject matters of other disciplines. While University of Chicago law and economics has produced useful insights, Medema argues that its limitations, as predicted by Coase, are increasingly apparent. This has meant more efforts to develop a genuine integration of law and economics and new attempts to bring noneconomic insights to bear on economic problems.

Joshua Cohen examines the debate among health economists, ethicists, psychologists, clinicians, and sociologists over the last two decades regarding the nature and purpose of the quality-adjusted-life year (QALY) measure of patient utility and well-being. He demonstrates that an adequate characterization of the concept requires an understanding of experience utility—a psychologist's concept originally conceived by Bentham, but one not often embraced by health economists. Health economics as a subdiscipline, then, depends on insights that originate in other disciplines and cannot be satisfactorily developed by using only the tools of economists. Paul Harrison charts the recent history of the development of financial economics as an applied field within economics, emphasizing the adjustment of questions studied to "core" theorizing strategies in economics. Specifically, by premising the notion of arbitrage, finance was legitimized as an economics field, and the concept of efficiency and deductive reasoning gained pride of place as essential to good financial economics. But success on this score also served to exclude insights from a more traditional inductive reasoning in finance, so that innovation in the field appears to have slowed.

Social-Contextual Perspectives on How Economists Reason

Since the emergence of the sociology of scientific knowledge as a methodology for economics and the history of economic thought, increased attention has been devoted to the social framework in which economists operate and do research. Given the broadness that reference to social context involves, it is not surprising that historians and methodologists who work from this perspective have generated a wide variety of investigative approaches—ranging from characterization of professional frameworks to analysis of class, gender, and national affiliations to examination of the personal dimensions of economists' lives. What unites these different approaches, however, is a shared conviction that ideas are not abstract, logical forms detached from their mode of production, but are embedded in historical settings that do much to account for their selection, organization, and defense.

Mary Hirschfeld focuses on recent feminist thinking that challenges the notion that economics is free from value commitments and background assumptions that direct the way theory develops. Economics has historically marginalized the contributions of women economists, and this has surely influenced the types of questions, methods of analysis, and sorts of issues that the study of economics has pursued. An important case is the development of consumption theory and the different paths of the old home economics that were initiated by Hazel Kyrk and Margaret Reid and the new home economics of Gary Becker. Timothy Alborn looks back to late-Victorian financial journalism to understand the impact of popular reasoning about published balance sheets on economics reasoning about business organization. Economists such as William Jevons and Alfred Marshall expressed ambivalence about the value of the data that appeared in locations such as the *Economist*, but they did not hesitate to incorporate it into their work when possible. Later economists retreated further, in efforts to protect their claims to expertise: this gave rise to a pure economics safe from political contest. Ross Emmett presents Frank Knight in a light rarely seen through five stories that exhibit the paradoxes of Knight as an individual. Using a rich account of Knight's life and Chicago environment to upend traditional views of Knight's intellectual development as a march of progress, Emmett displays an influential economist's scientific practice as the intersection of philosophical, religious, theoretical, and personal commitments. This picture calls into question historians' search for order and unity in their histories, as well as the concept of truth they employ.

Dynamics of the Development of Ideas

Closely related to questions regarding the framework in which ideas develop are questions regarding what brings about change in ideas. Since the work of Thomas Kuhn and Imre Lakatos, economic methodologists have looked upon the history of economic thought in terms of its dynamics, or of how sets of ideas maintain sway or are displaced by others. Attention to the embeddedness of ideas in social-historical contexts has expanded the ways in which these dynamics may be investigated. Indeed, recent recognition of the multiplicity of ways in which change in ideas may be explored has generated broad support for methodological pluralism in examining the history of economics (Salanti and Screpanti 1996). This arguably makes for a far more interesting history of recent economics, since often dramatically different approaches to charting this history can be found side by side with one another, each eliciting very different—sometimes complementary, sometimes conflicting—judgments.

Daniel Hausman and Philippe Mongin combine their recent research on preference-reversals and full-cost pricing, respectively, to compare the economics profession's responses to two historical episodes in which standard economic theory encountered what appeared as significant disconfirmations. Interestingly, while the latter, earlier anomaly provoked extensive controversy, the former, more recent anomaly generated very little controversy, though both can be argued to have been equally damaging. Hausman and Mongin consider alternative explanations for this change in responsiveness, and they draw the conclusion that the development of neoclassical economics in the intervening period has increasingly constrained economists' openness to challenges to the theory. S. Abu Turab Rizvi turns to another case in which the principal propositions of mainstream economics have been jeopardized, namely, the 1970s Sonnenschein-Mantel-Debreu demonstration that aggregate excess demand in general equilibrium theory is essentially arbitrary. Here, in contrast to the two cases above, economists have come to a realization that a major research program in contemporary mathematical economics has reached a dead end, and that a redirection of research is necessary. Rizvi examines the implications of one such new beginning in the efforts of Werner Hildenbrand, Jean-Michel Grandmont and others to find well-behaved aggregate excess demands by considering the economy-wide distribution of agents' characteristics. John Davis adapts the thinking of historian of science Andrew Pickering to an examination of recent macroeconomics. Pickering works in terms of a dynamics or dialectic of resistance and accomodation, rather than research programs and anomalies, and looks upon the development of science as an interaction with the material world. The crafting of models in economics may be thought analogous to experiments in laboratories, such that the development of economic ideas proceeds hand in hand with the exigencies of modeling.

The articles in this volume provide an excellent introduction to how investigation of recent economics is influencing horizons for the history of economic thought. The most tangible effects of this beginning reorientation of historical research are no doubt the development of new historiographic methodologies and a closer blending of the history of economic thought and the methodology of economics. Reading this volume should impress the reader that the history of economics is becoming a highly innovative domain of economics research driven by serious reflection on perspectives and methods. It is not unimportant that few today would claim the same for the bulk of standard economics research.

There, the rule seems more to continue what has customarily occupied well-placed individuals in the profession than to ask what explanatory power a given analysis offers. Indeed, if economists are accomplished at complex analysis, they often seem at a loss regarding its purpose. Thus a further and perhaps ultimately more significant effect of historians' new attention to recent economics may be to produce understanding about ongoing economics the profession itself appears unable to generate. As Robert Leonard's recent award-winning paper on the origins of game theory appears to illustrate, economists may be most prepared to learn from historians of thought when the latter succeed in showing just how present ideas are informed by the past.

References

Henderson, James. 1996. Emerging Learned Societies: A Context for Economic Ideas. *Journal of the History of Economic Thought* 18.1:186–206.

Leonard, Robert J. 1996. From Parlor Games to Social Science: von Neumann, Morgenstern, and the Creation of Game Theory 1928–1944. *Journal of Economic Literature* 33.2:730–61.

Pickering, Andrew. 1995. *The Mangle of Practice*. Chicago: University of Chicago Press.

Salanti, A., and E. Screpanti, eds. 1996. *Pluralism in Economics*. Aldershot: Edward Elgar.

Part 1

The Incursion of Noneconomic Methods into Economics

Machine Dreams: Economic Agents as Cyborgs

Philip Mirowski

1. Why Historians Should Become Acquainted with Cyborgs

How much of what has been written under the rubric of the "history of economic thought" is now obsolete? This question is posed not only because the secondary literature has become so drearily repetitive in its demonstrated inability to surprise and entertain us concerning our past but also, more distressingly, because it has proven incapable of speaking to the concerns of the tyro and the average economist, both of whom would like some basis from which they might initiate informed speculation and argument about where the discipline of economics is headed. The pathetically parochial and jejune responses of economics graduate students when asked to identify their heroes (Klamer and Colander 1990, 42), or their narrow career aspirations, which rarely venture beyond imitation of their teachers, barely six years their elders, are all symptoms of the catastrophic failure of historians of economics to provide some modicum of reflexive distance and perspective for their readers.

With the banishment of all residual traces of historical representation from the faculties of most departments of economics, I doubt there remain any reasonable grounds to think the situation can be reversed from within. Therefore, I will suggest that the next best hope for the reorientation of

I should like to thank Andy Pickering, Matthew Weagle, and Roy Weintraub for comments, and the participants of Economics 517 at the University of Notre Dame for accompanying me on some paths less taken.

the history of economics comes from without—namely, a coalition of writers from the social studies of science (Pickering 1995a; Heims 1991), anthropologists and philosophers of science (Latour 1993), and modern third-generation feminist thought (Fox Keller 1995; Haraway 1991), all of whom have recently recast the entire question of the post–World War II relationship of the natural and the social sciences. While they have not *specifically* addressed the situation of modern economics, their observations concerning biology, computer science, operations research, and other collateral disciplines can be readily extended to economics, with potentially far-reaching consequences.

It is the guiding principle of this novel coalition of historians and sociologists to insist that the conception of distinct self-sufficient free-standing academic sciences in the postwar period is obsolete and should be replaced by the more encompassing notion of a *cyborg science*. When one first encounters the term, a plausible initial reaction is to regard it as premature capitulation to a fin-de-siècle weakness for cute and empty phrase-mongering, which evokes childhood images of *Star Wars* or, if the auditor is a bit more experienced in popular culture, William Gibson's *Neuromancer*. The endless evocation of "cyberspace" has proven such a drug upon measured thought—with not the most ridiculous policy proposal suggesting that those below the poverty line trade their food stamps for a tax credit for laptops—that the reader may be easily forgiven if they are inclined to withdraw from such terminology in disgust. Yet, as these writers are the first to remind us, the term *cyborg* did not appear first in the aetherial realms of science fiction or frothings of facile futurologists; no, it was in a U.S. Air Force technical report in 1960 (Pickering 1995a; Gray 1995, 3), and this fact is of signal importance for the concept. *Cyborg science* will here serve as shorthand for both a specific transformation of the subject matter of a particular discipline and the manner by which the transformation is usually brought about.

We can begin with the definition of cyborg subject matters by Andrew Pickering: "Unlike the traditional natural sciences that find their ontological foundations in the natural world, or the traditional social sciences that speak of the distinctively human (or social), the ontology of [a science like] operations research was the operation, the performance of an heterogeneous assemblage of humans and machines" (1995a, 21). In other words, cyborg sciences do not generally respect the Great Divide between the Natural and the Social; indeed, they display a certain gleeful panache in violating those expectations. The paradigmatic cyborg object in the post–World War II period was and is the computer, while the paradigmatic cyborg science is computer or "cognitive" science. One can always recognize a cyborg science by such questions as "Can machines think?" or "How could you tell the difference between a genome and a binary string of digits?" or "Can lifeforms be patented?" (Office of Technology Assessment 1989). Cyborg sciences typically result from the invasion of one science, perhaps nominally dealing with the living or social world, by another putatively based in the inanimate world, which produces a curious hybrid that then takes on a certain life and momentum of its own. It is the achievement of science studies scholars such as Pickering, Lily Kay, and Evelyn Fox Keller to have made us aware that there now exist a whole range of cyborg sciences: molecular genetics, information theory, computer science, chaos theory, cybernetics, neural psychobiology, artificial life, systems theory, operations research, and game theory.

However, cyborg sciences are not simply distinguished by their subject matters. If one had to depend on that criterion alone, then the above list would be far too motley and heterogeneous to serve as a legitimate classification. The other primary distinguishing characteristic of cyborg sciences is that they were generally constructed by a new breed of science managers, extracting knowledge forged out of the fires of World War II and annealed by a few philanthropic foundations and military sponsors. *The new cyborg sciences did not simply spontaneously arise; they were consciously made.* The primary way this happened was that a science manager recruited some scientists concerned with the inanimate sphere and paired them off with collaborators from the life sciences or social sciences, then provided them with lavish funding in order to produce a hybrid that would fit the needs or prospective requirements of their sponsors. Thus the hoary chestnut of the lone scientist freely following his own muse wherever she might lead does *not* generally apply to the cyborg sciences. This was the case even though some of the preeminent cyborg science managers would publicly argue for the older laissez-faire images of science (Kay 1993, 223–25). Cyborg science is Big Science par excellence, the product of planned coordination of teams with structured hierarchical objectives, expensive discipline-flouting instrumentation, and explicitly retailed rationales. The structure of a cyborg science frequently displays the military fascination with "command, control, and information," at the levels of both conceptualization and implementation; it rapidly becomes the province of a narrowly defined technical elite—a group that maintains its status largely through its new position in the interlocking military/governmental/industrial structure.

Why should a historian of economic thought care about any of this? It is my thesis that what eventually came to be regarded as orthodox economics, especially in the later twentieth century, should be paired with computer science as the other paradigmatic locus of cyborg science, at least in the United States. However, an appreciation of this thesis requires another as prerequisite: that the cultural shift to cyborg sciences is accompanied by another late-twentieth-century shift—namely, away from physics proper as the paradigm of all effective human knowledge and toward an amalgam of evolutionary biology/computation theory/thermodynamics, a package which still is in the process of osmosis throughout the natural and human sciences. It is this relative subordination of physics to a nascent "general theory of information" that has previously misled various commentators about the relationship between neoclassical economics and the natural sciences in their understanding of modern trends (Ingrao and Israel 1990; Cohen 1994), causing them to suggest that "physics envy" is not an operant factor in the development of twentieth-century economics.

Once this recalibration of economics on the topography of intellectual endeavor is carried out, it will eventually provoke the complete revision of the canon of the history of economic thought. It may also serve to recoup the function that history used to play in the discipline: *it will provide a narrative that explains nascent developments in the present, as well as defunct developments in the past.* Let me suggest the primary reason for an economist to become more familiar with this literature. Every major transformation of the postwar orthodoxy in economics can be understood as a more or less direct function of a prior development in a related cyborg science; furthermore, the innovation was initiated by one of the premier actors in the existing cyborg science with the direct encouragement of a military or foundation sponsor. The first and most obvious instance is John von Neumann and Oscar Morgenstern's invention and nurturing of game theory (von Neumann and Morgenstern 1964). The next is Norbert Wiener's work on gunnery prediction, which eventually became the basis for the theory of rational expectations (1956). The third is Wiener's new science of "cybernetics" (1961; Galison 1994) and von Neumann's theory of automata (1996), which serve as the primary inspirations behind the modern Santa Fe Institute and its program of "complexity." The fourth is Claude Shannon and Warren Weaver's (1949) information theory, which inspired Friedrich von Hayek's 1969 "turn" from a conventional economist to a prophet of laissez-faire complexity theory. The fifth is Herbert Simon's 1982 theory of "bounded rationality," which became transformed into his version of "artificial intelligence" (1991). There are many more cyborg genealogies of modern economics (for example, the "experimental analysis of animal behavior" as in Kagel, Battalio, and Green 1995 or the "evolutionary" approaches to the Nash equilibrium in game theory), but I think these five cases sufficiently cover the waterfront in the 1990s to justify the following claim: *What is deemed "exciting" by the elite avant garde in American orthodox economics, not to mention the bright graduate student, is determined by what other cyborg sciences had precipitated a generation before.* This article is intended solely to sketch out some historical evidence for this claim. An evaluation of the implications of this claim for the philosophy of economics must await a separate venue.

2. From Clockwork to Dissipation, from Demons to Patrons

> The human body is a machine which winds its own springs. It is the living image of perpetual motion.—La Mettrie

> In Gibbs' universe order is least probable, chaos most probable. But while the universe as a whole . . . tends to run down, there are local enclaves whose direction seems opposed. . . . Life finds its home in some of these enclaves. It is with this point of view at its core that the new science of Cybernetics began its development.—Norbert Wiener

One reason that economics is such a magnet for cyborgs is that the concept of the division of labor is one of the primordial themes in the cyborg sciences. The metaphor of synchronic cooperation of the various organs of the body as exemplifying all manner of social organization dates back to the beginnings of written history (Mayr 1986), but the use of the metaphor to explain the synchronization of machines themselves is roughly contemporaneous with the rise of a self-conscious political economy. An elaborate history of the reciprocal interaction of the computer and the factory is just beginning to be written: the inspiration in Adam Smith for de Prony's calculators (Grattan-Guinness 1990); the impact of political economy on Babbage's calculating engine in the 1820s (Schaffer 1994); the contribution of William Stanley Jevons's logic machine (Grattan-Guinness 1991; Weagle forthcoming b).

Nevertheless, cyborg history is preeminently a twentieth-century phenomenon, not because automata and clockwork simulacra date from modern times but because of the way the simulacra were reconceptualized and realized in the modern era. This transformation is captured in the juxtaposition of the quotes from Julien La Mettrie and Norbert Wiener that preface this section. In the eighteenth century, when Jacques Vaucanson produced his automata—his mechanical duck and mechanical flautist—he intended to exemplify the virtues of regularity, order, and harmony through the integration of smoothly interacting parts, subject to a central power source, which "illustrated and thus reinforced the general world view of determinism" (Mayr 1986, 119). Life was regarded as essentially similar to other orderly natural phenomena, such as the solar system, or the well-functioning state. This pervasive determinism might create conceptual problems for notions of freedom and will, as Kant insisted, but such arguments were still carried out in the context of a presumption of a sort of timeless dynamics, an encounter of windowless monads in a featureless space. This mechanical approach to human encounters was initially given a boost by the rise of the energy concept in the mid-nineteenth century, as I have argued elsewhere (Mirowski 1989). The version that inscribed these laws as extremum principles subject to external constraints provided the inspiration for neoclassical economics.

The clockwork metaphor was transformed beyond recognition in the later nineteenth century, as has been noted by a number of historians:

> The eighteenth-century machine was a product of the Newtonian universe with its multiplicity of forces, disparate sources of motion, and reversible mechanism. By contrast, the nineteenth-century machine, modeled on the thermodynamic engine, was a "motor," the servant of a powerful nature conceived as a reservoir of motivating power. The machine was capable of work only when powered by some external source, whereas the motor was regulated by internal, dynamical principles, converting fuel into heat, and heat into mechanical work. The body, the steam engine, and the cosmos were connected by a single unbroken chain of energy. (Rabinbach 1990, 52)

Physics had embarked on a period of self-criticism in the late nineteenth century with respect to the earlier brand of determinism and its attendant treatment of life. If energy really was conserved, then what happened to the body, which seemed to run down over time? The answer was initially sought in the phenomenon of heat, the inevitable concomitant of life, and ultimately resulted in the novel field of thermodynamics. It is of critical importance for our story to observe that neoclassical economics split off from physics just prior to the full elaboration of the second law of thermodynamics (Mirowski 1989, 389–90), and never dealt adequately with the problems of dissipation and temporal orientation.[1] It was initially left to the physicists and their fellow travelers to tackle the problems of the place of life (and work) in the physical universe, and it is from the writings of James Clerk Maxwell that the historians cited here tend to date the rise of cyborg science.

The story of Maxwell's Demon has been told in many places (Brush 1983; Fox Keller 1995; Leff and Rex 1990), so we may just glance briefly at the genesis of the tiny progenitor of our narrative. The second law of thermodynamics states that heat will only move from a warmer to a cooler body, but Maxwell and others realized that if heat was molecular motion, then there should be some mechanical method to violate the second law at the microscopic level. In an 1867 letter to Peter Tait, Maxwell imagined a homunculus stationed at the door partitioning off a cooler from a hotter gas. Since the cooler gas was comprised of faster and slower molecules, the nimble Demon could wait till one of the faster molecules was headed toward the door, quickly whip it open to let the molecule pass to the warmer gas, and then close it with even more precise alacrity to prevent the "inevitable" back migration of faster molecules from the hotter gas. By this modus operandi, the Demon could make heat flow from a cooler to a hotter body and violate the second law. This possibility took on greater significance in the Victorian context, where the rise of entropy predicted by the second law of thermodynamics was represented in the popular mind by the eventual Heat Death of the Universe.[2] Note well: the dissipation of heat had become grimly conflated with death, for both

1. "We may safely accept as a satisfactory scientific hypothesis the doctrine so grandly put forth by Laplace, who asserted that a perfect knowledge of the universe, as it existed at any moment, would give perfect knowledge of what was to happen thenceforth and forever after. Scientific inference is impossible, unless we may regard the present as the outcome of what is past, and the cause of what is to come. To the perfect intelligence nothing is uncertain" (Jevons 1905, 738–39).

2. As late as 1905, Ernest Rutherford maintained, "science offers no escape from the conclusion of Kelvin and Helmholtz that the sun must ultimately grow cold and this earth will become a dead planet moving through the intense cold of empty space" (in Smith and Wise 1989, 551). Chapters 15 and 16 of Smith and Wise discuss this literature.

the individual body and the universe as a whole. This betokened further metaphorical calamities since circumventing the second law meant that, in principle, a perpetual motion machine was possible; cheating death was one thing, but cheating capitalism by getting something for nothing was quite another.

Laymen often think that science is about colorless facts and forbidding formulae; on the contrary, folklore protagonists like Maxwell's Demon are often just as important in the elaboration of scientific thought. The fact that an illustrious parade of physicists—from Maxwell to Kelvin to Schrodinger to Szilard to Brillouin to Landauer to Bennett—have taken such a fanciful conceit so very seriously is incontrovertible proof of that observation. As Harvey Leff and Andrew Rex (1990, vii) have observed, the Demon himself has often been pronounced dead, only to rise from the grave in some new guise. The twin images of the Demon and dissolution have stalked the dreams of physicists in the intervening century and spurred their intermittent search for a place for life in the now-hostile universe. As Fox Keller suggests, "between the promise of progressive development in Darwin's theory and the threat of inexorable decay and dissolution in the laws of thermodynamics, Maxwell foresaw a third possibility in the nature of molecular structures—neither of progress nor of decay but of stability" (1995, 52).

In the minds of many, the Demon came to represent the improbable triumph of Life over Death (if only temporarily); but the beauty of the synecdoche was how it left the essential character of life underdetermined. What was it that allowed life to prevail, or to maintain homeostasis in the face of entropic degradation? The answers were many and varied (Leff and Rex 1990), but we shall concentrate on only two of them since they provide the direct inspiration for the cyborg sciences: the image of life as voraciously feeding on pockets of negative or low entropy, and the image of life as the intelligent maintainance of "memory" in the face of dissipation. Both molecular genetic theory and the theory of information found their point of departure at the portal manned by the versatile Demon.

The linking of the Demon to the characterization of life is often traced to a "seminal" paper by Leo Szilard in 1929 whose objective was to "find the conditions which apparently allow the construction of a perpetual motion machine of the second kind, if one permits an intelligent being to intervene in a thermodynamic system" (in Leff and Rex 1990, 124–33). The curious apparatus described in the paper, in which a single gas molecule is made to do work on a piston, should not detain us here; it was, rather, the interpretation superimposed on the device that set off reverberations through the decades. Szilard suggested that one might save the Second Law from violation by associaton of measurements of velocity made by the Demon with the production of entropy.[3] Just like a physicist, Szilard insisted that "ignorance of the biological phenomena need not prevent us from understanding that which seems to us the essential thing" (in Leff and Rex 1990, 125). Brushing aside all sorts of quibbles one might bring to indict the smaller-than-life character—say, the energy dissipation of its nervous system or the implausibility of its own heat not influencing the motion of the molecules—Szilard postulated that the thing that allowed violation of the Second Law was the capacity for *memory* on the part of the Demon; furthermore, the thing that counteracts this capacity is the very act of measurement, which increases entropy by at least as much as the use of memory is able to diminish it. Here, in a nutshell, was a novel construction of the meaning of life: memory, which permitted the seeming bootstrapping of free energy, plus observation, which reimposed the discipline of scarcity by itself carrying a cost. While the conflation of life and cognition was new, the combination of memory plus observation left life pretty much where it had been before in physics: it was still inexplicable.

One possible answer to this conumdrum was provided by Erwin Schrodinger in his essay *What Is Life?* (1945). Schrodinger suggested (not implausibly) that there was "a precious something contained in our food which keeps us from death" ([1944] 1973, 75); as a physicist, however, he did not mean the same thing as your mother when she told you to eat your spinach. Schrodinger proposed that life does not violate the Second Law, but does cheat it, by managing to find itself "continually sucking orderliness from its environment" (75). It was convenient that this kind of cheating was perfectly compatible with a market system: at least no one would be getting something for nothing. While this was one way to prosecute the answer, by itself it did not manage to distinguish Life

3. "We show that it is a sort of a memory faculty, manifested by a system where measurements occur, that might cause a permanent decrease of entropy and thus a violation of the Second Law of Thermodynamics, were it not for the fact that the measurements themselves are necessarily accompanied by the production of entropy" (in Leff and Rex 1990, 124). The entry of "memory" into molecular physics, so soon after the inception of the "sciences of memory" in the late nineteenth century described by Ian Hacking (1995), is another branch of the geneaology of the cyborg sciences that requires further exploration.

from, say, a black hole. That required the next leap of imagination: "An organism's astonishing gift of concentrating a 'stream of order' on itself and thus escaping decay into atomic chaos . . . seems to be connected with the presence of the 'aperiodic solids,' the chromosome molecules" (1944, 82). As Fox Keller demonstrates, this was the beginning of the doctrine of the "master molecule" in molecular biology, the privileged proteins wherein "the ordinary laws of physics do not apply" (1995, 72).

Fox Keller does a wonderful job of tracing all the metaphors that went into the making of the "gene": military control center, masculine intelligence, Maxwell's Demon, vampire of negentropy, self-referential computer, and the only really important part of the cell. We would add that the story of the "race to the double helix" in the 1930s through the 1950s would only spin its wheels if it didn't include Warren Weaver. Weaver, the Svengali of the cyborg sciences, was the person who coined the term *molecular biology* and brought the field to life in the 1930s in his capacity as program officer for the Rockefeller Foundation (Kohler 1991; Kay 1993). Weaver felt that many conventionally defined disciplines—and especially biology—were not properly configured to make the great breakthroughs that he believed lay in wait there; so he encouraged all manner of physicists and chemists to jump disciplinary boundaries and shake up the biological community. As he later admitted, "I started out with genetics, not because I realized in 1932 the key role the subject was destined to play, but at least in part because it was a field congenial to one trained in mathematics" (Weaver 1970, 69). His love of interdisciplinarity, which in practice meant warm exhortations to physicists to venture where no physicist had gone before, a hallmark of cyborg sciences, was something Weaver was prepared to back up with cold hard cash; and when the double helix was at last found, Weaver was willing to regard it as a vindication of his enthusiasm (Kohler 1991, 330).

Molecular biology was only one possible elaboration of the narrative sequence of Maxwell's Demon; the theory of information was another. This set of events has yet to find its historian, though a good beginning can be found in Aspray 1985; Bennett 1987; Hayles 1990, ch. 2; Leff and Rex 1990; and Kay 1995. The narrative here would begin with the paper by Leo Szilard in 1929, but rapidly careens out of control into a number of seemingly unrelated developments, such as von Neumann's 1932 book on quantum mechanics, Claude Shannon's work on transmission channel capacity, Alan Turing's work on computation and code breaking, Norbert Wiener's cybernetics, and Henry Quastler's work on the genetic code. But before our own narrative threatens to succumb to entropic degradation, it may be prudent to restrict our account to the vicissitudes of the Demon himself, at least temporarily. What seems to have escaped most historians of physics is that the partisans of Demonology could be divided into those who believed the Demon (and therefore "life") embodied some principle that allowed thermodynamics to be thwarted or circumvented and those who thought this dispensation sheer vitalist nonsense. Curiously enough, this battle tended to be waged more and more over the meaning of intelligence and "information," probably because most of the combatants were physicists ignorant of the "wet" details of biology, and also due to the spin given the issue by Szilard, than over any other putative capacity or attribute of the Demon. For instance, in 1951 Leon Brillouin sought to link the entropy increase of measurement to the classical theory of black body radiation, insisting the Demon would be incapable of "seeing" the relative speeds of the molecules without an external source of photons. This suggested to Brillouin that the ultimate source of the diminution of entropy was information, or as he put it, "information is negentropy."

Something peculiar happened in this lineage sometime in the late 1940s: while entropy developed stronger links to "information," information itself was becoming progressively divorced from meaning. As Katherine Hayles notes, "From now on, control [of entropy] was increasingly seen not in terms of human will fighting universal dissipation, but as information exchanges processed through machines" (1990, 46). It seems that Szilard and Brillouin were talking about information as if it were literally commensurate with thermodynamic entropy, though confusion ensued because Szilard thought the sign was positive, whereas Brillouin insisted it was negative. The situation was further bedeviled when it became fashionable to abstract information further by isolating it in machines and treating its measure as *analagous* to the measure of entropy in thermodynamics.

The lead protagonist in this tendency, and perhaps the very model of a modern cyborg scientist, was Claude Shannon. Upon taking a job at MIT as research assistant to Vannevar Bush and helping him with his differential analyzer, Shannon wrote a 1938 master's thesis showing that electronic switching circuits can be described by Boolean algebra, a fact now taken as transparently obvious in our modern digitalized society. After writing a Ph.D. dissertation on a mathematical description of heredity, Shannon moved to Bell Labs and wrote his 1949 classic *Mathematical Theory of Communication* (with Warren Weaver). Predicated solely on the use of identical mathematics rather than any pronounced isomorphism with regard to theoretical thermodynamical content, Shannon wrote down a function of the probabilities of message codes in transmission lines and named this expression for transmission capacity "entropy."[4]

Of course, Shannon was primarily concerned with formalizing the question of the accuracy of transmission of digitalized information, but the wicked spin given to the term *entropy* resulted in all manner of confusion, excitement, and misapprehension concerning the range of applicability of this new "theory of information" (Georgescu-Roegen 1971, appendix B). Indeed, one can make a case that Shannon was a bit devious (if not Demonic) himself here since he clearly intended his ideas to extend beyond the limited ambit of error-correction codes and capacity constraints in telephone transmission lines. In this he shared a vaulting ambition with Alan Turing, who had spent time at Bell Labs in 1943: "Shannon had always been fascinated with the idea that a machine should be able to imitate the brain; he had studied neurology as well as mathematics and logic; and he had seen his work on the differential analyzer as a first step towards a thinking machine. They found their outlook to be the same: there was nothing sacred about the brain" (Hodges 1983, 251). He reported later: "I believe in evolutionary theory and that we are basically machines but of a very complex type. . . . We are the extreme case: a natural mechanical device" (Shannon 1987, 64).

But Shannon should not be given all the credit: the ubiquitous Warren Weaver was the first to comment on Shannon's theory, to the extent that he was listed as coauthor when the paper was republished in book format (Shannon and Weaver 1949). It seems that Weaver caught a whiff of that combination that proved so heady in the postwar years: a physicist

4. The equation, which was the same as Boltzmann's H-function, was

$$H = \sum_{i=1}^{s} P_i \ln P_i$$

where P represents the probabilities of a particular symbol in a set of s symbols showing up in an "average" string. "Information" or "entropy" is at a maximum when the symbols are neither too probable, and hence redundant from the viewpoint of transmission, nor too improbable, and therefore generally take too much code to transmit efficiently. As Hayles describes the conventional interpretation: "Maximum information [in this sense] is conveyed when there is a mixture of order and surprise, when the message is partly anticipated and partly surprising" (1990, 53). Notice this has *nothing* to do with the semantic content of the message.

who mathematized something potentially biological by combining issues of thermodynamics, computation, and electrical engineering. In this particular instance he did not need to fund the operation, since that side of things was already covered by Bell Labs; but he was responsible for promoting something that might have otherwise only interested some theoretically inclined telephone engineers into a transdisciplinary cause célèbre, the first rumblings of another new science which he alone glimpsed on the horizon, a science of "complexity." The beauty of Weaver's interpretation was that the whole thing was brought back round to a kind of "economics" once it became quantified:

> To be sure, this word *information* in communication theory relates not so much to what you do say, as to what you could say. That is, information is a measure of one's freedom of choice when one selects a message. . . . The concept of information applies not to the individual messages (as the concept of meaning would), but rather to the situation as a whole, the unit information indicating that in this situation one has an amount of freedom of choice, in selecting a message, which is convenient to regard as a standard or unit amount. (1949, 8–9)

Weaver, like Kilroy in World War II, had been everywhere that was going anywhere; he was the anonymous entity behind the lines who left his mark on most of the scientific developments that mattered in the postwar world. The inscription of the "command-control" military paradigm was something Weaver was not ashamed to openly admit: "It may be reasonable to use a still broader definition of communication, namely, one which includes the procedures by means of which one mechanism (say, automatic equipment to track an airplane and to compute its probable future positions) affects another mechanism (say, a guided missile chasing this airplane)" (3). Indeed, one could say he was one of the World War II triumverate who defined the triple helix of university-government-industrial science in the postwar United States, along with Vannevar Bush and James Conant. He was so effective in his role as the power behind the scenes—the facilitator and orchestrator of the research of others—that he hasn't even attracted a biographer,[5] nor has he gained admission among the elect in the *Dictionary of Scientific Biography*, unlike his fellow triumvers. Perhaps part of the reason for this neglect is that, unlike Bush or

5. The only partial exception is Rees 1987, which manages to be both uninformative and poorly organized.

Conant, he had the good taste not to become very involved with building the atomic bomb. More than anyone else, however, it was Warren Weaver whom we have to thank for opening doors for the cyborgs to find their way into our fin-de-siècle world.

Warren Weaver took degrees in civil engineering and mathematics from the University of Wisconsin, becoming the protégé of physicist Max Mason. After some war work and a brief stint at Cal Tech, he spent the decade of the 1920s on the mathematics faculty at Wisconsin. Mason brought him to New York in 1932 to head up the newly created Division of Natural Sciences, right at the time the depression was forcing the Rockefeller Foundation to reduce and consolidate its grants. Although he had no background in the area, Weaver managed to reorient the program toward his vision of "molecular biology," which also included mathematical and physiological approaches to psychology (Kohler 1991; Weaver 1970). Indeed, one historian has situated the whole reorientation of the Rockefeller philanthropies away from physics and toward "molecular biology" in the 1930s as part and parcel of its initiative to produce a new "Science of Man"; genetics was seen as a more suitable underpinning for the social sciences than the discredited eugenics (Kay 1993). In one of his earliest memos at the Foundation, Weaver stated: "In the social sciences, the institutional program must not only modify the attitude towards research, but must also modify the attitude as to what constitutes research" (in Kay 1993, 47). Rockefeller subventions in economics were likewise destined to transform the face of the discipline in the 1940s (Craver 1986).

In 1940, Vannevar Bush tapped Weaver to organize the gunnery-control group for the National Defense Research Committee (NDRC); in 1941 he was part of a U.S. mission to examine the successes of P. M. S. Blackett's Operational Research group (Bush 1970, 92; Fortun and Schweber 1993; Weaver 1970, 89–90); and in 1942 he was made head of the Applied Mathematics Panel (Owens 1989). The late 1940s was the period of his greatest interest in issues of computation, while he became part of the postwar military/academic complex: chair of the Naval Research Advisory Committee, member of the R&D Board of the Department of Defense; and in 1954 president of the American Association for the Advancement of Science. In the 1950s he turned the eleemosynary attention of the Rockefeller Foundation to another area of biology—namely, the agricultural breeding program that became known in retrospect as the Green Revolution.

In fact, Weaver is best understood as the latest incarnation of Maxwell's Demon. He was stationed strategically at the partition between disciplines, and maybe the partition between the Social and the Natural, and with his resources and his "information" about what went on in the differing chambers, he opened doors for a few selected "quick ones" to pass through. In the process he endowed a couple of scientific communities in some danger of entropic dissipation (due to an anachronistic belief in the efficacy of the "pure curiosity" of the scientist) with a renewed bout of life. Almost every cyborg science enumerated in the previous section owes a greater or lesser debt for its existence to Warren Weaver. In briefly touching on the nodes in Weaver's vast web of patronage, we will signpost many of the loci of development of the cyborg content of postwar economics.[6]

It may be best to start with the genius of cyberscience, John von Neumann. Von Neumann was well acquainted with Weaver by 1942, if not before, and depended on him for all manner of support in his role as "philanthrapoid" (Weaver's own term). Weaver had been instrumental in bringing Operations Research to America, and Weaver's Applied Mathematical Panel (AMP) did not often distinguish between linear programming, statistical optimization, and game theory as their tools of choice when his mathematicians were put to work on submarine warfare, antiaircraft gunfire control, and optimal torpedo salvos (Leonard in Weintraub 1992, 62–64). Since the response to von Neumann and Morgenstern's newfangled game theory was not wildly enthusiastic in economics, the military developments were the primary source of new blood and ideas in the first two decades after its inception (Mirowski 1991). Even though game theory has come to be employed in biological contexts in the more recent past (Smith 1982), it seems von Neumann's own interests did not turn in a more cybernetic direction until just after the publication of the game theory book—that is, precisely when his dependence on Weaver and the military nexus became more acute. The earliest evidence of von Neumann's interest in the computer comes in a letter to Weaver in January 1944, when he solicited Weaver's expertise about the various computing technologies that could be commandeered

6. In portraying Weaver as a Demon, it should not be inferred that we intend also to "demonize" him. The overriding impression one gains from reading his own memoir (1970) and those of others in retrospect is of a rather lackluster character, a good organization man, someone who was best at smoothing over the waves created by others more histrionic and more talented than he (Hager 1995).

for the effort to build the bomb (Aspray 1990, 30). Weaver complied and delegated a subordinate to scare up some IBM equipment for von Neumann's use. When von Neumann decided to have his own computer built at the Institute for Advanced Study in 1946, Weaver was one of the first he approached for funding (54). "By the spring of 1945 the NDRC had become seriously interested in computers, and Warren Weaver asked von Neumann to write a report for the AMP surveying past, present and future computing machines" (240). Few have noted, however, that von Neumann's "biological turn" happened right at the same time (189)—something that resonates rather conveniently with Weaver's effect on other physical scientists. It was in late 1944 that von Neumann banded together with such figures as Norbert Wiener, W. Edwards Deming, Warren McCulloch, and Herman Goldstine to foster development of a field which "as yet is not even named," though the cabal provisionally called it the Teleological Society. Although the organization did not get off the ground immediately, Wiener wrote in a letter to one of the participants: "We are also getting good backing from Warren Weaver, and he has said to me this is just the sort of thing that the Rockefeller should consider pushing. In addition, McCulloch and von Neumann are very slick organizers, and I have heard from von Neumann mysterious words concerning a some thirty megabucks which is likely to be available for scientific research. Von Neumann is quite confident that he can siphon some of it off."[7]

Lest we give the impression that cyborgs could only be found lurking about in postwar America, it would be prudent to remember that many of the same parallel developments could be found in Britain, perhaps even slightly ahead of developments in the United States. In Britain, the preeminent cyberscientist was Alan Turing, inventor of the Turing Machine, a cyberobject par excellence. Turing is credited by some with sketching the outlines of the computer well before von Neumann, though the two were in early and repeated contact: "Turing's analysis can be seen as part of the general movement, already in evidence in the 17th century, towards a mechanistic—or physicalistic—account of human behavior" (Gandy 1988, 87). Turing was heavily involved with the military for support of his unorthodox approach, in particular with regard to cryptanalysis, but he moved effortlessly between game theory, probability theory, computer design, and biological morphogenesis (Hodges 1983; Mirowski in

7. Wiener to Arturo Rosenblueth, 24 January 1945; quoted in Aspray 1990, 316.

Weintraub 1992, 123–26). Turing would have been the British von Neumann, except for the fact that he lacked von Neumann's willingness to subordinate himself to bureaucratic and military figures.

Von Neumann went on to do pathbreaking work on the architecture of the computer, cellular automata, and the structure of the brain; but the other major heritage of his later years was the institution of the Macy Conferences, which their historian has dubbed "the cybernetics group" (Heims 1991). These were the first hopeful manifestations of the new science that Wiener later named "cybernetics." Citing Schrodinger and Maxwell's Demon as precursors, Wiener had great hopes of the new science transforming statistical mechanics into an information framework that would encompass all self-regulating systems (Wiener 1961, 11; Kay 1996). The explicit purpose of these conferences was to extend the new machine/brain developments to the social sciences—at first, primarily psychology and anthropology. However, the statistical/thermodynamical orientation of the participants was construed broadly to include the work of Leonard Savage on Bayesian/utilitarian decision theory, as well as the information theory of Claude Shannon.

The importance of the conferences was not so much in the synergy they engendered—that was not such a clear outcome—but, rather, in promoting the conviction that some important developments had come out of the war work and that they were fraught with implications for many "social" disciplines. The primary enthusiast was Wiener, who had been led to cybernetics by his work on gun-control sevomechanisms during the war "under the supervision of Dr. Warren Weaver" (Wiener 1956, 249). Wiener's innovation did not simply consist of the Wiener-Hopf prediciton theorem, but in the reconceptualization of antiaircraft gunnery as a pure problem of information: "The concept of predicting the future of a message with a disturbing noise on the basis of simultaneous statistics of the noise and the message turned out to contain in itself the whole idea of a new method for separating noise and messages in what would be in some sense the best possible way. . . . Bigelow and I started up a little laboratory to explore the possibility of predictors . . . [to] put our ideas into metal almost as fast as we could conceive them" (246, 248). The pilot and the gunner might be thought of as engaged in a living duel, but Wiener insisted that their activities could be reduced to semimechanical feedback motions, and therefore the entire process could be mechanized: "The work I did on the statistical treatment of antiaircraft control has led eventually to a general statistical point of view in communication engineering. . . . This is passing over to less orthodox fields such as meteorology, sociology and economics" (255). As Shannon later admitted: "Communication theory is heavily indebted to Wiener for much of its basic philosophy and theory. His classic NDRC report *The Interpolation, Extrapolation and Smoothing of Stationary Time Series* (1949) contains the first clear-cut formulation of communications theory as a statistical problem" (1949, 85n).

The characteristic moves of the cyborg sciences—capturing feedback motions in metal, framing biological reproduction in equations of automata, reducing thought to the Boolean logic of electrical circuits, leaching the problem of meaning out of the definition of information, treating probability theory as though it had somehow solved the problem of induction, blurring the distinction between hardware and wetware, summarizing the endless regress of strategy in a few dynamic optimality conditions, and subordinaing the lot to the explanation of the emergence of "order" out of chaos—could be multiplied by numerous further examples, most of them linked in one way or another to Warren Weaver.[8] This is a history that is only beginning to be written (Pickering 1995a; Galison 1994; Kay 1996). But our more immediate task is to indicate how these developments made their way into economics.

3. Invasion of the Body Snatchers

The purpose of this section is to suggest the broad shape of the histories of the invasion of the cyborgs in economics, not to do justice to the topic according to the stringent standards of the historian. While we shall point to various texts that might be considered forerunners of the genre, most of the hard historical work still remains to be done. This is just a first halting gesture in the direction of a thick description of how neoclassical economics slowly abandoned its nineteenth-century center of gravity in the palpable bodily experience of scarcity and moved progressively to conceptualize the core of the market experience as one of the processing of information.[9]

8. For instance, apparently Weaver introduced Brillouin to Szilard before he wrote his paper on Maxwell's Demon (Lanouette 1992, 332, 535n). There is also the connection that many of the people involved in postwar Operations Research went on to work in linear programming, combinatorics, graph theory, matroids, and thus eventually the theory of computational complexity. (See Lenstra, Kan, and Schrijver 1991).

9. A beginning toward this work can be found in Weagle forthcoming b. There we learn that computational themes had been present since the inception of neoclassicism, but that as

The point of departure is the realization that economics did not exactly lock up its doors and set the guard dogs loose when the cyborgs came to town; that would have gone against the grain of nearly seventy years of qualified adherence to a model of man that was based fairly openly on the motion of mass points in space (Mirowski 1989). Neoclassical economics often conflated man and machine—witness Jevons's logical piano, Pareto's endorsement of an economic mechanics, Fisher's portrayal of mind as water flow in cisterns, and Harold Hotelling's wish to treat human migration like heat flow. Economists welcomed physicists exiled by war and unemployment with open arms into the discipline in the 1930s and 1940s; these had always been the sort of people they wanted to encourage to live in their neighborhood. The difference in the 1940s was that, when the cyborgs came to town, the ideas they brought with them did not seem to resemble those that had represented "science" to previous generations. In a nutshell, the machine no longer signified the silent orbits of celestial mechanics or the conduits of hydraulic flow to the interlopers. The tensions were expressed along many different dimensions. For instance, the neoclassical characterization of "energy" was a perfectly reversible and deterministic world with a unique, stable, well-defined "equilibrium" where there was no free lunch; in contrast, the cyborgs talked of entropy and loss, dissipation, and irreversibility. The neoclassicals displayed an aversion to probability theory in the first decades of the century, whereas the cyborgs were adamant that the contrast between chaos and order had to be cast in probabalistic terms. The neoclassicals were wedded to their Panglossian stories of optimality; the cyborgs wanted to jabber about feedback mechanisms where one just made do. Neoclassicals, of course, tried to circumvent the problem of knowledge by simply asserting it was always already perfect; in contrast, the cyborgs regarded knowledge more like information—something transmitted with error and sometimes confused with background noise. For neoclassicals, redundancy was equated with inefficiency; for cyborgs, however, some redundancy was required to ward off noise. *Pace* Marshall, neoclassicals knew little or no biology and didn't care to learn any more, while the cyborgs insisted that biology would be the main arena of action in the twentieth century. When neoclassicals were attracted to formal logic, it was always the most austere and foundationalist sort, like Gérard De-

they came increasingly to the fore, they served to undermine the key notion of equilibrium as constrained optimization.

breu's championing of the Bourbakist approach, but logic for the cyborgs meant exploration of its more intractable or paradoxical corners—like Turing's work on computable numbers or von Neumann's work on effective algorithms and computational architectures. Neoclassicals got a warm glow from their existence proofs; cyborgs needed to *calculate*.

Thus the cyborgs were not initially welcomed with open arms when they came marching, stiff-gaited and military, into economics. Each of the later cyborg manifestations—such as game theory, information theory, cybernetics, automata theory, and theories of bounded rationality—were resisted and ridiculed by the then-regnant neoclassical orthodoxy. In the last decade of the twentieth century, when game theory has come to define graduate microeconomics and the Santa Fe "complexity" approach is all the rage, it might be salutary to be reminded that the rise of this new wave was neither smooth nor continuous. It is also worthwhile to remember that this internal opposition cannot be simply written off as a matter of tastes: the delayed acceptance was primarily due to changes in the fundamental images of "science" and the slow diffusion of the computer. This change only becomes more apparent when we realize that the cyborg scientists themselves regarded economics as one of their obvious next conquests in their Long March across the sciences. As physicist Alvin Weinberg wrote in 1982: "The market system is a social Maxwell's Demon; by sending price signals to the consumer, it causes him to use energy more efficiently. As the scale of the demon increases, so does the ratio of the energy saved to the energy used by the demon" ([1982] 1990, 116).

Let us start in order of recent significance, with von Neumann's game theory. It is now agreed among historians of game theory that the neoclassical orthodoxy met the 1944 book with indifference and incomprehension, forcing von Neumann to resort to the incipient "defense analyst" community as the group to nurture and develop it further (Mirowski 1991; Weintraub 1992; Leonard 1995). Although his ties with the military (especially at RAND) permitted von Neumann to recruit new enthusiasts and make sure they were well funded, it is noteworthy that he did not feel impelled to do much more work in this area in the last decade of his life. The reasons von Neumann thought the theory potentially promising—that it was intriniscally stochastic; that it highlighted certain feedback conceptions of accomodation; that it mimicked certain activities of the brain—were not the reasons neoclassicals thought it worth their notice. Neoclassicists were more fascinated with the idea of axiomatizing what they thought of as their "basic theory"—especially the expected utility theory—an exercise which for von Neumann was a mere detour. Von Neumann instead chose to focus his attention on the promise of cyborg science much more directly, by altering his research program starting in 1944: computer theory, the theory of automata, and stylized descriptions of the brain (Aspray 1990; von Neumann 1958). It is perhaps not unexpected that orthodox economic theorists became hung up on the premature and incomplete realization of the cyborg in game theory, finding themselves still unable or unwilling to follow von Neumann fully into the promised land. Recent fascination with a putative "evolutionary game theory" may signal another major cyborg accomodation, however.[10]

It is not just microeconomics that has become a stomping ground for cyborgs; macroeconomics has proven at least as vulnerable to invasion. While much effort has been expended on the examination of the provenance of the theory of rational expectations, only one author to my knowledge has located its inspiration in cyborg theory (Sent forthcoming). One of the protagonists of the movement, Thomas Sargent, has admitted the importance of Wiener's theory of prediction in underwriting the formal possibility of separating signal from noise; the trick of rational expectations then comes in projecting this capacity onto the cognitive equipment of the representative economic actor, rendering it the very essence of "rationality." The centrality of "information" as a species of meaning-indifferent valuation is the mark of the cyborg that rational expectations economists wear proudly on their brows. If Shannon had defined information as "logical instructions to select," then the extension of choice functions to the processing of information appeared an obvious next step. Yet the sampling of the fruits might be regarded as a prelude to expulsion from the paradise of an optimally functioning system. For one, Thomas Sargent became famous for setting himself the impossible task of reconciling static mechanistic neoclassical theory with these cyborg imperatives; under the pressure of failure, however, there are some recent signs that he feels impelled to engage in cyborg science much more unreservedly (Sargent 1993; Weagle forthcoming a).

Both game theorists and rational expectations theorists epitomize the fascination with formal models that inhabits the economics profession; but a fondness for mathematics is not a necessary prerequisite for falling

10. The finest image of cyborgism one can cite in recent literature is the spectacle of two or more Turing machines playing one another in a stylized game-theoretic context—the purpose of this science fiction being a metajustification for some refinement of the Nash equilibrium concept (see Binmore 1987–88).

under the sway of the cyborg sciences. Our exemplar in this regard is the Nobel prize–winning economist Friedrich von Hayek. It is now well known that prior to the late 1930s Hayek was a more or less conventional Austrian economist, constructing relatively mechanical business cycle models. Under the pressures of the war and a bruising battle with Keynes over whose version of macroeconomics could explain the depression, Hayek underwent a "transformation" (Caldwell 1988), changing from being a supporter of the neoclassical orthodoxy to being a critic. He came to believe that the way forward was to propose a novel theory of complex phenomena, which would explain why a decentralized market would always outperform a centrally planned economy. Although it is not much read outside the circles of Austrian afficianados, Hayek even proceeded to publish his own theory of the brain in his *Sensory Order* (1952). The cyborg provenance of Hayek's enthusiasms are clear in his later writings: "Even in such relatively simple constituents of biological phenomena as feedback (or cybernetic) systems, in which a certain combination of physical structures produces an overall structure possessing distinct characteristic properties, require for their description something much more elaborate than anything describing the general laws of mechanics" (1969, 26). And who does Hayek cite as his authority on such weighty matters? Why, none other than . . . Warren Weaver (4, 26, 40)!

My final example of a cyborg scientist is Herbert Simon, best known elsewhere as one of the "fathers" of artificial intelligence (AI) (Crevier 1993), but in economics remembered as the theorist of "bounded rationality." From game theory to computers to feedback theory to military strategy, there is no one who has lived the cyborg creed more faithfully, more consistently, and more successfully than Simon. His theory of bounded rationality did not meet with much welcome or comprehension in economics; like so many other cyborg scientists, however, he simply moved to another department (psychology at Carnegie Mellon) when the economists proved too obtuse or recalcitrant. He, too, wears his cyborg credentials proudly on his sleeve:

> Information theory, statistical decision theory, and game theory had roused new interest in concept formation. . . . The war had produced a vast increase of research in human skills and performance. . . . Because much of this work was concerned with the human members of the complex man-machine system—pilots, gunners, radar personnel—the researchers could observe the analogies between human information

> processing and the behaviors of servomechanisms and computers. . . . The completely new turn that my life took in 1955 was the unanticipated result of the work with the Systems Research Lab at RAND and my contact there with the computer. (1991, 196, 198)

Orthodox economists, as is their wont, tried to tame bounded rationality as a special case of their optimization models, but Simon stuck to his guns, insisting that the meaning of "rationality" could not remain the same under the new cyborg regime: "To the subject who perceives the situation as one in which the probabilities may change, and who is more intent upon outwitting the experimenter (or nature) than on maximizing expected gain, rationality is something quite different" (1982, 271). What better way to describe the predicament of a Life faced with persistent and inexorable entropic degradation?

4. Order out of Chaos

In section 1 of this article I raised the issue of a particular payoff to this proposed reorientation of the history of modern economics. If it results in little else, I would hope this brief foray into cyborg history will prompt some serious reflection on the part of those who find the prospect of the Santa Fe Institute or the rise of an "evolutionary economics" or the allure of complexity theory as holding out exceptional opportunity for the thoroughgoing transformation of the discipline. In the absence of any historical dimension, waves of enthusiasm that sweep economics have all the charm of paid political campaign advertisements and commensurate staying power. This problem of understanding the content of a research strategy in economics may become more insistent as it becomes more difficult to attract qualified candidates into the discipline. What is the promise that economics holds for the tyro at the end of this millenium?

The advantage of the reorientation of the history of economic thought as producing an account of the cyborg sciences is that it can provide an occasion for raising these questions in a newer and less supercharged arena. One can begin the discussion by asking the following questions. Is economics now grown more interested in constructing little simulacra of information processors than in describing market transactions? Has "rationality," for all practical purposes, become a purely algorithmic notion? Has the meaning of "economizing" changed dramatically over the last century? Is economics in the process of repudiating physics and embracing biology as a source of fruitful metaphors and formalisms? What precisely has been the intellectual impact of the computer that now sits on everyone's office desk? Would it be better for the tyro to skip that course in topology in favor of a course in recursive function theory in the computer science department? Is all this talk about "evolution" anything more than a dreary recrudescence of Social Darwinism? What is it that economics seeks to achieve in reorienting its vision of the role and functions of markets?

I fully expect that economists will become more infatuated with the cyborg sciences in the immediate future; indeed, I think it inevitable. The reasons for this belief should now be a little clearer. Economics has persistently lagged behind the truly exciting developments in the physical sciences, only to take them up later in a distorted and distended version. This is happening right now, to a certain extent, at the Santa Fe Institute (Mirowski 1996; Horgan 1995; Weagle forthcoming a). Economists don't practice this debased form of mimesis simply to try and arrogate for themselves the trappings and glittering prizes of "science," although some of that does go on. It would behoove historians and philosophers of economics to seriously entertain the notion that modern economics is as much concerned with producing simulacra—or better yet, automata—as it is with understanding "the economy." In this sense, economists have always been closet cyberneticians, at least ever since François Quesnay produced a model of the circulatory system out of tubes of tin and then rendered the same model numerical in his *Tableau oeconomique*.

The conviction that there is a hidden order of things "behind" or "underneath" the market is of course an important theme in the history of political economy. This theme has repeatedly become entangled or intertwined with the conviction that the order to be found there is Natural or, better yet, of the same general character as the Laws of Nature. In the eighteenth and nineteenth centuries, this convinced any number of important figures that the market was more or less like a machine; machines were the highest form of order they knew—human artifacts governed by impersonal laws of science. But the twentieth century is the century of biology and of information. As Wiener wrote: "Organism is opposed to chaos, to disintegration, to death, as message is to noise" (1954, 95). The fact that there is a machine, a computer, on nearly every desktop only intensifies such convictions, curiously enough. Is it any wonder that, when denizens of the late twentieth century want to assert that the market conjures order out of chaos, their minds turn to abstract models of bits of information, which are taken from simulacra of genes or Turing machines?

References

Arrow, Kenneth, and David Pines, eds. 1988. *The Economy as an Evolving Complex System*. Redwood City, Calif.: Addison-Wesley.

Aspray, William. 1985. The Scientific Conceptualization of Information: A Survey. *Annals of the History of Computing* 7:117–40.

———. 1990. *John von Neumann and the Origins of Modern Computing*. Cambridge: MIT Press.

Bennett, Charles. 1987. Demons, Engines and the Second Law. *Scientific American* (November) 258:108–16.

Binmore, Ken. 1987–88. Modelling Rational Players, I, II. *Economics and Philosophy* 3:179–214; 4:9–55.

Bowker, Geof. 1993. How to Be Universal: Some Cybernetic Strategies, 1943–70. *Social Studies of Science* 23:107–27.

Brillouin, Leon. 1951. Maxwell's Demon Cannot Operate: Information and Entropy I. *Journal of Applied Physics* 22:334–57.

Brush, Stephen. 1983. *Statistical Physics and the Atomic Theory of Matter*. Princeton, N.J.: Princeton University Press.

Caldwell, Bruce. 1988. Hayek's Transformation. *HOPE* 20:513–41.

Cohen, I. B. 1994. *Interactions*. Cambridge: MIT Press.

Craver, Earlene. 1986. Patronage and the Direction of Research in Economics. *Minerva* 24:205–22.

Crevier, Daniel. 1993. *AI: A History*. New York: Basic.

Fortun M., and S. Schweber. 1993. Scientists and the Legacy of WWII: The Case of Operations Research. *Social Studies of Science* 23:595–642.

Fox Keller, Evelyn. 1995. *Refiguring Life*. New York: Columbia University Press.

Galison, Peter. 1994. The Ontology of the Enemy: Norbert Wiener and the Cybernetic Vision. *Critical Inquiry* 21:228–66.

Gandy, Robin. 1988. The Confluence of Ideas in 1936. In *The Universal Turing Machine: A Half-Century Survey*, edited by Rolf Herken. Oxford: Oxford University Press.

Georgescu-Rögen, Nicholas. 1971. *The Entropy Law and the Economic Process*. Cambridge: Harvard University Press.

Goodwin, Craufurd, ed. 1991. *Economics and National Security*. Supplement to vol. 23, *History of Political Economy*. Durham, N.C.: Duke University Press.

Goodwin, Craufurd, and Alex Rogers. Forthcoming. Cyberpunk and Chicago. In *History of Economics Society Proceedings*, edited by James Henderson. London: Routledge.

Grattan-Guinness, Ivor. 1990. Work for the Hairdressers: The Production of de Prony's Tables. *Annals of the History of Computing* 12:177–85.

———. 1991. The Correspondence between George Boole and Stanley Jevons, 1863–4. *History and Philosophy of Logic* 12:15–35.

Gray, Chris, ed. 1995. *The Cyborg Handbook*. London: Routledge.

Hacking, Ian. 1995. *Rewriting the Soul*. Princeton, N.J.: Princeton University Press.

Hager, Thomas. 1995. *Force of Nature*. New York: Simon and Schuster.

Haraway, Donna. 1991. *Simians, Cyborgs and Women*. New York: Routledge.

Hayek, Friedrich von. 1952. *The Sensory Order*. Chicago: University of Chicago Press.

———. 1969. *Studies in Philosophy, Politics and Economics*. New York: Simon and Schuster.

Hayles, Katherine. 1990. *Chaos Bound*. Ithaca, N.Y.: Cornell University Press.

Heims, Steve. 1980. *John von Neumann and Norbert Wiener: From Mathematics to the Technologies of Life and Death*. Cambridge: MIT Press.

———. 1991. *The Cybernetics Group*. Cambridge: MIT Press.

Hodges, Alan. 1983. *The Enigma*. New York: Simon and Schuster.

Horgan, John. 1995. From Complexity to Perplexity. *Scientific American* 272.6:104–9.

Houthakker, Hendrik. 1956. Economics and Biology: Specialization and Speciation. Stanford University Technical Report, no. 30. Bethesda, Md.: Office of Naval Research.

Ingrao, B., and G. Israel. 1990. *The Invisible Hand*. Cambridge: MIT Press.

Jevons, William. 1905. *The Principles of Science*. 2d ed. London: Macmillan.

Kagel, John, Raymond Battalio, and Leonard Green. 1995. *Economic Choice Theory: An Experimental Analysis of Animal Behavior*. New York: Cambridge University Press.

Kauffman, Stuart. 1993. *The Origins of Order*. New York: Oxford University Press.

Kay, Lily. 1993. *The Molecular Vision of Life*. Oxford: Oxford University Press.

———. 1995. Who Wrote the Book of Life? *Science in Context* 8.4:609–34.

———. 1996. Cybernetics, Information, Life: The Emergence of Scriptural Representations of Heredity. Program in Science and Technology Studies working paper. Cambridge: MIT Press.

Klamer, Arjo, and David Colander. 1990. *The Making of an Economist*. Boulder: Westview.

Kohler, Robert. 1991. *Partners in Science*. Chicago: University of Chicago Press.

Landauer, Rolf. 1991. Information Is Physical. *Physics Today* (May): 23–29.

Langton, Chris. 1992. Life at the Edge of Chaos. In *Artificial Life II*. Reading, Mass.: Addison-Wesley.

Lanouette, William. 1992. *Genius in the Shadows: A Biography of Leo Szilard*. New York: Scribners.

Latour, Bruno. 1993. *We Have Never Been Modern*. Cambridge: Harvard University Press.

Leff, Harvey, and Andrew Rex, eds. 1990. *Maxwell's Demon*. Princeton, N.J.: Princeton University Press.

Lenstra, J., A. Kan, and A. Schrijver, eds. 1991. *History of Mathematical Programming*. Amsterdam: North-Holland.

Leonard, Robert. 1995. From Parlor Games to Social Science. *Journal of Economic Literature* 33:730–61.

Maxwell, James Clerk. 1927. *Collected Scientific Papers*. Paris: J. Hermann.

Mayr, Otto. 1986. *Authority, Liberty and Automatic Machinery in Early Modern Europe*. Baltimore, Md.: Johns Hopkins University Press.

Mirowski, Philip. 1989. *More Heat than Light: Economics as Social Physics, Physics as Nature's Economics*. New York: Cambridge University Press.

———. 1991. When Games Grow Deadly Serious. In Goodwin 1991.

———. 1994. *Natural Images in Economic Thought: Markets Read in Tooth and Claw*. New York: Cambridge University Press.

———. 1996. Do You Know the Way to Santa Fe? In *New Directions in Political Economy: Malvern after Ten Years*, edited by Steve Pressman. London: Routledge.

Office of Technology Assessment. 1989. *New Developments in Biotechnology—Patenting Life*. Washington, D.C.: U.S. Government Printing Office.

Owens, Larry. 1989. Mathematicians at War: Warren Weaver and the AMP. In *History of Modern Mathematics*, vol. 2, edited by David Rowe and John McCleary. San Diego: Academic Press.

Pickering, Andrew. 1995a. Cyborg History and the World War II Regime. *Perspectives in Science* 3:1–45.

———. 1995b. *The Mangle of Practice*. Chicago: University of Chicago Press.

Quastler, Henry. 1964. *The Emergence of Biological Organization*. New Haven, Conn.: Yale University Press.

Rabinbach, Anson. 1990. *The Human Motor*. New York: Basic.

Rees, Mina. 1987. Warren Weaver (1894–1978). *Biographical Memoirs of the National Academy of Sciences* 57:493–530.

Romano, Richard. 1982. The Economic Ideas of Charles Babbage. *HOPE* 14:385–405.

Sargent, Thomas. 1993. *Bounded Rationality in Macroeconomics*. Oxford: Clarendon.

Schaffer, Simon. 1994. Babbage's Intelligence: Calculating Engines and the Factory System. *Critical Inquiry* 21:203–27.

Schrodinger, Ervin. [1944] 1967. *What Is Life?* Cambridge: Cambridge University Press.

Sent, Esther-Mirjam. Forthcoming. *Resisting Sargent*. New York: Cambridge University Press.

Shannon, Claude. 1987. Interview. *Omni* (August): 61–66, 110.

Shannon, Claude, and Warren Weaver. 1949. *The Mathematical Theory of Communication*. Urbana: University of Illinois Press.

Sheehan, J., and M. Sosna, eds. 1991. *The Boundaries of Humanity: Humans, Machines, Animals*. Berkeley: University of California Press.

Simon, Herbert. 1982. *Models of Bounded Rationality*, vol. 2. Cambridge: MIT Press.

———. 1991. *Models of My Life*. New York: Basic.

Smith, C., and M. Wise. 1989. *Energy and Empire*. Cambridge: Cambridge University Press.

Smith, John Maynard. 1982. *Evolution and the Theory of Games*. Cambridge: Cambridge University Press.

Szilard, Leo. 1929. Uber die Entropieverminderung in einem thermodynamischen System. *Zeitschrift für Physik* 53:840–56.

Turing, Alan. 1970. Machine Intelligence. In vol. 5 of *The Collected Papers of Alan Turing*. Amsterdam: Elsevier.

von Neumann, John. 1932. *Mathematische Grundlagen der Quantenmechanik*. Berlin: J. Springer.

———. 1958. *The Computer and the Brain*. New Haven, Conn.: Yale University Press.

———. 1966. *The Theory of Self-Reproducing Automata*. Urbana: University of Illinois Press.

von Neumann, John, and Oskar Morgenstern. 1964. *Theory of Games and Economic Behavior*. New York: Wiley.

Waldrop, Mitchell. 1992. *Complexity*. New York: Simon and Schuster.

Weagle, Matt. Forthcoming a. Innoculating Neoclassicism against the Genetic Algorithm.

———. Forthcoming b. Architects of Automata: Synthesizers of Simulacra. Ph.D. diss. University of Notre Dame.

Weaver, Warren. 1947. Science and Complexity. *American Scientist* 36:536–44.

———. 1970. *Scenes of Change*. New York: Scribners.

Weinberg, Alvin. [1982] 1990. On the Relationship between Information and Energy Systems. In *Maxwell's Demon*, edited by Harvey Leff and Andrew Rex. Princeton, N.J.: Princeton University Press.

Weintraub, E. R., ed. 1992. *Towards a History of Game Theory*. Durham and London: Duke University Press.

Wiener, Norbert. 1949. *The Interpolation, Extrapolation and Smoothing of Stationary Time Series*. Cambridge: MIT Press.

———. 1954. *The Human Use of Human Beings*. 2d ed. New York: Doubleday Anchor.

———. 1956. *I Am a Mathematician*. New York: Doubleday.

———. 1961. *Cybernetics*. 2d ed. New York: Wiley.

Engineering Dynamic Economics

Esther-Mirjam Sent

One way of understanding twentieth-century developments in economics is by analyzing how they were influenced by other disciplines. The twentieth century witnessed an increasing degree of mutual dependence between scientific fields and the rise of big science (see Galison and Hevley 1992; Hughes 1989; Whitley 1984). As World War I approached, scientific research became involved in inventing for and was partly funded by the military. During the interwar period, there was a massive increase in state and industrial employment organizations. As a result, research became less dictated by purely academic interests and more by external research support. Scientists became part of large systems of production that expanded immensely during the interwar years. During World War II, the development of radar and nuclear weapons led to an unparalleled position of prestige and power for the sciences. At the same time, weapons projects—like guided missiles and space programs of moon missions and unmanned interplanetary aircraft—led to an increase of public and political support for the sciences.[1] During the Cold War, these processes were

Thanks to Philip Mirowski and E. Roy Weintraub in particular and to the participants of the HOPE conference in general for many helpful comments and suggestions. Thanks to Steve Tradewell for research assistance.

1. I should note that technological enthusiasm was also somewhat dampened by the Great Depression and the violence and destruction made possible by modern technology during World War II.

extended and intensified through a massive growth of external funding for the sciences.

One field that benefited in particular from these developments was engineering (see Vincenti 1990). Throughout the ages, engineering has been a moving force in shaping our society. While engineers traditionally engaged in either civil or mechanical engineering, two new fields emerged around the turn of the century: chemical and electrical engineering. The twentieth century witnessed a further broadening of interest in fields such as aerospace, control systems, and computer engineering. Driven partly by the establishment of an engineering curriculum and the increased employment opportunities for engineers, partly by broad public support resulting in increased external funding for its projects, and partly by broad political support for its defense-related research, engineering has assumed an increasingly vital role in our society during the twentieth century. Its techniques not only were used in the engineering field but also were applied to other realms of social activity, such as economics.

During the twentieth century, engineering conceptions of the world dominated economists' quests for a more scientific analysis of economic dynamics. While economists claimed to be using rigorous mathematics as a universal language, their techniques were, in fact, mostly popularized by and borrowed from engineering. Engineering mathematics did not function as mere language, for it led economists to model the economy in specific ways. At the same time, it helped solve some problems as it generated other problems.

This article discusses how engineering mathematics initially made its way into the economics vocabulary. The next section examines the first phase in this development, which was the initial attempt to model agents who solve rich intertemporal problems. This approach can be linked to the techniques in the calculus of variations, which were used in engineering for analyzing aerospace systems, hydrodynamics, and thermodynamics. The second development, discussed in the second section, was the attempt to analyze more complicated environments and to model agents as choosing a sequence of actions through time. This analysis can be linked to general optimal control techniques used in engineering for designing mechanical, electrical, electromechanical, electronic, and other devices and to L. S. Pontryagin's (1962) and R. E. Bellman's (1957) procedures used in missile guidance. The third phase, the application of the theory of maximizing agents to expectations about the future, are covered in the third section. This interpretation had its roots in the optimal prediction and filtering techniques that were used in the field of communications engineering and the prediction of signals. The fourth section analyzes the attempts to link optimal control and optimal prediction through a focus on quadratic objective functions, linear transition functions, and Gaussian noise in economics. This interpretation can be linked to the linear control techniques that were used for feedback control systems in electrical, communications, and control engineering.[2]

1. Phase One: Calculus of Variations

1.1. Economics

Calculus of variations deals with choosing a time path for a so-called state variable that connects given initial and terminal points in order to maximize the value of the integral of a given function of the state variable, the time rate of change of the state variable, and time. A typical calculus of variations problem is of the form (see Kamien and Schwartz 1991)

$$\max_{x(t)} \int_{t_0}^{t_1} F[t, x(t), x'(t)]\,\mathrm{d}t \tag{1}$$

subject to

$$x(t_0) = x_0, \tag{2}$$

where $x'(t) = \mathrm{d}x/\mathrm{d}t$, and t, $x(t)$, and $x'(t)$ are regarded as independent arguments of the function F. The necessary conditions for $x^*(t)$ to maximize (1) subject to (2) are the Euler equation

$$F_x = \mathrm{d}F_{x'}/\mathrm{d}t, \tag{3}$$

the Legendre condition

$$F_{x'x'} \leq 0 \tag{4}$$

and the transversality conditions

$$\begin{cases} \text{a. } F_{x'} = 0 \text{ at } t_1, \text{ if } x(t_1) \text{ is free,} \\ \text{b. } F - x'F_{x'} = 0 \text{ at } t_1, \text{ if } t_1 \text{ is free,} \end{cases} \tag{5}$$

2. After having completed the first draft of this article, I discovered two essays by Nancy Wulwick (1990, 1995) that discussed the engineering and physics roots of optimal growth theory. I have subsequently incorporated some of the background information provided in these two essays.

where F_x and $F_{x'}$ refer to the partial derivatives of F with respect to x and x', respectively, and $F_{x'x'}$ is the second partial derivative of F with respect to x'.

The earliest application of the calculus of variations to economics was attempted by F. Y. Edgeworth ([1881] 1967), who was quite explicit about the roots of his approach in physics and sought to find a way to maximize total social welfare through the use of a function for distributing income and assigning work. Next, F. P. Ramsey (1928), a teacher of mathematical logic who came to economics with a strong interest in philosophy and mathematics, used calculus of variations in his analysis of how much a nation should save out of its national income through time in order to maximize its overall welfare over time. Since economics was largely literary in style, many economists did not appreciate Ramsey's contribution. The Ramsey model was rediscovered when economics became more mathematical partly due to the influx of former physicists and the promotion of mathematical economics by the Cowles Commission (see Wulwick 1990, 1995). It subsequently became the basis for the optimal growth theory of the late 1950s and 1960s. This research effort was sponsored partly by the U.S. Air Force and partly by the U.S. Office of Naval Research.

While Ramsey implicitly applied the conservation law associated with calculus of variations to the problem of dynamic optimization in economics, P. A. Samuelson (1947) was the first to explicitly apply this law. Samuelson, trained in mathematical physics, and his MIT colleague R. S. Solow subsequently wrote out the correspondence between the conservation of energy and the optimal theory of capital (Samuelson and Solow 1956).[3] Samuelson and Solow's work was financed by the RAND corporation, which saw a sound program of economics as an important part of national defense in the Cold War period. Initially consisting of physicists, engineers, and mathematicians, RAND quickly recruited economists who eventually rose to the top of the pecking order (see Leonard 1991).

A principal weakness of calculus of variations is that it cannot cope directly with problems in which there are constraints on the derivatives of the functions sought. As shown in section 2, these problems can be handled by optimal control theory. However, before moving to

3. From its inception, MIT was designed to work with industry. In fact, the MIT program in economics attracted many failed engineers.

that topic, we will explore the roots of calculus of variations methods in engineering.

1.2. Engineering

Some of the main results in calculus of variations were already established by L. Euler and J. L. Lagrange in the eighteenth century in an attempt to solve certain problems in mechanics (see Goldstine 1980; Lancos 1986; Weinstock 1974). While Euler started the systematic investigation of variational problems, Lagrange gave an explicit solution to these problems quite independently of Euler's implicit procedures, and with entirely new methods. He developed for this purpose a new calculus, the calculus of variations. During the nineteenth century, new methods were developed and important contributions were made by W. R. Hamilton and C. G. J. Jacobi. While Hamilton transformed Lagrange's complicated differential equations into "canonical equations," Jacobi developed the transformation theory of the canonical equations, the theory of "canonical transformations."[4] These developments started a new era in the development of many branches of physics, the most notable examples being mechanics, both classical and quantum, and thermodynamics. While calculus of variations originated as a study of certain isolated maximum and minimum problems not treatable by the techniques of elementary calculus, it is at present a powerful method for the solution of problems in dynamics.

Although economists used calculus of variations in an attempt to become more scientific, the development of the variational principles ironically never aroused much enthusiasm in scientific circles. Instead, it was merely tolerated as an efficient tool for describing mechanical phenomena. While the actual solution of the differential equations in calculus of variations is possible only for a restricted class of problems, it so happens that many important problems of applied engineering belong precisely to this class. As a result, calculus of variations has assumed an increasingly important role in the field of engineering. The applications of variational calculus to engineering can be divided into three broad categories. First, we find problems that require the determination of some best design or strategy, where "best" has a well-defined sense. In this context, engineers have applied calculus of variations to problems in aerodynamics, thermo-

4. As a by-product of his study of the variational properties of the optical system, Hamilton also crystallized the concept of energy (Wulwick 1990, 1995).

dynamics, and hydrodynamics. Second, engineers have used methods of approximating certain differential equations by direct calculations based on the variational "analog" to differential equations. Third, engineers have found variational formulations are useful in finding approximate solutions.

Wulwick (1990, 1995) criticizes the use of these formalisms by economists on the grounds that economists have not discussed the substantial negative analogies between the conservation of energy that is central to the calculus of variations system and the theory of economic dynamics (see also Mirowski 1989). In particular, economists have not addressed what the analog of energy conservation would be in an economic system. Moreover, while the conservation of energy played an important theoretical role, the conservation of utility has had no theoretical significance. Furthermore, there is no influence for history in conservative systems.

2. Phase Two: Optimal Control and Dynamic Programming

2.1. Economics

Optimal control gives equivalent results to the calculus of variations, but it sometimes affords insights into a problem that might be less readily apparent through the calculus of variations. It also applies to problems for which the calculus of variations is not convenient, such as those involving constraints on the derivatives of functions sought. In optimal control problems, variables are divided into two classes, control variables and state variables. While state variables summarize the past history of a system, the time paths of control variables are chosen to maximize a given functional depending on the time paths for the control and the state variables. There are two distinct ways of approaching this class of problems, one using Pontryagin's maximum principle (Pontryagin et al. 1962) and one relying on Bellman's principle of optimality (Bellman 1957).

First, Pontryagin's maximum principle can be illustrated in the context of a simple control problem (see Kamien and Schwartz 1991). Suppose the problem is one of selecting a piece-wise continuous control function $u(t)$, $t_0 \leq t \leq t_1$, to

$$\max \int_{t_0}^{t_1} f(t, x(t), u(t))\, \mathrm{d}t \tag{6}$$

subject to

$$x'(t) = g(t, x(t), u(t)), \tag{7}$$

$$t_0, t_1, x(t_0) = x_0 \text{ fixed; } x(t_1) \text{ free.} \tag{8}$$

Here f and g are assumed to be continuously differentiable functions of three independent arguments, none of which is a derivative. The control variable $u(t)$ must be a piece-wise continuous function of time. The state variable $x(t)$ changes over time according to the differential equation (7) governing its movement. This equation is called the state or transition equation. The control u influences the objective (6) both directly (through its own value) and indirectly through its impact on the evolution of the state variable x.[5]

Next, Bellman's principle of optimality is the basic principle of dynamic programming and can be illustrated as follows (Kamien and Schwartz 1991). An optimal path has the property that whatever the initial conditions and control values over some initial period are, the control (or decision variables) over the remaining period must be optimal for the remaining problem, with the state resulting from the early decisions considered as the initial condition. Consider

$$\max \int_0^T f(t, x, u)\, \mathrm{d}t + \phi(x(T), T) \tag{9}$$

subject to

$$x' = g(t, x, u), \ x(0) = a. \tag{10}$$

Define the optimal value function $J(t_0, x_0)$ as the best value that can be obtained starting at time t_0 in state x_0. This function is defined for all $0 \leq t_0 \leq T$ and for any feasible state x_0 that may arise. Thus,

$$J(t_0, x_0) = \max_u \int_{t_0}^T f(t, x, u)\, \mathrm{d}t + \phi(x(T), T) \tag{11}$$

subject to

$$x' = g(t, x, u), \ x(t_0) = x_0. \tag{12}$$

Manipulating these expressions, we get that

$$-J_t(t, x) = \max_u [f(t, x, u) + J_x(t, x) g(t, x, u)]. \tag{13}$$

5. The calculus of variations problem in (1) and (2) is readily transformed into an equivalent problem of optimal control by letting $u(t) = x'(t)$.

This is the fundamental partial differential equation obeyed by the optimal value function $J(t, x)$. It is often referred to as the Hamilton-Jacobi-Bellman equation.

Control methods have been used in economics for about forty years. A. Tustin (1953), a British electrical engineer, was the first to spot a possible analogy between the control of industrial and engineering processes and postwar macroeconomic policy making. He showed that in its simplest form the Keynesian system is analogous to a partially self-exciting generator and that many variations of Keynesian theory can be formulated as direct analogs of electrical systems. A. W. Phillips (1954, 1957) took up the ideas of Tustin. He was trained as an electrical engineer and then enrolled at the London School of Economics as a sociology student, where his imagination was caught by the concept of circular flow and the notion of the economic system as a hydraulic machine.

Despite the interest of economists in the contributions of Tustin and Phillips, the use of dynamics in applied and theoretical work was still relatively rudimentary, and there were practically no applications of control theory in the 1950s. This changed in the 1960s, with the rise of large-scale macroeconometric models for forecasting, the availability of powerful computers, and the development of software techniques needed to solve the large number of computational problems that arise in econometric applications of control theory. Inspired by these developments, economists, with the help of a number of control engineers, began to encourage the use of control techniques for the analysis of economic planning, macroeconomic policy, optimal growth theory, and other aspects of the theory of firms.

Applications of Pontryagin's maximum principle have led to a flourishing of models for studying capital accumulation, as well as to optimization theory in general.[6] This is partly because K. J. Arrow brought the mathematician H. Uzawa from Japan to Stanford University through a grant from the U.S. Office of Naval Research. Uzawa subsequently inspired Arrow's graduate students D. Cass, K. Shell, and H. Ryder to use Pontryagin's maximum principle (see Wulwick 1990, 1995). Applications of Bellman's dynamic programming, also known as recursive theory, have led to much progress during the 1960s in devising methods of estimating systems of interdependent relationships in macroeconomics,

6. Wulwick (1990, 1995) notes that Pontryagin's maximum principle was originally used in economic planning in Europe in the 1940s and that it became more fashionable when it was given a marginalist interpretation.

in applying them to construct econometric models of national economies, and in designing optimal policies. Recursive theory has also been used extensively in dynamic game theory.

M. Aoki, one of the popularizers of optimal control theory, wrote the first edition of his book (1989) mainly for audiences with physical science and engineering backgrounds. Nevertheless, it reached some readers with economic and management science training. P. Miller observes that "macroeconomic policy-making was viewed as an engineering problem. . . . Guiding the economy is similar to guiding a rocket ship" (1994, xiii). Let us, then, take a closer look at the analysis of guiding rocket ships in engineering.

2.2. Engineering

A systematic development of "classical" optimal control techniques began in the United States around 1930. The migration of German scientists to the United States in the interwar period, the military problems during World War II, and the missile race during the Cold War gave a substantial boost to the research in this field (see Wulwick 1990, 1995). Control engineering was involved in connection with power-assisted gun turrets in bombers, and in guidance systems for acoustic and magnetic torpedoes, and for the V-weapons. Starting in the late 1950s and early 1960s, optimal control theorists (Bellman 1957; Pontryagin et al. 1962) developed the first methods for dynamic optimization based on the time-domain, state-space representation of dynamic systems (see Bertsekas 1976; Bertsekas and Shreve 1978; Blackwell 1965). It was also during this period that the most important applications of optimal control techniques in the U.S. space program took place. All these new advances now form the core of the so-called modern control theory.

Control theory is often regarded as a branch of the general subject of systems theory. Systems engineering has been successfully applied to the design of many large-scale engineering systems, including industrial process control systems, factory automation, resource allocation systems, and spacecraft guidance and control systems. Control theory is mostly concerned with the physical behavior of systems. Control may be achieved by means of mechanical, electrical, electromechanical, electronic, and other devices, which should function without direct human intervention or supervision. A classic example of optimal control is the servomechanism problem in which optimal missile trajectories are determined. An application in the field of minimum energy problems is the maximization of range for a given amount of fuel and payload in a rocket mission. Finally, optimal control techniques provide the tools needed to design guidance systems to send satellites into space and to assure a soft landing for a spacecraft.

The Soviet Union started specializing in engineering control theory after the Russian Revolution. During the height of the Cold War, Pontryagin and three engineers developed their maximum principle, which was used as a general basis for programming missile guidance. Bellman's research was funded by the U.S. Air Force as part of a research program on the control of the trajectory of air weapons, and his dynamic programming approach was used to analyze the optimal policy for missiles (see Wulwick 1990, 1995).

Wulwick (1990, 1995) summarizes the limitations of optimal control in economics. In contrast to economists, defense strategists recognized the gap between mathematical and physical models. Instead, economists concentrated increasingly on abstraction and formalism rather than the real world. In contrast to optimization in aeronautical engineering, the objective function in economics lacked an empirical counterpart. Instead, economists ignored the underpinning of the maximum principle and dynamic programming.

3. Phase Three: Optimal Prediction and Filtering

3.1. Economics

Optimal control theory has come under severe attack from new classical economics quarters. It was R. E. Lucas (1976) who first pointed out that optimal control simulations or evaluations may be seriously flawed. While the optimal control paradigm requires that the relationships that determine how the economy moves over time be invariant to changes in policy rules, rational expectations may cause these relationships to change when relevant policy rules change. The flaws of optimal control theory were further elaborated by F. E. Kydland and E. C. Prescott (1981) and G. A. Calvo (1981), who showed that optimal policy in some optimal control models was "inconsistent."[7] Furthermore, the neutrality proposition of T. J. Sargent and N. Wallace (1975) suggested that there

7. In essence, policymakers may have an incentive to cheat, and it appeared that traditional optimal control theory dictates this type of behavior.

is no systematic role for stabilization policy when expectations are rational. Hence, it became clear that traditional control theory, which treated expectations as predetermined, was not suited for dealing with models in which expectations were formed rationally.

One reaction to these problems has been to assert that only the parameters of preferences and technology (deep structure) will be regime-invariant and that macroeconomists should therefore estimate these. This research methodology is discussed in the next section; here I discuss the other reaction, consisting of a focus on linear prediction and filtering, either through the use of Wiener-Kolmogorov techniques or based on Kalman filtering.[8]

First, for the purpose of using the Wiener-Kolmogorov formula for prediction, let us start with a moving average, covariance stationary process (see Whittle 1983)

$$y_t = \sum_{j=0}^{\infty} d_j u_{t-j} \text{ or } y_t = d(L)u_t,\ d(L) = \sum_{j=0}^{\infty} d_j L^j \tag{14}$$

where $\{u_t\}$ is the sequence of one-step-ahead linear least-squares forecasting errors (innovations) in predicting y_t as a linear function of $\{y_{t-1}, y_{t-2}, \ldots\}$. Using the Wiener-Kolmogorov prediction formulas, we get the following expression for the k-step ahead linear least-squares forecast

$$\begin{aligned} P_{t-k}y_t &= \sum_{j=k}^{\infty} d_j u_{t-j} = \left(\frac{d(L)}{L^k}\right)_+ u_{t-k} \\ P_{t-k}y_t &= \left(\frac{d(L)}{L^k}\right)_+ \frac{1}{d(L)} y_{t-k} \end{aligned} \tag{15}$$

where $(\ )_+$ means "ignore negative powers of L."

Next, for the purpose of using the Kalman filter technique for prediction, suppose that the process variable x_t obeys a first-order vector autoregression (see Whittle 1983)

$$x_t = Ax_{t-1} + \varepsilon_t \tag{16}$$

where ε_t is a vector white noise. Suppose that the observation y_t that

8. Nonlinear models played an important role in modeling econometric dynamics during the first part of this century. By the 1960s, however, the profession had largely switched to the linear approach, using B. Slutsky's observation that stable low-order linear stochastic difference equations could generate cyclic processes that mimicked actual business cycles (see, for example, Granger and Teräsvirta 1993).

becomes available at time t is correspondingly given by

$$y_t = Cx_{t-1} + \eta_t. \tag{17}$$

Assume that the compound noise vector

$$\begin{pmatrix} \varepsilon_t \\ \eta_t \end{pmatrix} \tag{18}$$

has zero mean, covariance matrix

$$\operatorname{cov}\begin{pmatrix} \varepsilon_t \\ \eta_t \end{pmatrix} = \begin{pmatrix} N & L \\ L' & M \end{pmatrix}, \tag{19}$$

and zero auto-correlations at non-zero lag.

Further assume that all random variables are jointly normal and denote the conditional mean and covariance of the current state by

$$\begin{aligned} \hat{x}_t &= E(x_t | W_t) \\ V_t &= \operatorname{cov}(x_t | W_t). \end{aligned} \tag{20}$$

It can then be shown that the quantities $\hat{x}_t$ and V_t obey the forward recursions

$$\hat{x}_t = A\hat{x}_{t-1} + H(y_t - C\hat{x}_{t-1}) \tag{21}$$

$$\begin{aligned} V_t = {} & N + AV_{t-1}A' - (L + AV_{t-1}C')(M + CV_{t-1}C')^{-1} \\ & \times (L' + CV_{t-1}A') \end{aligned} \tag{22}$$

where

$$H_t = (L + AV_{t-1}C')(M + CV_{t-1}C')^{-1}. \tag{23}$$

Relation (21) constitutes the celebrated Kalman filter, used for generating state estimates recursively.

Among economists, it was J. F. Muth (1960) who first explicitly and extensively exploited the tools of linear optimal prediction for modeling random dynamical systems. Muth had studied at the Graduate School of Industrial Administration at Carnegie-Mellon University. This program was designed mainly to provide engineers and scientists with business degrees. In 1963, Whittle ([1963] 1983) published the first edition of a book that made the linear theory that Muth had used more accessible to economists. M. L. Nerlove (1967) used the material in Whittle's book extensively to work out additional examples along the lines of Muth.

Today, economics abounds with applications of linear prediction and filtering. In particular, the Wiener-Kolmogorov prediction formula has been used to analyze linear rational expectations models of consumption, investment, and the demand for money. It also provided the setting for C. W. J. Granger's (1969) and C. A. Sims's (1972) discussions of causality and exogeneity. The Kalman filter, finally, has been interpreted as a form of adaptive expectations and has been used to deal with the so-called signal extraction problem.

3.2. Engineering

Linear prediction and filtering theory is vital for communications and control (see Anderson and Moore 1979; Whittle [1963] 1983). Communication systems typically have unwanted signals, or noise, entering into them. Filtering may then be used to minimize the inaccuracies caused by the presence of this noise. In control systems, measurements will frequently contain random inaccuracies or may be contaminated by unwanted signals. In such a situation, filtering is necessary to make the control close to that desired.

A. N. Kolmogorov was the first to formulate the problem of extrapolating (predicting) and filtering stationary stochastic processes clearly. Subsequently, many attempts at a practical investigation of such stochastic processes occurred in engineering. According to P. Galison, "it was the mass development and deployment of guided missiles, torpedoes, and antiaircraft fire that centralized the technology to scientists and engineers" (1994, 263). Norbert Wiener, for example, considered problems similar to those of Kolmogorov and tried to use them in building an antiaircraft predictor aimed at destroying enemy warplanes during World War II (see Galison 1994). Though this device never worked, Wiener did show the practical significance of prediction and filtering for the fields of radio and communications engineering (see Wiener 1964). He analyzed not only the theory of linear extrapolation but also the theory of linear filtering of stationary random functions. The latter was very important in communications engineering, prediction of signals, and separation of signals from noise.

Some have criticized Wiener for simplifying and making Kolmogorov's general theory somewhat more concrete by diluting the content of Kolmogorov's general investigations through a focus on a much narrower class of processes (see Bartlett 1966; Yaglom 1962). I should also note that Wiener did not think his techniques were particularly useful in economics. According to Wiener: "In economics, the so-called econometric science of economic dynamics suffers under the radical difficulty that the numerical quantities which are put into the dynamics are not well-defined and must be treated as gross statistical estimates. . . . Econometrics will never get very far until [certain] steps are taken" (1956, 260).

One of the problems associated with Wiener's approach was that it had difficulty coming up with numerical answers. It was not until the late 1950s and early 1960s that the Kalman filter theory was developed to deal with some of these problem cases (see Kalman 1960). While Wiener-Kolmogorov prediction theory assumes that the underlying signal and noise processes are stationary, the Kalman filter does not require this stationarity assumption. One reason is that the former approach was developed and thought of in frequency-domain terms, while the latter was developed in time-domain terms. As a result, Wiener filters were implementable with amplifiers and time-invariant network elements such as resistors and capacitors, while Kalman filters could be implemented with digital integrated circuit modules. Kalman's analysis of linear filtering was similar to Wiener's in the sense that he stressed engineering applications. Like Wiener, he addressed theoretical and practical problems in communication and control engineering.

4. Phase Four: Linear Control and Prediction

4.1. Economics

After having criticized the use of control methods for econometric policy evaluation, new classical economists realized that the use of control techniques for the evaluation of economic policies and the estimation of macroeconomic models is not only possible but essential under rational expectations. In response, they tried to link linear prediction to linear optimal control techniques. This attempt was facilitated by the introduction of certainty equivalence by H. A. Simon (1956) and the subsequent application of this concept by H. Theil (1957, 1958) to the macroeconomic policy problem. It is applicable when the objective function is quadratic, the constraints are linear, and the noise is Gaussian.

Suppose the control variables x_t are to be chosen to minimize the equation (see Whittle [1963] 1983)

$$V = EQ(x_1, x_2, \ldots, x_n; u_1, u_2, \ldots, u_n; v_1, v_2, \ldots, v_n), \quad (24)$$

where Q is a positive definite quadratic form. The series $\{u\}, \{v\}$ are sequences of random variables whose unconditional means are zero, and x_t is restricted to being a linear function of $u_1, u_2, \ldots, u_t$. Then, $x_1, x_2, \ldots, x_{t-1}$ having been determined, x_t should be determined by minimizing the quadratic form

$$Q(x_1 \ldots x_n; u_1 \ldots u_t, u_{t+1}^{(t)} \ldots u_n^{(t)}; v_1^{(t)} \ldots v_n^{(t)}) \tag{25}$$

with respect to $x_t, x_{t+1}, \ldots, x_n$. Here $u_j^{(t)}, v_j^{(t)}$ are the estimates of u_j and v_j in terms of $u_1, u_2, \ldots, u_t$ and $x_1, x_2, \ldots, x_n$.

Certainty equivalence, sometimes called the separation principle, permitted the separation of the maximum problem facing an agent into two parts, an optimization or control part and a forecasting part (see Lucas and Sargent 1981). "Classical" procedures could then be used to solve the control problem via calculus of variations and the prediction problem via the Wiener-Kolmogorov method. Alternatively, "recursive" procedures could be applied to solve the control problem via Bellman's dynamic programming techniques and the prediction problem via the Kalman filter. Hence, certainty equivalence allowed new classical economists to establish a connection between linear-quadratic optimal control problems and linear prediction and filtering problems through a two-stage procedure. The first stage consists of solving the deterministic version of the model, and the second step consists of adding uncertainty.

One very desirable feature of linear-quadratic models was that they allowed the easy calculation of equilibria. Except for linear models, Bellman's "curse of dimensionality" makes it difficult to compute an equilibrium. Hence, these specifications were adopted for their convenient analytical properties rather than for their relationship to economic reality.[9] Another "advantage" associated with the solution methods for linear-quadratic models was that the deterministic version of the model was solved first and uncertainty was added later. The irony here is that new classical economists had earlier criticized pre-rational expectations economics for adding uncertainty. However, their approach did not get much further, since it assumed that the decision maker knows the future with certainty even if her environment is stochastic.

9. Interestingly enough, one of the early defenders of linear models in economics, Granger, is now arguing that economists should move away from the linearity assumption: "My personal beliefs, which I think are widely shared by other econometricians, are that . . . relationships should be nonlinear and that the models should be truly stochastic rather than deterministic" (1994, 532).

Simon, in fact, was particularly aware of all these limitations. After having developed the certainty equivalence proposition for linear-quadratic models, Simon, who helped establish Carnegie-Mellon's Graduate School of Industrial Administration, illustrated its use in a collaboration with the electrical engineer turned economist C. C. Holt and other fellow travelers from Carnegie-Mellon University (Holt, Modigliani, Muth, and Simon 1960). He noted that the team was able to find the optimal policy only for a gross approximation to the real world and argued that it satisficed by making these special assumptions (Simon 1991, 167). He was also aware of the engineering roots of his work. Simon, whose father was an engineer, noted in his autobiography: "It gradually dawned on me that the path I was following in my professional maze was returning me to the parental calling, and not only because I had chosen to teach at an engineering school. . . . I decided I had been a closet engineer since the beginning of my career" (1991, 108–9).

4.2. Engineering

Linear systems have been under study for a long time, and from several different points of view, in physics, mathematics, and engineering (see Anderson and Moore 1979; Kailath 1980; Kwakernaak and Sivan 1972). While linear systems have been extensively studied especially since the early 1930s, the frequency-domain techniques used during that time did not specifically exploit the underlying linearity of the systems involved. Moreover, these techniques were unable to analyze the kind of systems that became increasingly important in aerospace and process control in the late 1950s. This fact, plus the importance of time-variant systems and time-domain characteristics in aerospace problems, led to a resurgence of interest, sparked by the work of Bellman and Kalman, in the state-space description of linear systems. For a variety of reasons, as illustrated in section 2, the state-space approach has been largely developed in control theory, and not communication theory.

Linear system analysis is important primarily because of its utility, for even though physical systems are never completely linear, a linear model is often appropriate over certain ranges of application. Also, a large body of mathematical theory is available for engineers to use in the analysis of such systems. The range of processes in the "real world" for which linear systems serve as effective models encompass elementary electrical networks, communications systems, signal processing systems, and control systems, along with complicated mechanical processes, most notably those that arise in aerospace applications. Input-output linear systems may also be used as models for processes that have associated with them no well-defined concept of what constitutes an internal situation. A great number of the mathematical problems of engineering fit into this category, including the functioning of an amplifier, a digital computer, and a quantum-mechanical system.

5. Conclusion

The four phases of dynamic economic theory illustrate that there were no neoclassical dynamics that commanded much consensus anywhere. Attempts were made to unify and create a new language through the use of engineering techniques. First, calculus of variations was introduced in economics by Edgeworth, who explicitly acknowledged the physics roots of his approach, and Ramsey, a teacher of mathematical logic, in an attempt to make economics more scientific. Ironically, however, variational principles were merely tolerated as an efficient tool in engineering and never aroused much enthusiasm in scientific circles. Furthermore, economists have not discussed the substantial negative analogies between the conservation of energy that is central to the calculus of variations system and the theory of economic dynamics.

Second, optimal control techniques were first used by Tustin, a British electrical engineer. These ideas were taken up by Phillips, who was also trained as an electrical engineer. Inspired by subsequent developments, economists, with the help of a number of control engineers, began to encourage the use of control techniques for the analysis of economic planning, macroeconomic policy, optimal growth theory, and other aspects of the theory of firms. However, while defense strategists recognized the gap between mathematical and physical models, economists did not. While the objective function in aeronautical engineering had an empirical counterpart, that in economics did not.

Third, new classical economists criticized the use of control engineering in economics and adopted other engineering techniques instead. The tools of optimal prediction and filtering were introduced in economics by Muth, who had earlier collaborated with the electrical engineer turned economist Holt and who had studied at the Graduate School of Industrial Administration at Carnegie-Mellon University; a program was designed mainly to provide engineers and scientists with business degrees. However, the prediction and filtering theory adopted by economists was applicable to only a narrow class of processes. Furthermore, one of the inventors of this theory, Wiener, did not think his techniques were particularly useful in economics.

Fourth, new classical economists realized that the use of control techniques was not only possible but essential under rational expectations. As a result, they attempted to connect control and prediction through a focus on linear systems. Simon, who helped establish Carnegie-Mellon's Graduate School of Industrial Administration, showed how control and prediction could be separated in problems with quadratic objective functions, linear constraints, and Gaussian noise. This idea was taken up by new classical economists. However, these specifications were not adopted for economic reasons at all and did not allow a full discussion of uncertainty.

Engineering mathematics helped solve, but also generated, problems for economists. In using engineering mathematics in an attempt to unify the disparity in economic dynamics, economists ended up with the view of an economy as an engineering system. While economists claimed to be examining the real world, their engineering techniques were developed to analyze idealizations. In fact, engineers are concerned with bending the fundamental laws of nature to their own purposes. While economists attempted to develop scientific knowledge, their engineering techniques were focused on producing an artifact. In fact, a considerable amount of good, practical engineering has been done in complete ignorance of underlying scientific principles, or through the application of principles that were simply wrong. While economists sought to develop optimal policies, their engineering techniques were rooted in satisficing. In fact, engineers are practical people who are concerned with getting specific jobs done and who seek satisfactory solutions in the face of complexities and uncertainties. Engineers are known to use trial-and-error empiricisms and rule-of thumb techniques that could not be generalized to a wide range of problems. The value of engineering technology is centered on this technology's ability to provide convenience. Where does this leave the rationality postulate that is so central to most of economics? Engineering conceptions not only dominated economists' quest for a more scientific economics but also provided an interpretation of rationality driven by convenience.

References

Anderson, B. D. O., and J. B. Moore. 1979. *Optimal Filtering*. Englewood Cliffs, N.J.: Prentice Hall.

Aoki, M. 1987. *State Space Modeling of Time Series*. Berlin: Springer-Verlag.

———. 1989. *Optimization of Stochastic Systems*. San Diego: Academic.

Arrow, K. J., and M. Kurz. 1970. *Public Investment, the Rate of Return, and Optimal Fiscal Policy*. Baltimore, Md.: Johns Hopkins University Press.

Bartlett, M. S. 1966. *Stochastic Processes*. Cambridge: Cambridge University Press.

Bellman, R. E. 1957. *Dynamic Programming*. Princeton, N.J.: Princeton University Press.

Bellman, R. E., and S. E. Dreyfus. 1962. *Applied Dynamic Programming*. Princeton, N.J.: Princeton University Press.

Bertsekas, D. P. 1976. *Dynamic Programming and Stochastic Control*. New York: Academic.

Bertsekas, D. P., and S. E. Shreve. 1978. *Stochastic Optimal Control*. New York: Academic.

Blackwell, D. 1965. Discounted Dynamic Programming. *Annals of Mathematical Statistics* 36:226–35.

Box, G. E. P., G. M. Jenkins, and G. C. Reinsel. 1994. *Time Series Analysis*. Englewood Cliffs, N.J.: Prentice Hall.

Calvo, G. A. 1981. On the Time Consistency of Optimal Policy in a Monetary Economy. In *Rational Expectations and Econometric Practice*, edited by R. E. Lucas and T. J. Sargent. Minneapolis: University of Minnesota Press.

Cass, D. 1965. Optimal Growth in an Aggregative Model of Capital Accumulation: A Turnpike Theorem. *Econometrica* 34:833–50.

Cass, D., and K. Shell. 1976. The Structure and Stability of Competitive Dynamical Systems. *Journal of Economic Theory* 12 (February): 31–70.

Chow, G. C. 1975. *Analysis and Control of Dynamic Economic Systems*. New York: Wiley.

———. 1981. *Econometric Analysis by Control Methods*. New York: Wiley.

Dorfman, R. 1969. An Economic Interpretation of Optimal Control Theory. *American Economic Review* 59 (December): 817–31.

Edgeworth, F. Y. [1881] 1967. *Mathematical Physics*. New York: Augustus M. Kelley.

Fleming, W. H., and R. W. Rishel. 1975. *Deterministic and Stochastic Optimal Control*. Berlin: Springer-Verlag.

Galison, P. 1994. The Ontology of the Enemy: Norbert Wiener and the Cybernetic Vision. *Critical Inquiry* 21:228–66.

Galison, P., and B. Hevley, eds. 1992. *Big Science*. Stanford: Stanford University Press.

Goldstine, H. H. 1980. *A History of the Calculus of Variations*. New York: Springer-Verlag.

Granger, C. W. J. 1969. Investigating Causal Relations by Econometric Models and Cross-Spectral Methods. *Econometrica* 37:424–35.

———. 1994. Forecasting in Economics. In *Time Series Prediction*, edited by N. A. Gershenfeld and A. S. Weigend. Reading, Mass.: Addison-Wesley.

Granger, C. W. J., and T. Teräsvirta. 1993. *Modeling Nonlinear Economic Relationships*. Oxford: Oxford University Press.

Hansen, L. P., and T. J. Sargent. 1990. Recursive Linear Models of Dynamic Economies. Working Paper, no. 3479. National Bureau of Economic Research, Washington, D.C.

Harris, M. 1987. *Dynamic Economic Analysis*. Oxford: Oxford University Press.

Holly, S., and A. Hughes Hallett. 1989. *Optimal Control, Expectations, and Uncertainty*. Cambridge: Cambridge University Press.

Holly, S., B. Rüstem, and M. B. Zarrop, eds. 1979. *Optimal Control for Econometric Models*. New York: St. Martin's.

Holt, C. C., F. Modigliani, J. F. Muth, and H. A. Simon. 1960. *Planning Production, Inventories, and Work Force*. Englewood Cliffs, N.J.: Prentice Hall.

Hughes, T. P. 1989. *American Genesis*. New York: Viking.

Intrilligator, M. D. 1971. *Mathematical Optimization and Economic Theory*. Englewood Cliffs, N.J.: Prentice Hall.

Kailath, T. 1980. *Linear Systems*. Englewood Cliffs, N.J.: Prentice Hall.

Kalman, R. E. 1960. A New Approach to Linear Filtering and Prediction Problems. *Journal of Basic Engineering* 82 (March): 35–45.

Kamien, M. I., and N. L. Schwartz. 1991. *Dynamic Optimization*. Amsterdam: Elsevier Science.

Kendrick, D. A. 1981a. Control Theory with Applications to Economics. In vol. 1 of *Handbook of Mathematical Economics*, edited by K. J. Arrow and M. D. Intrilligator. Amsterdam: North-Holland.

———. 1981b. *Stochastic Control for Economic Models*. New York: McGraw-Hill.

Kwakernaak, H., and R. Sivan. 1972. *Linear Optimal Control Systems*. New York: Wiley.

Kydland, F. E., and E. C. Prescott. 1981. Rules Rather than Discretion: The Inconsistency of Optimal Plans. *Journal of Political Economy* 85:473–91.

Lancos, C. 1986. *The Variational Principles of Mechanics*. New York: Dover.

Léonard, D., and N. V. Long. 1992. *Optimal Control Theory and Static Optimization in Economics*. Cambridge: Cambridge University Press.

Leonard, R. J. 1991. War as a "Simple Economic Problem." In *Economics and National Security*, edited by C. D. Goodwin. Durham, N.C.: Duke University Press.

Liu, P.-T., ed. 1980. *Dynamic Optimization and Mathematical Economics*. New York: Plenum.

Lucas, R. E. 1976. Econometric Policy Evaluation: A Critique. In *The Phillips Curve and Labor Markets*, edited by K. Brunner and A. H. Meltzer. Carnegie-Rochester Conference Series on Public Policy, vol. 1. Amsterdam: North-Holland.

Lucas, R. E., and T. J. Sargent. 1979. After Keynesian Macroeconomics. *Federal Reserve Bank of Minneapolis Quarterly Review* 3.2:1–16.

———. 1981. Introduction to *Rational Expectations and Econometric Practice*, edited by R. E. Lucas and T. J. Sargent. Minneapolis: University of Minnesota Press.

Mayr, O. 1970. *The Origins of Feedback Control*. Cambridge: MIT Press.

Miller, P. J. 1994. Introduction to *The Rational Expectations Revolution*, edited by P. J. Miller. Cambridge: MIT Press.

Mirowski, P. E. 1989. *More Heat than Light*. Cambridge: Cambridge University Press.

Muth, J. F. 1960. Optimal Properties of Exponentially Weighted Forecasts. *Journal of the American Statistical Association* 55.290:299–306.

———. 1961. Rational Expectations and the Theory of Price Movements. *Econometrica* 29.3:315–35.

Nerlove, M. L. 1967. Distributed Lags and Unobserved Components in Economic Time Series. In *Ten Economic Studies in the Tradition of Irving Fisher*, edited by W. J. Fellner. New York: Wiley.

———. 1972. Lags in Economic Behavior. *Econometrica* 40.2:221–52.

Petit, M. L. 1990. *Control Theory and Dynamic Games in Economic Policy Analysis*. Cambridge: Cambridge University Press.

Phillips, A. W. 1954. Stabilization Policy in a Closed Economy. *Economic Journal* 64 (June): 290–323.

———. 1957. Stabilization Policy and the Time Form of the Lagged Responses. *Economic Journal* 67 (June): 265–77.

Pontryagin, L. S., V. G. Boltyanskii, R. V. Gamkrelidze, and E. F. Mishchenko. 1962. *The Mathematical Theory of Optimal Processes*. New York: Wiley.

Ramsey, F. P. 1928. A Mathematical Theory of Saving. *Economic Journal* 38:543–59.

Ryder, H. 1967. Optimal Accumulation and Trade in an Open Economy of Moderate Size. In *Essays on the Theory of Optimal Economic Growth*, edited by K. Shell. Cambridge: MIT Press.

Samuelson, P. A. 1947. *Foundations of Economic Analysis*. Cambridge: Harvard University Press.

Samuelson, P. A., and R. S. Solow. 1956. A Complete Capital Model Involving Heterogeneous Capital Goods. *Quarterly Journal of Economics* 70:537–62.

Sargent, T. J. 1983. An Economist's Foreword to Prediction and Regulation by Linear Least-Square Methods. In P. Whittle, *Prediction and Regulation by Linear Least-Square Methods*, 2d rev. ed. Minneapolis: University of Minnesota Press.

———. 1988. Linear Optimal Control, Filtering, and Rational Expectations. Unpublished manuscript. Stanford University, Hoover Institution.

Sargent, T. J., and N. Wallace. 1975. Rational Expectations, the Optimal Monetary Instrument, and the Optimal Money Supply Rule. *Journal of Political Economy* 83.2:241–54.

Seierstad, A., and K. Sydsaeter. 1987. *Optimal Control Theory with Economic Applications*. Amsterdam: North-Holland.

Sent, E.-M. 1996. Convenience: The Mother of All Rationality in Sargent. *Journal of Post Keynesian Economics* 19.1:3–34.

———. In press. *Resisting Sargent*. Cambridge: Cambridge University Press.

Simon, H. A. 1956. Dynamic Programming under Uncertainty with a Quadratic

Objective Function. *Econometrica* 24.1:74–81.
———. 1991. *Models of My Life*. New York: Basic Books.
Sims, C. A. 1972. Money, Income, and Causality. *American Economic Review* 62:540–52.
Stokey, N., and R. E. Lucas. 1989. *Recursive Methods in Economics*. Cambridge: Harvard University Press.
Theil, H. 1957. A Note on Certainty Equivalence in Dynamic Planning. *Econometrica* 25 (April): 346–49.
———. 1958. *Economic Forecasts and Policy*. Amsterdam: North-Holland.
Tinbergen, J. 1952. *On the Theory of Economic Policy*. Amsterdam: North-Holland.
———. 1956. *Economic Policy*. Amsterdam: North-Holland.
Tustin, A. 1953. *The Mechanism of Economic Systems*. Cambridge: Harvard University Press.
Uzawa, H. 1965. Optimal Technical Change in an Aggregative Model of Economic Growth. *International Economic Review* 6:18–31.
Vincenti, W. G. 1990. *What Engineers Know and How They Know It*. Baltimore, Md.: Johns Hopkins University Press.
Weinstock, R. 1974. *Calculus of Variations*. New York: Dover.
Whiteman, C. 1983. *Linear Rational Expectations Models*. Minneapolis: University of Minnesota Press.
Whitley, R. 1984. *The Intellectual and Social Organization of the Sciences*. Oxford: Oxford University Press.
Whittle, P. [1963] 1983. *Prediction and Regulation by Linear Least-Square Methods*, 2d rev. ed. Minneapolis: University of Minnesota Press.
Wiener, N. 1956. *I Am a Mathematician*. New York: Doubleday.
———. 1964. *Extrapolation, Interpolation, and Smoothing of Stationary Time Series*. Cambridge: MIT Press.
Wold, H. 1938. *A Study in the Analysis of Stationary Time Series*. Stockholm: Almqvist and Wiksell.
Wulwick, N. J. 1990. The Mathematics of Economic Growth. Working Paper, no. 38. Jerome Levy Economics Institute, Bard College.
———. 1995. The Hamiltonian Formalism and Optimal Growth Theory. In *Measurement, Quantification, and Economic Analysis*, edited by I. H. Rima. London: Routledge
Yaglom, A. M. 1962. *An Introduction to the Theory of Stationary Random Functions*. Englewood Cliffs, N.J.: Prentice Hall.

Lucas and Artificial Worlds

Marcel Boumans

> In general, I believe that one who claims to understand the principles of flight can reasonably be expected to be able to make a flying machine, and that understanding business cycles means the ability to make them too, in roughly the same sense.—Robert E. Lucas, *Studies in Business-Cycle Theory*

It is a long and hard way from understanding the principles of a complex system to a technically manageable instrument. In the case of flying machines, having the disposal of mechanics and hydrodynamics at the end of the nineteenth century was not enough to build these machines. The necessary analytical techniques to solve the theoretical equations under the relevant restrictions were lacking, and, without further restrictions, the system of equations was not solvable. Furthermore, solutions that worked on paper or even under laboratory conditions failed under real conditions. Because of the gap between theory, which described fundamental processes and mechanisms, and the application of this knowledge, further technical-scientific research was needed.

I am grateful to Mary Morgan, Margie Morrison, Hans Amman, and the research group colleagues at the University of Amsterdam and at the Centre for the Philosophy of the Natural and Social Sciences, London School of Economics, for their comments on earlier drafts of this article. I thank Phil Mirowksi and the other participants of the *HOPE* Conference "New Economics and Its Writings" for their very critical remarks.

Because an economy is a complex system, economists encounter a gap between theory and application. To do justice to the complexity of the economy, more and more comprehensive models were built. This development was not justified by its results: more comprehensiveness did not lead to better predictions, which was seen as essential for policy evaluation. There is a gap between understanding the economic principles and the use of economic models as instruments for economic policy. To deal with this difficulty, two strategies are possible. First, the project of building more and more comprehensive models may be eliminated, because one is convinced that in principle this project does not lead to satisfying results. Then two directions are possible. One possibility is to develop and use only very simple models, which perform as well as complicated models in forecasting tests but are cheaper and more manageable to work with. The other possibility is to examine only subsystems of the economy, without believing that these studies can be integrated into a picture of the whole economy. Second, a new criterium to assess models may be proposed—one more useful for policy evaluation, namely, to verify whether they mimic the relevant characteristics of an economy. This new test criterion implies a new methodology for model building.

This article explores the development of the second strategy and its methodology, which is influenced by the insights of artificial intelligence (AI) into both model building and tests. While Robert Lucas advocates this methodology without applying it to model building, in the work of Herbert Simon—the "father of Artificial Intelligence"—one can find a strategy to build models to analyze complexity. Because both men are very explicit in advocating this new methodology, it is mainly with the aid of their contributions that this new methodology will be expounded.

Section 1 exposes the central problem which induced this new methodology, namely, the so-called Cournot problem. Section 2 shows that in the discussion of the proper strategy to deal with this problem, naive models have played a particular role. The strategy advocated by Lucas implied new criteria for testing; in section 3 these criteria are explored. Bringing Lucas and Simon together in the context of this discussion is not self-evident; section 4 shows what they have in common and in what sense they differ. Section 5 is an exposition of Simon's AI approach to help understand the modeling element in this new methodology. In section 6 some conclusions are made.

1. The Problem of Complexity

The economic system is complex in that it consists of a large number of agents that interact with each other in various ways. A consequence of this complexity is the difficulty labeled by Kevin D. Hoover (1988, 135) as the Cournot problem after its lucid, early formulation by Augustin Cournot:

> The economic system is a whole of which all the parts are connected and react on each other. . . . It seems, therefore, as if, for a complete and rigorous solution of the problems relative to some parts of the economic system, it were indispensable to take the entire system into consideration. But this would surpass the powers of mathematical analysis and of our practical methods of calculations, even if the values of all the constants could be assigned to them numerically. ([1838] 1971, 127)

Cournot displayed a technical problem. The Walrasian program was the answer to this problem by setting up a manageable interdependent system of a whole economy. A modern version of this program is the Cowles approach: a combination of the Walrasian method to construct a mathematical system without empirical content and econometrics to put empirical flesh and blood on this system. The optimism was fostered by the successful development of macroeconometric modeling in the late 1940s and early 1950s, which culminated in the Klein-Goldberger model of the United States (1955). Seen as a research program in strict Lakatosian sense, the hard core contains the following elements:

a. that the economy may be characterized as a set of autonomous and simultaneous behavioral (causal) relations with structural features captured by the parameters of these relations;
b. that these relations are essentially stochastic. The positive heuristic corresponding to this hard core is: "build, identify, estimate and assess the parameter estimates of structural models conforming to the theory of optimizing agent behavior, stochastically formulated." (De Marchi and Gilbert 1989, 5–6)

A sharp critique of the Cowles approach came from Milton Friedman (1951), who severely doubted the validity of these econometric models on the basis of the poor results of post-model forecasting tests by Andrew

Marshall (1950a, 1950b) and Carl Christ (1951). These tests were conducted on Klein's model III. An important part of these tests was a comparison of the predictive power of Klein's model against that of simple extrapolation models, the so-called naive models.

2. Naive Models

The concept of "naive models" was introduced into econometrics by Andrew W. Marshall at a joint session of the Econometric Society and the American Statistical Association in New York, December 29, 1949 (Report of the New York Meeting 1950, 264–67; Littauer 1950, 151–55). It seems that Friedman went about with the same idea, though not under this name (Christ 1951, 57n). During that session Marshall presented the results of his M.A. thesis, "A Test of Klein's Model III for Changes of Structure" which has—unfortunately—never been published, except for the two short abstracts (Marshall 1950a,b; see Qin 1993, 138n). He had tested Klein's model III in two ways (see Christ 1951, 55–59; Qin 1993, 137–38). Both ways used the calculated residuals for Klein's structural equations for the postsample period of 1946-47.

Marshall's first test examined each residual for 1946 and for 1947 to see whether they were larger than would be expected under the hypothesis that Klein's model described 1946 and 1947 equally as well as it did the sample period (1921–47). This was done for each structural equation separately by means of a tolerance interval for the calculated residuals. Because of this procedure, Christ called this test the structural equation tolerance interval test, or SETI test for short.

The second test examined each calculated residual for 1946 and 1947 to see whether it was larger than the error one would expect to make by using the naive models. Two naive models were used for testing. Naive model I says that next year's value of any variable will equal this year's value plus a random normal disturbance; naive model II says it will equal this year's value plus the change from last year to this year plus a random normal disturbance. The results of these tests were that three equations were rejected on the basis of his naive model tests and two equations on the basis of the SETI test.

Christ (1951) revised Klein's model, estimated it with the data for 1921–47, and tested the results against 1948 data. He distinguished between two groups of tests: "tests of internal consistency" and "tests of success in extrapolation and prediction." The first group comprised tests dependent only on data available for use in the estimation process; the second group comprised tests that used postsample and "therefore are of higher authority" (67). This second group consisted of the SETI test, the naive model test, and an additional comparative test of the goodness of fit of different estimation methods on the grounds of their predictive abilities.

The result of the naive model tests were remarkable. Each of the two naive models predicted seven out of thirteen endogenous variables better than did the reduced-form equations, as estimated by the ordinary least-squares method. Naive model I predicted better in fifteen cases out of twenty-one, and naive model II predicted better in thirteen cases out of twenty-one than the reduced form as estimated by the restricted least-squares method (78, 80). So, "the econometric model used here has failed, at least in our sample consisting of the one year 1948, to be a better predicting device than the incomparably cheaper naive models" (80).

In defense of the macroeconometric model, Christ used an argument that became an important criterion in justifying macroeconometric model building—namely, the policy evaluation argument. Macroeconometric models are preferred over naive models because they better predict the effects of alternative policy measures; naive models can only say that there will be no effect (80).

Friedman's "Comment" (1951) on Christ's paper was very critical toward the Cowles program but favored the postmodel tests of Marshall and Christ, in particular the naive model tests. Friedman saw them not as competing theories of short-time change, but as standards of comparison, "the 'natural' alternative hypotheses—or 'null' hypotheses—against which to text the hypothesis that the econometric model makes good predictions" (109). On the basis of Christ's exercise, then, one should reject the latter hypothesis. Against Christ's argument that these models are preferable to naive models because of their ability to predict consequences of alternative policy measures, Friedman claims that naive models can make such predictions, too. One can simply assert that a proposed change in policy will have no effect:

> the assertion that the econometric model can be used to predict the consequences of policy changes implicitly assumes that the theory of change implicit in the econometric model abstracts some of the essential forces determining economic change; states loosely, that the model is an approximation to the 'correct' one, and that the parame-

> ters are better estimated by giving them the values obtained from the estimated econometric structure than by setting them equal to zero. Now it is precisely these propositions that the naive model test contradicts. (111)

The assertion that the econometric model can predict the consequences of policy changes, according to Friedman, is a "pure act of faith." And because of "the fact that the model fails to predict one kind of change is reason to have less rather than more faith in its ability to predict a related kind of change" (111).

Friedman interpreted the disappointing test results as evidence of the prematurity of macromodeling of a whole economy, before dynamic models of parts of an economy were well developed:

> As I am sure those who have tried to do so will agree, we now know so little about the dynamic mechanisms at work that there is enormous arbitrariness in any system set down. Limitations of resources—mental, computational, and statistical—enforce a model that although complicated enough for our capacities, is yet enormously simple relative to the present state of understanding of the world we seek to explain. Until we can develop a simpler picture of the world, by an understanding of interrelations within sections of the economy, the construction of a model for the economy as a whole is bound to be almost a complete groping in the dark. The probability that such a process will yield a meaningful result seems to me almost negligible. (112–13)

Friedman's lack of faith in the macroeconometric program sent him in another research direction (naive models were no theoretical alternatives to him)—namely, that of partitioning, the so-called Marshallian approach (see Hoover 1988, 218–25): "The direction of work that seems to me to offer most hope for laying a foundation for a workable theory of change is the analysis of parts of the economy in the hope that we can find bits of order here and there and gradually combine these bits into a systematic picture of the whole" (Friedman 1951, 114). This opinion became increasingly shared in the applied circle. Many applied modelers shifted their interest in macromodeling away from a whole economy to parts of economic activities in which economic theories were relatively well developed (Qin 1993, 138–39).

As mentioned, Friedman considered a naive model not a theoretical alternative but a standard of comparison in model testing. However, besides the Cowles program and Friedman's program, there exists a third alternative—namely, a program that develops macroeconomic models that contain just one or a very few dynamic relations. When they predict better than macroeconometric models, they are preferred. They could be called "simple models" in the sense that they only admit one or two dynamic relations to be essential and so deny the complex interweaving of the many economic forces, which a macroeconomic model tries to cover. A nice example is Harvey's term *structure model* (1991); this model contains a single equation with only one forecasting variable to forecast economic growth. The forecasting variable is the term structure—the difference between long-term and short-term interest rates—so that "one needs only a hand-calculator and a copy of a financial newspaper" to obtain forecasts of economic growth (Harvey 1991, 8).

Of course, it is not necessary to lose faith in the Cowles program, as Friedman did, because of the poor short-term forecasting abilities of the early macroeconometric models. In the first place, one can be confident that the forecasting abilities will steadily improve—and, in fact, they did. In the second place, one may wonder whether a test of success in extrapolation and prediction is the most suitable standard to judge these models. When such models are built to gain insight into the mechanism of business fluctuations, a more adequate postmodel test could be to verify whether the model mimics the relevant characteristics of these fluctuations. For example, Jan Tinbergen's last stage of valuing the U.S. model (1939) was to check whether the model as a whole would represent the cycles (Morgan 1990, 116). As a matter of fact, it was this kind of postmodel test that provided the Cowles program with strong support. Irma and Frank Adelman's computer simulation showed that the Klein-Goldberger model of the U.S. economy, when shocked by disturbances, could generate cycles comparable in their properties to those of the United State economy (1959). Indeed, the Klein-Goldberger model cycles were remarkably similar to those described by the National Bureau of Economic Research (NBER) as characterizing the U.S. economy. From this they concluded that the Klein-Goldberger model was "not very far wrong" (Adelman and Adelman 1959, 621).

3. Characteristics Tests

To Friedman, the poor forecasting abilities of the early macroeconometric models were due to the limitations of mental, computational, and statistical resources. These limitations enforced models that were "enormously simple relative to the present state of understanding of the world we seek to explain" (Friedman 1951, 112). However, within ten years there was considerable progress in the development of computer capacities. An important achievement with respect to the subject of this article is the introduction of the IBM Magnetic Drum Calculator Type 650. The IBM 650, as it is usually called, was not the first electronic computer, nor was it the largest or the fastest; it was the first computer to be used extensively in universities. Its popularity was due to the price, its ease of use, and its robustness—you could do almost anything without causing harm. The IBM 650 became available to universities around 1955. Because of its immediate acceptance and availability to faculty and students at almost every large university in the United States, it had a major impact on the evolution of computing, computer education, and computer science and engineering research. For example, but more of it later, the IBM 650 at Carnegie Institute of Technology played a significant role in the early research on artificial intelligence and cognitive science because it provided Herbert Simon and Allen Newell the opportunity to develop the first widely used list-processing language, IPL-V.[1]

In 1959, Irma and Frank Adelman used the IBM 650 calculator of the University of California Radiation Laboratory to examine the dynamic properties of the Klein-Goldberger model of the United States economy. Both were interested in an endogenous explanation of the persistent business fluctuations so characteristic of Western capitalism. Existing theories led to either damped or explosive cycles. Exogenous shocks or externally imposed constraints seemed to them "rather artificial," so they were looking for a "more satisfactory mechanism for the internal generation of a persistent cyclical process" (Adelman and Adelman 1959, 596). The purpose of their essay was to investigate whether the Klein-Goldberger model was a good candidate.

The model consisted of twenty-five difference equations in a corresponding number of endogenous variables; it was nonlinear in character, including lags up to the fifth order. The model had been applied to yearly projections of economic activity in the United States with some success, but its dynamic properties had been analyzed only under highly simplifying assumptions, like Arthur S. Goldberger's (1958) and John Cornwall's (1958) investigations of linearized versions of the model. The innovative

1. For more about IPL-V and about the IBM 650, see a special issue of the *Annals of the History of Computing*, vol. 8 (1986), no. 1.

element of the research of the Adelmans was that, rather than making simplifying assumptions, the complexity of the Klein-Goldberger model was left intact and the equations were programmed for the IBM 650 and run for one hundred years. The reason this work had not previously been done was that until then there hadn't been the technical ability to do it.

> The complexity of the model requires the use of modern high-speed computers for the long-run solution of the system in a reasonable length of time. Since the problem is about the right size for the IBM 650 calculator, and since the appropriate computing facilities exist at the University of California Radiation Laboratory, we programmed the equations for the machine. (Adelman and Adelman 1959, 597)

The first step of the research was to run the program in the absence of additional external constraints and shocks. The exogenous variables were extrapolated by fitting a least-squares straight line to the postwar data. The result was that the variables in the Klein-Goldberger model grow almost linearly with time. Thus, the endogenous part of the model did not contain an explanation of the oscillatory process. However, because the Klein-Goldberger model did present a detailed description of the U.S. economy, the Adelmans found it worthwhile to continue their examination by investigating the model's response to shocks.

Because it appeared that the model was stable even under large exogenous displacements, the next step was to see whether the introduction of relatively minor uncorrelated perturbations into the model would generate cyclical fluctuations analogous to the observed ones. Two types of shocks were introduced. Shocks of type I were random shocks superimposed on the extrapolated values of the exogenous quantities, and shocks of type II were random perturbations introduced into each nondefinitional model equation. Shocks of type I induced cycles with three to four year periods in the variables of the model, but the average amplitude of these cycles appeared too small. Shocks of type II also induced cycles with three to four year periods, but now the amplitudes were more realistic. Since the effects of shocks of type II were much larger than those of type I, and because either type of shock may be present in an actual economy, further analysis was carried out for the case in which both shocks are present.

To find that the amplitudes and the periods of the cycles were "roughly the same as those which are found in practice" (611) was seen by the

Adelmans as "merely a necessary condition for an adequate simulation of the cyclical fluctuations of a real industrial economy" (611). The question now was whether the shocked model produces business cycles in the "technical" sense:

> If a business cycle analyst were asked whether or not the results of a shocked Klein-Goldberger computation could reasonably represent a United States-type economy, how would he respond? To answer these questions we shall apply to the data techniques developed by the National Bureau of Economic Research (NBER) for the analysis of business cycles. (Adelman and Adelman 1959, 612)

Comparison of the characteristics of the cycles generated by the shocked model with those described by the NBER was seen by the Adelmans as "quite a stringent test of the validity of the model" (612).

The striking result was that when random shocks of a "realistic order of magnitude" (620) are superimposed on the Klein-Goldberger equations, the resulting cyclical fluctuations are remarkably similar to those described by the NBER as characterizing the U.S. economy:

> The average duration of a cycle, the mean length of the expansion and contraction phases, and the degree of clustering of individual peaks and troughs around reference dates all agree with the corresponding data for the United States economy. Furthermore, the lead-lag relations of the endogenous variables included in the model and the indices of conformity of the specific series to the overall business cycle also resemble closely the analogous features of our society. (Adelman and Adelman 1959, 620)

So, they concluded that "it is not unreasonable to suggest that the gross characteristics of the interactions among the real variables described in the Klein-Goldberger equations may represent good approximations to the behavioral relationships in a practical economy" (620).

To Robert Lucas this achievement of the Adelmans signaled a new standard of testing models (Lucas 1977, 11). However, Lucas paraphrased the above question as follows:

> The Adelmans posed, in a precise way, the question of whether an observer armed with the methods of Burns and Mitchell (1946) could distinguish between a collection of economic series generated artificially by a computer programmed to follow the Klein-Goldberger equations and the analogous series generated by an actual economy. (11)

This paraphrasing is important because the characteristics test of the Adelmans is thereby reinterpreted as a Turing test.

Alan Turing was a British mathematician. Among his many accomplishments was basic research in computing science. In 1950, in the article "Computing Machinery and Intelligence," which appeared in the philosophical journal *Mind*, Turing asked the question, "Can machines think?" Turing didn't answer this question directly but replaced it by another:

> The new form of the problem can be described in terms of a game which we call the "imitation game." It is played with three people, a man (A), a woman (B), and an interrogator (C) who may be of either sex. The interrogator stays in a room apart from the other two. The object of the game for the interrogator is to determine which of the other two is the man and which is the woman. . . . The interrogator is allowed to put questions to A and B. . . . The ideal arrangement is to have a teleprinter communicating between the two rooms. . . . We now ask the question, "What will happen when a machine takes the part of A in this game?" Will the interrogator decide wrongly as often when the game is played like this as he does when the game is played between a man and a woman? These questions replace our original, "Can machines think?" (433–34)

As one can see, the test is in principle the same: an observer (interrogator) has to decide whether a distinction can be made between a computer output or something from the "real" world. However, the experiment has to be designed so that the test output really can distinguish between the two.

Kim, De Marchi, and Morgan (1995) identify four notions of testing in the econometric literature and criticize the last one, characteristics testing. Characteristics testing is matching the presence of certain rather specific characteristics in an empirical model with features of selected data sets (82). Their main criticism is that inference from characteristics tests normally cannot feed back to confirm the empirical model when the particular characteristics tested for are not unique or essential to the empirical model. Several different empirical models may result in the same characteristics in the data, and it may not always be clear what is an essential characteristic. Characteristics tests do not capture the essential characteristics that would enable discrimination.

The cases discussed in their essay are the natural rate hypothesis tests of the 1970s that had been carried out by Lucas, Sargent, and Barro;

in these cases, the characteristics tests failed to work to provide reverse inference. However, in each case the theory was reduced to a simple test relation or single-data characteristics. In my view, this element was one main reason that the characteristics test failed to provide reverse inference. The Adelman-Adelman test was "quite a stringent test" of the validity of the Klein-Goldberger model because the number of matched characteristics was pretty large and the test did go beyond the comparison of cycle lengths and amplitudes. Some years after his NRH tests, in his 1977 essay and in his account of these business-cycle papers (1981), Lucas realized that the facts that require explanation should be more detailed in their characteristics:

> Naturally, my earlier papers recognized to some extent which qualitative facts, because of their central importance, required explanation; but for the most part these were second-hand facts for me, picked up from Phelps or Allan Meltzer or "common knowledge" around Chicago and Carnegie-Mellon. I was beginning to be concerned that the particular theoretical line I was following might be focused on explaining "coffee-break" facts only. (Lucas 1981, 16)

Another reason for the failure of characteristics testing in the NRH examples is that the model as a whole is judged. If the models could be partitioned into submodels in such a way that each submodel responsible for a particular characteristic can be located, reverse inference would be possible. This is not the case with Lucas's models. But the issue is clearly related to how complexity is dealt with.

4. Lucas and Simon

To Robert Lucas this achievement of the Adelmans also signaled a new standard for what it means to understand business cycles (see also the quotation at the beginning of this article): "One exhibits understanding of business cycles by constructing a *model* in the most literal sense: a fully articulated artificial economy which behaves through time so as to imitate closely the times series behavior of actual economics" (1977, 11). However, in Lucas's view, the ability of models to imitate actual behavior in the way tested by the Adelmans is a necessary but not a sufficient condition to use these kind of major econometric models for policy evaluation: "simulations using these models can, in principle, provide *no* useful information as to the actual consequences of alternative economic policies (1976, 20). The underlying idea, known as the Lucas Critique, is that parameters may change when policy changes (Lucas 1976). The only parameters Lucas "hopes" to be invariant under policy changes are the parameters describing tastes and technology (Lucas 1981, 11–12; 1977, 12). This is reason enough for Lucas to start from equilibrium models: "An equilibrium model is, by definition, constructed so as to predict how agents with stable tastes and technology will *choose* to respond to a new situation" (Lucas 1977, 12). Although no such equilibrium model had been developed at that time which could pass the Adelmans' test, Lucas expected that "success in this sense is five, but not twenty-five years off" (25).

To answer the question, Why is Milton Friedman not a rational expectationist?, Kevin Hoover (1988) shows that Friedman differs from the new classicals on a fundamental point of methodology. Both agree that at root the economy is a complex interdependent system. In the face of its consequential Cournot problem, Friedman is a pessimist; he believes that only the Marshallian method of partitioning the problem produces fruitful results. In contrast, the new classicals are optimists; they believe that a Walrasian program of fully specifying the optimization problem which agents face is a real possibility (Hoover 1988, 224).

Lucas's optimism is based on a mixture of his expectations of future technological developments and his conception of economic theory:

> A "theory" is not a collection of assertions about the behavior of the actual economy but rather an explicit set of instructions for building a parallel or analogue system—a mechanical, imitation economy. A "good" model, from this point of view, will not be exactly more "real" than a poor one, but will provide better imitations. Of course, what one means by a "better imitation" will depend on the particular questions to which one wishes answers. (1980, 697)

As a result, Lucas expects developments in business-cycle theory to arise from "forces" outside economics, consisting of "purely technical developments that enlarge our abilities to construct analogue economies": improvements in mathematical methods and improvements in computational capacity (697).

Lucas's advocacy of "superficiality" in economic theory rested on Herbert Simon's 1969 publication, *The Sciences of the Artificial*. In a footnote to the above statement, he mentions this book as its "immediate ancestor." Also on other occasions when dealing with the idea of superficiality: "I think it is exactly this superficiality that gives economics much of the power that it has: its ability to predict human behavior without knowing very much about the makeup and the lives of the people whose behavior we are trying to understand" (Lucas 1986, 425; see also Klamer 1984, 47). Lucas refers to Simon (1969). In following up this reference, Hoover (1995) shows that Simon (1969) provided the materials from which to construct a methodological foundation for calibration (the choice of the model parameters to guarantee that the model precisely mimics some characteristics; see Hoover 1995, 25), of which Lucas is an articulate advocate.

The roles are reversed in underlining the need for empirical inquiry at the micro level. Then it is Simon's turn to refer to Lucas (1980): "Support for this thesis comes from surprising directions" (Simon 1984, 40), referring to Lucas's statement:

> Our task as I see it . . . is to write a FORTRAN program that will accept specific economic policy rules as "input" and will generate as "output" statistics describing the operating characteristics of time series we care about, which are predicted to result from these policies. . . . The central idea is that *individual* responses can be documented relatively cheaply, occasionally by direct experimentation, but more commonly by means of the vast number of well-documented instances of individual reactions to well-specified environmental changes made available "naturally" via censuses, panels, other surveys, and the (inappropriately maligned as "casual empiricism") method of keeping one's eye open. Without such means of documenting patterns of behavior, it seems clear that the FORTRAN program proposed above cannot be written. (Lucas 1980, 709–10)

It is interesting to see that Lucas's more recent definition of a model given in his "On the Mechanics of Economic Development" (1988) refers to a special class of models called "artificial worlds": "This is what I mean by the 'mechanics' of economic development—the construction of a mechanical, artificial world, populated by the interacting robots that economics typically studies, that is capable of exhibiting behavior the gross features of which resemble those of the actual world that I have just described" (Lucas 1988, 5). Artificial worlds (AWs) are computer-implementable stochastic models, which consist of a set of "microlevel entities" that interact with each other and an "environment" in prescribed ways. AWs are designed to give insight into processes of emergent organization (see Lane 1993). In his survey, Lane provides an example of an artificial economy. An artificial economy is an artificial world whose microentities represent economic agents and products. Interactions between these microentities model fundamental economic activities—production, exchange, and consumption. The purpose of an artificial economy experiment is to discover what kinds of structured economic regimes can occur and to see how they depend on system parameters and the characteristics of the constituent agents. For example, one of the problems of a general equilibrium model is the problem of coordination: Where does this order come from? While general equilibrium modelers start by assuming a Walrasian equilibrium, the designer of an artificial economy is first of all concerned to model how economic agents interact. Whether a Walrasian equilibrium will emerge depends on the system parameters and the agent's characteristics. Another example is Nicolaas J. Vriend's 1995 essay, of which the main objective was "to present an example of a computational approach to address the following question: How do self-organized markets emerge in the economy, and what are their characteristics?" (205).

To everyone who knows the works of Simon and Lucas, the differences in their works are more striking than the agreements. Lucas is a general equilibrium modeler who solved the Cournot problem by adopting the representative-agent model, in which one agent or a few types of agents, stand in for the behavior of all (Hoover 1995, 39). Even the paper from which the above quotation on artificial worlds is taken contains three models, which are, in fact, representative-agent models. Therefore it is very interesting to learn from Hoover that Lucas's *advocated* methodology leans on Simon's. An obvious labeling of this paradox is that Lucas's work is an example of methodological schizophrenia, in which methodological pronouncements and practice contradict one another (Hausman 1992; see, for another example, Cohen 1995). Whereas Lucas bypasses the Cournot problem with his representative-agent model, Simon has explicitly dealt with complexity. The procedure of Simon (1969) to consider systems as hierarchic, thus facilitating the investigation of complex systems, is the point of departure of much research dealing with complexity. For example, David Lane's artificial worlds are designed to study hierarchic systems in particular (1993, 90).

One way of dealing with this problem is to solve it with the concept of a "representative agent," as Lucas does. An alternative is to use artificial intelligence techniques to build computer simulations—the so-called computational approach.

5. The AI Approach to Complexity

To avoid discussions about the correct naming of the techniques and methodology discussed here—the candidates are artificial intelligence, artificial life, sciences of the artificial, and others—the original name is chosen: artificial intelligence. Artificial intelligence can briefly be characterized as the discipline that tries to gain an understanding of systems of such complexity (like the mind) that we can't expect mathematics to do the whole job. The relevant point is the following: "Given a certain model with a certain parameterization, can one reason, i.e. without running a simulation, *which* functions of the parameterization the outcomes are?" (Vriend 1995, 212n). If not, computer simulations are appropriate.

> My own hunch is that the tools . . . —the approach to philosophical questions by writing computer programs, seeing how the computers then behave, analyzing the structures of the programs—is going to be particularly useful in gaining an understanding of complex or ultracomplex systems. This is not really a radical hypothesis. In almost every field of science today scientists are finding that they can get very useful, if not always elegant, answers from computers to a wide range of questions where they can't solve the equations in closed form. As a result, we find a proliferation today of scientific analysis by computer simulation. (Simon 1990,[2] 59)

Typical of the AI method is the top-down approach to deal with complexity. John von Neumann's essay "The General and Logical Theory of Automata" is paradigmatic to this approach. He introduces what he calls the "axiomatic procedure":

> The natural systems are of enormous complexity, and it is clearly necessary to subdivide the problem that they represent into several parts. One method of subdivision, which is particularly significant in the present context, is this: The organisms can be viewed as made up of parts which to a certain extent are independent, elementary units. We may, therefore, to this extent, view as the first part of the problem the structure and functioning of such elementary units individually. The second part of the problem consists of understanding how these

2. In the fall of 1985 Carnegie Mellon University established a department of philosophy. To mark the inauguration of the department, a daylong celebration was held. In his contribution "Progress in Philosophy," Simon emphasized the powerful approach computers offer us to complex philosophical problems.

> elements are organized into a whole, and how the functioning of the whole is expressed in terms of these elements. (von Neumann [1951] 1963, 289).

The first part of the problem belonging to the relating discipline, in this case physiology, could be removed by the "process of axiomatization":

> We assume that the elements have certain well-defined, outside, functional characteristics; that is, they are to be treated as "black boxes." They are viewed as automatisms, the inner structure of which need not to be disclosed, but which are assumed to react to certain unambiguously defined stimuli, by certain unambiguously defined responses. (209)

The last chapter in Simon's 1969 book was entitled "The Architecture of Complexity"; it was an elaboration of von Neumann's paradigmatic axiomatic procedure. The central thesis was that complex systems frequently take the form of hierarchic systems (Simon 1969, 87). A hierarchic system is composed of interrelated subsystems, each of the latter being, in turn, hierarchic in structure until we reach some lowest level of elementary subsystem (87). There is some arbitrariness, depending on the researcher's interest, as to where the partitioning is left off and what subsystems are taken as elementary. A system is decomposable when the subsystems are independent of each other. Decomposable systems are much easier to investigate, but complex systems are by definition not decomposable. For the description and comprehension of complex systems, however, it is useful to approximate hierarchic systems by near-decomposable systems. Near-decomposable systems are systems in which the interactions among the subsystems are weak but not negligible.

The contributions of Simon are extremely vast and diverse, ranging from the philosophy and methodology of science; through applied mathematics; through various aspects of economics, computer science, management science, political science, and cognitive psychology; to the study of human problem-solving behavior. Reviewing Simon's contributions to economics, Ando formulates a theme that runs consistently throughout Simon's writings: "To construct a comprehensive framework for modelling and analyzing the behavior of man and his organizations faced with a complex environment, recognizing the limitation of his ability to comprehend, describe, analyze and to act, while allowing for his ability to learn and to adopt" (1979, 83). One of the research areas was therefore to find a description of that complex environment so that it is both comprehensible and manageable for decision makers. Very early in his career Simon already found that the description of a very complex system can be simplified by dividing it into a number of subsystems in such a way that each subsystem can be analyzed independently of one another—in other words, to describe them as hierarchic. This strategy can be found in several of Simon's articles that deal with complexity. Ando refers to two economic contributions, which are discussed below; first, one example from outside economics is treated because of the explicitness of its top-down approach.

5.1. Information Processing Language V

In late 1954, Simon and Allen Newell[3] began a collaboration with J. Cliff Shaw in research on complex information processing with computers. The initial goal was to develop a computer program that could learn to play chess; this target was displaced by the interim goal of writing a program that could prove theorems in the propositional calculus of *Principia Mathematica*. To achieve these goals, Simon and Newell decided it was essential to devise a programming language capable of handling large, complex symbol structures whose size and configuration would be extremely difficult to predict in advance and would have to be modified during run time. Their solution was to organize memory in terms of list structures and to construct a language designed to operate on lists. By the end of 1955, the first list-processing language, IPL-II, had taken shape. IPL-V was developed for the IBM 650 and was provided with a manual (first edition 1961); this became the first list-processing language to be made available for public use. Subsequently, IPL-V was brought up on a substantial number of other computers and continued for a decade to be an important language, both for research in AI and cognitive science and for teaching the basic concepts of list processing.

The IPL-V manual is quite explicit in its advocacy of top-down programming and independent closed subroutines:

> One programming strategy, often called the "top-down" approach, is to divide each large process, no matter how complicated, into a small

3. This subsection is drawn from an account of the development of IPL-V given by the originators themselves (Simon and Newell 1985). For a more eleborate account, see Simon 1991, ch. 13, pp. 198–214.

> number of subprocesses. Each of these subroutines is given a name, and its function—the processing it accomplishes—is defined precisely by specifying exactly what inputs it requires and what outputs it produces. How the subprocess will carry on this processing does not matter at this stage. . . .
>
> Once any process is coded, attention can be directed to developing and coding each of its subprocesses, using exactly the same strategy of decomposing these into subprocesses. Ultimately, subprocesses are reached that can be defined directly in terms of the IPL primitive processes, so that the decomposition comes to a stop. Although apparently at each stage all the complexities are being relegated to the subprocesses and only codes for trivial processes are being written, it will be found at last that nothing complicated remains to be done at the bottom of the hierarchy. . . .
>
> Another principle may be called the principle of isolation. The flexibility in hierarchical organization depends on each subroutine being isolated from the rest of the program, except for a small number of well-defined connections. (Simon and Newell 1986, 49)

5.2. Causal Ordering

A more implicit application of the top-down approach can be found in Simon's (1953) "Causal Ordering and Identifiability," an article written for the Cowles Foundation. The context of this essay was a debate between the Cowles Commission, as proponent of simultaneous equations models, and Herman Wold as proponent of recursive chain models.[4] One of the issues in the debate was causality and its representation and interpretation in economic models. Although the Cowles Commission group mainly ignored the issue, it was taken seriously and discussed in greater depth by Simon (1953). While Simon and Wold disagreed on certain notions about causal systems—asymmetries and relationships versus time sequences and variables—they came closer to each other with respect to the need for causal chain system models: "In order to know how a policy change would affect the equations in the structure, it is necessary to know the causal ordering" (Morgan 1991, 249).

The aim of the article was to provide "a clear and rigorous basis for determining when a causal ordering can be said to hold between two variables or groups of variables in a model" (Simon 1953, 51). The

4. For a more comprehensive discussion of this debate, see Morgan 1991.

discussion was limited to systems of linear equations without random disturbances. To introduce the notion of causal ordering, it appeared to be essential that the structure is complete ("self-contained" in Simon's terminology). A linear structure is complete when the number of variables in the structure equals the number of structural equations.

The first step was to show that a complete linear structure can be decomposed into a sum of distinct "minimal" complete subsets and a remainder. Minimal subsets were defined as complete subsets of a linear structure that do not themselves contain complete (proper) subsets. When there are one or more minimal complete proper subsets of the structure and the remainder is not null, the structure is said to be "causally ordered." The next step was to repeat the partitioning as follows. The equations of the minimal subsets are solved and substituted in the equations of the remainder. The result is again a complete structure, called the "derived structure of first order." When this structure is also causally ordered, the process can be repeated. The derived structure is of second order. Et cetera. Finally the point will be reached that the remainder of the nth decomposition is null. The result of this process is a complete ordering of disjunct subsets of the equations of the original structure. A consequence of this ordering is that each variable appears as an endogenous variable in one and only one complete subset, and that it appears in a structure of higher order as an exogenous variable. Thus, there exists a one-to-one correspondence between the minimal subsets of equations and the subsets of variables that occur as endogenous variables in these equations. From this, Simon defined a causal ordering of the sets of variables endogenous to the corresponding complete subsets of equations:

> Let β designate the set of variables endogenous to a complete subset B, and let γ designate the set endogenous to a complete subset C. Then the variables of γ are *directly causally dependent* on the variable of $\beta(\beta \rightarrow \gamma)$ if at least one member of β appears as an exogenous variable in C. (Simon 1953, 57)

The second part of Simon's article was to show how the concept of causal ordering was connected with the concept of identifiability, which lies beyond the scope here. More relevant to the discussion of the top-down approach in Simon's work is that the preceding definition of causal ordering is based on a particular partitioning of a system into subsystems and that causal ordering is a special chain of asymmetrical connections between these subsystems.

By interpreting the Lucas Critique as a late variation on the theme of identification and causality, Simon (1953) can, according to Hoover (1995, 191), be considered one of the precursors of Lucas. By defining "causality" in terms of controllability and therefore as invariance under interventions of control, one can see that Simon puts it in exactly such words:

> We found that we could provide the [causal] ordering with an operational basis if we could associate with each equation of a structure a specific power of intervention, or "direct control." That is, any such intervention would alter the structure but leave the model (and hence the causal ordering) invariant. Hence causal ordering is a property of models that is invariant with respect to interventions within the model. (Simon 1953, 66)

5.3. Aggregation of Variables

The third and last example of Simon's approach to complexity is also a partitioning of a linear equation system, now represented by matrices, to discuss the links among the parts. The aim of his 1961 essay, jointly written with Albert Ando, "Aggregation of Variables in Dynamic Systems," was "to determine conditions that if satisfied by a (linear) dynamic system, will permit approximate aggregation of variables" (114). This discussion of aggregation was actuated by the disappointing facilities of computer capacities.

> It was hoped at first, perhaps, that modern computers would handle matrices of about any desired size, and hence would obviate the need for aggregation. By now it is clear that our ambitions have outstripped the computers, for the time required to invert a matrix by known methods increases with the cube of the number of rows and columns. The high cost of inverting large matrices has led to a number of experiments to determine whether aggregation can be used to obtain approximate inverses more economically. (Simon and Ando 1961, 112)

It appeared that in "nearly decomposable" systems aggregation can be performed. The notion of near decomposability was clarified by the definition of a decomposable matrix. When a matrix can be arranged in the following form,

$$P^* = \begin{Vmatrix} P_1^* & & \\ & \cdot P_i^* & \\ & & \cdot P_n^* \end{Vmatrix}$$

where the P_i^*'s are square submatrices and the remaining elements, not displayed, are all zero, then the matrix is said to be completely decomposable. A nearly decomposable matrix is the slightly altered matrix P: $P = P^* + \varepsilon C$, where ε is a very small real number, and C is an arbitrary matrix of the same dimension as P^*.

With the aid of both definitions, the dynamic behavior of the following systems was investigated: $x(t+1) = x(t)P$ and $x^*(t+1) = x^*(t)P^*$. To present Simon's result, the following notations for the vector $x(t)$ on which P operates, and the vector $x^*(t)$ on which P^* operates, should be adopted: $x(t) = \{x_1(t), \ldots, x_i(t), \ldots, x_n(t)\}$ and $x^*(t) = \{x_1^*(t), \ldots, x_i^*(t), \ldots, x_n^*(t)\}$ where $x_i(t)$ and $x_i^*(t)$ are row vectors of a subset of components of $x(t)$ and $x^*(t)$, respectively.

The results were the following:

1. In the short run, the behavior of $x_i(t)$ will be dominated by roots belonging to P_i, so that the time path of $x_i(t)$ will be very close to the time path of $x_i^*(t)$ and almost independent of $x_j(t)$ and P_j. "If we are interested in the behavior of the system at this stage, we can treat the system as though it were completely decomposable" (116).
2. Unlike P^*, P is not completely decomposable, so that weak links among the subsystems will eventually make their influence felt. But the time required for these influences to appear is long enough so that when they do become visible, within each subsystem the largest root will have dominated all other roots. Thus, at this stage, the variables within each subset, $x_i(t)$, will move proportionally, and the behavior of the whole system will be dominated by largest roots of each subsystem.
3. At the end, however, the behavior of $x(t)$ will be dominated by the largest root of P, as in any linear dynamic system (116–17).

Since the variables in each subsystem, after a while, move roughly proportionately according to no. 2, they may be aggregated into a single variable.

The main theoretical findings of the analysis of the structure of dynamic systems represented by nearly decomposable matrices were summed up in two propositions, which were also mentioned in slightly more general terms in the last chapter of Simon's *Sciences of the Artificial*: "(a) in a nearly decomposable system, the short-run behavior of each of the component subsystems is approximately independent of the short-run behavior of the other components; (b) in the long run, the behavior of any one of the components depends in only an aggregate way on the behavior of the other components" (1969, 100). By considering a complex system as nearly decomposable, the description of the system can be simplified: only aggregative properties of its parts enter into the description of the interactions of those parts (110).

6. Conclusion

I have shown here that Lucas mainly adopts the AI test methodology without applying its approach to complexity. The AI approach to complexity is a top-down decomposition of the complex system till a certain level is reached, on which the subsystems are treated as black boxes, and of which the input-output relation is well-defined. The purpose of AI simulation is to discover what kind of organization will emerge and how it depends on the input-output specifications.

The point is to find an adequate partitioning and the choice of the elementary systems that can be treated as black boxes. When models are only meant to be forecasting devices, it is possible to consider the whole economy as a black box and to use naive models that contain only a set of rules of thumb. An example is Harvey's (controversial) term-structure model (1991) to forecast economic growth. In this context, Lucas's representative-agent model can also be considered a black box. The heuristic of his model consists of a simple optimization algorithm with respect to macroeconomic aggregates. When partitioning is carried out further, one comes closer to the Marshallian method of partitioning the Cournot problem. One example, of course, is the Friedman-Marshallian distinction between the long run and the short run: "The essence of much of Friedman's work is that much may be known about the long run, yet little about the short run" (Hoover, 1988, 226). Another nice example is Tinbergen's use of the adiabatic method: sufficient slowly (adiabatically) changing parameters are replaced by constants to facilitate the analysis of a complex system (Boumans 1993, 132–33).

To use macroeconometric models for policy evaluation, one has to know the properties of the model that are invariant under policy changes. Because Lucas and Simon differ in belief where the invariance of the model is located, they differ in methodology of model building. According to Lucas, the model invariance is located on the level of the parameters describing tastes and technology, and equilibrium models are—by definition—constructed to predict outcomes of interventions. So, Lucas was not interested in the coordination problem—namely, how equilibrium depends on system parameters and the agent's characteristics; he just assumed equilibrium. Thus, it was no problem to bypass the problem of interactions between microentities with his representative-agent model. As we have seen, Simon located the model invariance on the level of the causal ordering. The causal ordering of the model was uncovered by a specific method of partitioning.

References

Adelman, Irma, and Frank Adelman. 1959. The Dynamic Properties of the Klein-Goldberger Model. *Econometrica* 27:596–625.

Ando, Albert. 1979. On the Contributions of Herbert A. Simon to Economics. *Scandinavian Journal of Economics* 21:81–114.

Annals of the History of Computing, special issue. 1986. *IBM 650: IBM Expands the Computing World*, edited by Cuthbert C. Hurd.

Boumans Marcel. 1993. Paul Ehrenfest and Jan Tinbergen: A Case of Limited Physics Transfer. In *Non-Natural Social Science*, edited by Neil De Marchi. Durham and London: Duke University Press.

Burns, A. F., and W. C. Mitchell. 1946. Measuring Business Cycles. New York: National Bureau of Economic Research.

Christ, Carl F. 1951. A Test of an Econometric Model for the United States, 1921–1947. In *Conference on Business Cycles*. New York: National Bureau of Economic Research.

———. 1966. *Econometric Models and Methods*. New York: Wiley.

Cohen, Joshua. 1995. Samuelson's Operationalist-Decriptivist Thesis. *Journal of Economic Methodology* 2:53–78.

Cornwall, John. 1958. Economic Implications of the Klein and Goldberger Model (Abstract). *Econometrica* 26:621.

Cournot, Augustin. [1838] 1971. *Researches into the Mathematical Principles of the Theory of Wealth*. Translated by N. T. Bacon. New York: Augustus M. Kelley.

De Marchi, Neil, and Christopher Gilbert. 1989. *History and Methodology of Econometrics*. Oxford: Clarendon.

Friedman, Milton. 1951. Comment [on Christ 1951]. In *Conference on Business Cycles*. New York: National Bureau of Economic Research.

Goldberger, Arthur S. 1958. Properties of an Econometric Model of the United States (Abstract). *Econometrica* 26:620.

Harvey, Campbell R. 1991. The Term Structure and World Economic Growth. *Journal of Fixed Income* 1:7–19.

Hausman, Daniel M. 1992. *The Inexact and Separate Science of Economics*. Cambridge: Cambridge University Press.

Hoover, Kevin D. 1988. *The New Classical Macroeconomics: A Sceptical Inquiry*. Oxford: Basil Blackwell.

———. 1995. Facts and Artifacts: Calibration and the Empirical Assessment of Real-Business-Cycle Models. *Oxford Economic Papers* 47:24–44.

Kim, Jinbang, Neil De Marchi, and Mary S. Morgan. 1995. Empirical Model Particularities and Belief in the Natural Rate Hypothesis. *Journal of Econometrics* 67:81–102.

Klamer, Arjo. 1984. *The New Classical Macroeconomics*. Brighton, Sussex: Harvester.

Klein, L. R., and A. S. Goldberger. 1955. *An Econometric Model of the United States, 1929–1952*. Amsterdam: North-Holland.

Lane, David A. 1993. Artificial Worlds and Economics. *Journal of Evolutionary Economics* 3:89–107, 177-97.

Littauer, S. B. 1950. Report of the New York Meeting of the Institute. *Annals of Mathematical Statistics* 21:151–55.

Lucas, Robert E. 1976. Econometric Policy Evaluation: A Critique. In *The Phillips Curve and Labor Markets*, edited by Karl Brunner and Allan Meltzer. Amsterdam: North-Holland.

———. 1977. Understanding Business Cycles. In *Stabilization of the Domestic and International Economy*, edited by Karl Brunner and Allan Meltzer. Amsterdam: North-Holland.

———. 1980. Methods and Problems in Business Cycle Theory. *Journal of Money, Credit, and Banking* 12.4:696–715.

———. 1981. *Studies in Business-Cycle Theory*. Oxford: Basil Blackwell.

———. 1986. Adaptive Behavior and Economic Theory. *Journal of Business* 59.4:401–26.

———. 1988. On the Mechanics of Economic Development. *Journal of Monetary Economics* 22:3–42.

Marshall, Andrew W. 1950a. A Test of Klein's Model III for Changes of Structure (Abstract). *Annals of Mathematical Statistics* 21:141.

———. 1950b. A Test of Klein's Model III for Changes of Structure (Abstract). *Econometrica* 18:291.

Morgan, Mary S. 1990. *The History of Econometric Ideas*. Cambridge: Cambridge University Press.

———. 1991. The Stamping Out of Process Analysis in Econometrics. In *Appraising Economic Theories: Studies in the Methodology of Research Programs*, edited by N. De Marchi and M. Blaug, Aldershot: Edward Elgar.

Qin, Duo. 1993. *The Formation of Econometrics: A Historical Perspective*. Oxford: Clarendon.

Report of the New York Meeting. 1950. (Meeting held December 21–30, 1949.) *Econometrica* 18:264–67.

Simon, Herbert A. 1953. Causal Ordering and Identifiability. *Studies in Econometric*

Method, edited by W. C. Hood and T. C. Koopmans. Cowles Foundation Monograph 14. New Haven and London: Yale Unviersity Press.
———. 1969. *The Sciences of the Artificial*. Cambridge: MIT Press.
———. 1984. On the Behavioral and Rational Foundations of Economic Dynamics. *Journal of Economic Behavior and Organization* 5.1:35–55.
———. 1990. Progress in Philosophy. In *Acting and Reflecting: The Interdisciplinary Turn in Philosophy*, edited by Wilfried Sieg. Dordrect: Kluwer.
———. 1991. *Models of My Life*. New York: Basic.
Simon, H., and Albert Ando. 1961. Aggregation of Variables in Dynamic Systems. *Econometrica* 29:111–37.
Simon, H., and A. Newell. 1986. Information Processing Language V on the IBM 650. In *Annals of the History of Computing*.
Tinbergen, Jan. 1939. *Statistical Testing of Business Cycle Theories*. Geneva: League of Nations.
Turing, Alan M. 1950. Computing Machinery and Intelligence. *Mind* 59:433–60.
von Neumann, John. [1951] 1963. The General and Logical Theory of Automata. In vol. 5 of John von Neumann: Collected Works, edited by A. H. Taub. 6 vols. Oxford: Pergamon.
Vriend, Nicolaas J. 1995. Self-Organization of Markets: An Example of a Computational Approach. *Computational Economics* 8:205–31.

Part 2

Fields and Subdisciplines

A Historical Perspective on the Common Methodological Heritage of Contemporary Law, Economics, and Organizational Theory

S. Todd Lowry

1. Jurisprudential Methodological Process and Economic Theory: The Rational Process Enshrined

Conceptual Background

One of the most effective ways to discuss an extended and amorphous body of interdisciplinary material is to retreat to a point where one can see the various presumptions and approaches in terms of common methodological perspectives. In this study, we focus our primary attention on the concept of rationality and on process.

The current discussions that go under this name date from the late 1950s with the founding of the *Journal of Law and Economics* at the University of Chicago. The interdisciplinary term and concept, however, predated this apparent nascence by several decades. It was previously directed primarily toward policy and analysis of problems in government regulation of business (Samuels 1993). The conceptual and methodological issues associated with the neoclassical economic orientation of this post 1960s economic interest and with classical jurisprudence, however, are traceable into the distant past.

Although a comparative legal and economic methodological approach may involve some analytical gymanstics, it offers the possibility of a functional overview of important characteristics and parallelisms between jurisprudential and economic concepts. In a very real sense, the movement over the past several decades by some legal scholars to embrace the insights put forward by neoclassical economists, practitioners of the *hardest* of the social sciences, is the reverse of the previous movement of institutional economists and legal realists to embrace regulation and legislative dynamics (Samuels 1993). The new subdiscipline can be characterized by its apparent desire to provide a generalizing method that would give coherence and consistency to the treatment of complex modern legal problems. The appeal of a formal social science dedicated to reducing all production and exchange processes to a common abstraction emphasizing rational efficiency cannot be underestimated.

One of the appeals of modern economics has been its alleged standing as a value-free science. According to this view, given a body of factual and institutional premises and value limitations, the economist can prescribe, in a microeconomic mode, a program for rationally achieving optimum efficiency for any given end. In this mode the economist claims the same rational purity as the mathematician or engineer. This appeal, however, does not easily translate into the search for a justice-free or justice-transcending jurisprudence. To the extent that *justice* as a legal end corresponds to the maximization of economic welfare with certain *values implicit in the economic process*, law and economics can be methodologically correlated. However, since rationality is the classical operative concept in both of these formulations, two critical distinctions must be made. First, we must keep track of the protean concept of *rationality* that can refer to an operational process participated in by individuals—be they judges or traders—on the one hand, and *rationality* as an existing potential or vision toward which we strive, on the other. Second, we must be conscious of the varying concepts of *rationality* as a human or social creation, on the one hand, and *rationality* as an extant natural phenomenon, on the other.

The emphasis on rationality has a parallel role in economic and legal thought, including the two procedural and substantive ambiguities raised here. Whether based on mathematics or on rigorous logic, rationality in neoclassical economics coincides with a legal tradition that justice is coterminous with or at least consistent with rationality. If we begin with this commonality, we can, perhaps, better abstract and compare the various legal approaches to economics, and vice-versa.

In the Beginning: A "Brooding Omnipresence in the Sky"

At the threshold of the current law and economics movement, Roscoe Pound, an eminent legal philosopher, pinpointed the beginning of legal philosophy with the Roman jurisconsults. As he recognized, the Greeks had worked out some general principles of law to be applied on a case by case basis. The Roman jurists, however, were faced with the challenge of "satisfying the wants of a whole world while . . . insuring uniformity and predictability" (Pound [1922] 1954, 11). This juridical philosophy, as Pound interpreted it—unconsciously paraphrasing Platonism—was the belief that the universe, including human society, was a seamless web of "forms," or "ideal types," that represented the potential perfection of being. Earthly processes properly strove for replication of these forms, and the human decision-making processes that could give insight into these proper forms were rationality and mathematics. As Pound put it, "The technique was one of legal reason; . . . identified with natural reason and worked out and applied under the influence of a philosophical ideal" (11). Developed with maxims and broad principles, this juridical system "was a process very like that by which Anglo-American judicial empiricism has been able to make a law of the world on the basis of the legal precepts of seventeenth century England" (11). Pointing out that the Greeks had established the principle of law as a protection of the orderly status quo, Pound says, "When the theory of the natural law is applied to that conception, we get the notion of an ideal form of the social *status quo*—a form which expresses its nature, a perfect form of the social organization of a given civilization—as that which the legal order is to further and maintain" (12). Unfortunately, in both law and economics, close attention is seldom given to this fundamental Platonic tradition that rationality and its rigorous formulation, mathematics, have a *real* existence and are to be discovered or approached. The contrasting view that rationality and mathematics are synthetic processes—organizing techniques to correlate and systemize ideas and activities—is frequently followed without comprehending the fundamental ontological dichotomy. For example, in economics, the question is whether the rational market is the result of the human capacity, under certain conditions, to implement reasonably consistent exchanges within the confines of culturally accepted bounds, or a necessary expression of natural material realities and human nature. In the latter case, market-type processes are inherent in all cultures and at all times in human history. Such issues are dealt with in economic anthropology and in the Polanyi literature.

In jurisprudence, the naturalistic tradition takes its modern form as the idea that we should recognize a government of law, not of men. This implies that the courts should be drawing on some immutable reference base that they discern through rationality and apply to the problems before them. The Platonic imagery in this tradition is caught and challenged by Justice Oliver Wendell Holmes Jr.'s observation "that the Common Law is not a brooding omnipresence in the sky and that the U.S. is not subject to some mystic overlaw that it is bound to obey" ([1926] 1953, 822–23). This basic tension is reflected in the principle that, on the one hand, the courts should draw their "core of authority" from the political sector or from the legislature and, on the other hand, that the constitution carries some inviolable authority derived from some omnipresence or "original position" (Halper 1993).

Rational Objectivism and Rational Equilibrium in Law and Economics

We can recognize the Platonist echoes in Pound's image of the Roman law and its American Common Law parallels—the rational objective "brooding omnipresence in the sky" rejected by Holmes. We can also compare it with the parallel image of general equilibrium economics. In this economic formulation, ideally, all forces will move toward a perfect mathematically definable harmony. The visions of an extant rational and perfectible body of law and an implicit equilibrium in the economy are cut from the same Platonic cloth. Putting aside any problems of resolving disparate values or ends, a concept of an implicit rationality or optimum of economic allocation would be possible. However, since a consensus of values and ends is usually expressed as a status quo power structure, a Platonic philosopher king is a common ideal type for human implementation of perfect rationality and wisdom.

Both economists and jurisprudents may consider a perfectible order of forces, interests, or legal rules to be too elusive in practice to be other than an ideal. It is a moving target because of constantly changing social values and technological capacities. Nevertheless, the viability of the image of a rational system guiding a dynamic continuum is just below the surface in the minds of many practitioners. The question is how does rationality actually function as a process in both economics and law?

For Plato, the issue was simple: right reason applied by the superior intellect would most effectively approach or approximate justice, which was defined as both order and efficiency (Lowry 1987, ch. 4). For Plato, justice was the optimum political order; individuals were assigned to their proper roles, which were commensurate with their natural talents, thereby optimizing public welfare. There was only one appropriate end, and the social objective was to rationally optimize its implementation. To many, including Pound, the Roman law with its jurisconsults was a replication of this Platonist ideal defined as natural law. This perspective is also congenial to Pigouvian welfare theory, which was used as the reference base by Ronald Coase in his article "The Problem of Social Cost" (1960). This article was the "eye of the storm" of controversy that stimulated much of the recent discussion in the field of law and economics. The neoclassical economist may assume a rationally efficient adjustment process that can optimize social welfare. Pigou thought the process was flawed in places and required administrative rational intervention. Coase thought the ideal system perfect, but identified frictions—transaction costs—that altered the process and expected outcomes. This concern with *process* cannot be overemphasized. It is here that we can extrapolate the fundamental parallelism between economic analysis and jurisprudence.

The ultimate problem is to disentangle concepts of process from visions or images of ideal states. The analysis of interactive processes that promote desired ends and values is common to both law and economics.

Coase's basic thesis in "The Problem of Social Cost" was that, under ideal conditions, unfettered rational bargaining between individuals would optimize the social efficiency—welfare. By thus nominally democratizing rational decision making, Coase, consistent with neoclassical economic theory, defined a process that optimized social welfare, building from the idealized unit individual. According to Coase, except for transaction costs, individual bargaining could provide the process by which optimum welfare is achieved. The secondary jurisprudential appeal of Coase's theorem was that it obviated the need for ponderous tort actions that were designed to redress grievances based on rights that permitted individuals to obstruct the optimum use of property. This compressed emphasis on the commercial process essentially negates the individual's vested interest in long-term property rights since infringements, according to Coase, should be commercially bought off. This aspect of process is dealt with in more detail below.

The corresponding image in jurisprudence is that litigants or panels of judges contend rationally and build a justice that also corresponds with some optimum omnipresent system. Ultimately, individual rationality outside of some context of process is an empty concept (see Ellickson 1989).

Past Concepts of the Legal and Economic Process

It is a simple truism to say that whatever given individuals do is rational—necessarily consistent with their values as expressed by their voluntary free choices. Jurists and economists, however, must define an objective or a public rationality when dealing with conflicting or incompatible individual interests. An emphasis on the integrity of a process, however, permits such frictions to work themselves out as in markets, legislatures, and appellate courts. In antiquity, the Sophists taught that subjective impressions were the only source of valid information. Discrepancies had to be worked out by rational discourse to achieve consensus. This was the closest one could get to natural law—that is, the law worked out by the citizenry of each community for themselves (see Lowry 1987, chap. 6). Donald R. Kelley, in *The Human Measure: Social Thought in the Western Legal Tradition* (1990), has traced this legal perspective through the Roman law. His work, of course, cuts deeper than the Platonist pattern accepted by many scholars, Pound included.

The braiding together of apparently conflicting views of rationality and intuition into theories of ultimate sources of law and of process is succinctly developed by Peter Stein (1995). Two academic schools of Roman jurisprudence emerged in the early empire. The Proculian school, elaborated by Labeo, promoted the thesis that law was a science and used rigorous rationality and analogy, along with grammar, to enforce the laws and precedents, wills and contracts, according to their wording. While this tradition gave rise to considerable "logic chopping" and pedantry, it applied scientific rigor to the statutory and documentary choices of the populus. Celsus, a Proculian, wrote the definition of law in the *Justinian Digest*: "the science (or technique) of the good and the fair" (D.1.1.1) (Stein 1995, 1554). This formulation permitted the rigorous application of a scientific process or art to a body of socially established rules, giving nominal stability and predictability to the law.

The opposing school's major proponent was Sabinus, who defended historical tradition and accepted inconsistencies in the interest of a case by case concern for justice. Stein concludes that Sabinus was the source of the doctrine of natural reason (*naturalis ratio*) that was an argument for commonsense justice in cases where precedent was absent (D.5.1.28.5; Stein 1995, 1552). Stein points out that "Later Sabinians substituted 'the general convenience' (*utilitas communis*) for nature as a criterion to set against Proculian logic" (1553). Of course, economists cannot ignore this parturition of a *general welfare* criterion.

While the Roman jurists' controversies seem to anticipate modern confrontations between "formalists versus substantivists," or "theoretical economists versus institutionalists," the issue of greater interest is that these debates were over process by practitioners whose responsibility it was to provide the stabilizing fabric for the economy. Stein documents the indirect influence of this Roman law literature on Oliver Wendell Holmes Jr.'s famous statement that "the life of the law has not been logic: it has been experience." Holmes added, "The law . . . cannot be dealt with as if it contained only the axioms and corollaries of a book of mathematics" (Stein 1995, 1556). While these inquiries into Roman law and Holmes's views expressed in his 1881 book, *The Common Law*, bring out the affinity between these ideas and those of the American institutionalist economists, my interest is in the issues of process they raise for the mainstream economist.

In the Judaic literature, "Shikul-Da'at" represents this tradition of "balanced reasoning." A third-century Talmudic account tells of a group of elders who were seeking the truth between two conflicting points of religious law. They rejected the authority of an individual who claimed direct divine insight authenticated by his ability to cause miracles. They contended that rational discourse, and "ROV" (majority rule) and "Rubba" (probability) were the only legitimate sources of truth (Ohrenstein 1996).

This tradition was reinforced by sixteenth- and seventeenth-century Spanish Scholastics with similar conclusions that natural law, as it operates among human beings, is accessible by *recta ratio*, or right reason (Gomez-Camacho 1996, 7, n. 1). This traditional assumption—that there is an objective or natural truth *optimally accessible* by observation, rational analytical discourse, or market bargaining—is subjectivist in orientation. The Spanish thinkers felt that panels of both officials and bargaining merchants could approach rational just price through this interactive process. The objectivist tradition reflected in neoclassical economic thought, however, presumes a perfectible equilibrium price approached through natural forces involving rational economic man and market bargaining—not men trained in rational thought and economic theory.

In the laissez-faire tradition, what do economists do? Is there a process in which they participate that is parallel to the role of the jurist? Jurisprudence laid claim to being a science long before economics did, based on its rigorous, near-mathematical analyses in imposing rules to resolve conflicts among the citizenry. The modern institutional economist has a great deal in common with the jurisprudent, analyzing the economic process in order to recommend appropriate interventionist policies where desired social needs or objectives are not being met by the market bargaining process. The neoclassical formalist actually has no participative role to play, except to serve as an advocate of pure market procedures and to provide rigorous analyses of the optimum outcomes that will result from the bargaining process. In reality, however, most mainstream microeconomists recognize that the complexity of the calculable refinements that will maximize profitability in the economic process is beyond the practical understanding of traditional participants. The academic economist is therefore in the position of training individuals to effectuate the rational and mathematical optima that the discipline teaches are implicit in the bargaining process when left to itself.

Paralleling late-nineteenth-century economics and neoclassicism, and their twentieth-century perpetuations, we find in jurisprudence what is called by Horwitz "classical legal thought" (1992). This perspective is committed to an objectivist theory of law and is approachable by judicial reasoning. It is in the light of this dichotomy and tension between an agnostic methodological individualism rationally constructing just price or laws, on the one hand, and rationally discovering it, on the other, that we can appreciate the ambiguities shared by law and economics.

The operative assumption in classical legal thought is that "core principles" can be abstractly defined and accepted as working truths or just principles through rational analysis. The problem emerges when these core principles have to be rationally extended to cover cases that fall between their clearly defined scope. There tends to be a problem with the "brooding omniscience" of the law when basic proto-natural principles do not quite meet or seem to overlap. These zones of *indeterminacy* between core principles must be worked out by judicial reasoning or deduction, assuming an objective body of law. Otherwise, judges are using reason to "make law" to fill in gaps. A colorful noncommmercial illustration of this rationalization of legal indeterminacy between principles is found in an old Texas case. "A" entered his house and found his wife sitting on "B's" lap—"B," having his hand under her skirt. There is a well-established legal principle that a husband, surprising his wife with a paramour, can kill "in the heat of passion" without being culpable. There is also a well-established principle that a man can kill in self-defense without being culpable. "A" drew his gun and fired at "B." "B," the paramour, drew his gun and fired back at "A," killing him. Was

"B" able to claim self defense since "A" was within his rights in firing at him? Extending the *core* principles into such a *fringe* case is conceived, by classical legal thought as rational analysis, not judicial legislation (Horwitz 1992, 18). The court concluded that this was "imperfect self defense" and that "B" was guilty of a crime. Was this decision the rational elaboration of one of these core principles, or was it the judicial creation of a new law?

Painting with a broad brush, we can say that the "legal realism" (not to be confused with the near contemporary philosophical Realists) that flourished in the 1920s and the current critical legal studies movements tend to argue that the unique aspects and predominance of fringe elements in many cases mean that justice has to be approached on more of a case by case basis. They rely less on a drive toward rational coherence of the law and more on a concern for justice as viewed in a broader social context of values, legal intent, and processes (Altman 1990). The Realists, perhaps, were more inclined to augment justice with institutional considerations and endorsed legislative innovation. They were part of the same social movement as the institutional economists of the first half of this century (Samuels 1993). John R. Commons, the "Old Institutionalist" most relevant in this discussion, had a more systematic view of law and economics than contemporary scholars generally recognize (Gonce 1979). H. H. Liebhafsky—one of the few scholars formally prepared in institutional economics, neoclassical price theory, and law—has made a cogent case (1979) for a clearly articulated law, economics, and industrial organization theory that evolved in the 1920s under the influence of Commons and Clark. Commons's sense of *process*, however, was at the general evolutionary economics level. He dealt with the *transaction* as framed in the context of broader economic forces—efficiency, scarcity, sovereignty, legal and customary rules, and futurity (Liebhafsky 1979). It should be kept in mind, of course, that the old institutionalists were dealing with policy crises in the macroeconomic process where a rapidly expanding industrial economy was characterized by such major market imperfections as to discourage any faith in eventual inherent competitive tendencies leading to self-regulation.

Despite the ideological commitment by the economic mainstream to a natural economic process built up from individual interactions, Bernard Mandeville, one of the patron saints of laissez-faire, had a surprising grasp of the role of law and economics. He spoke of the cumulative development of cultural capacity for social organization and leadership "that can make every Frailty of the Members add Strength to the whole Body, and by dexterous Management turn *private vices into publick benefits*" ([1924] 1988, 319). Drawing on the illustration of the cumulative development of the technological components of the mechanical clock, Mandeville extended it to the legal background for the political economy: "Look into the History and Antiquity of any such city, . . . the Changes, Repeals, Additions and Amendments [388], that have been made in and to its Laws and Ordinances by which it is ruled, are in Number prodigious: But that when once they are brought to as much Perfection, as Art and human Wisdom can carry them, the whole Machine may be made to play of itself, with as little Skill, as is required to wind up a Clock. [With such order,] the Magestrates only following their Noses, will continue to go right" (323).

It is unfortunate, of course, that such a well-articulated insight into the importance of a legal and institutional infrastructure or bureaucracy and of the setting for apparently unregulated activity was ignored during the ideological repudiation of mercantilism. This cannot be said, however, of Adam Smith who, according to Jeffrey T. Young, held a legal-recognition concept of property rights with a remedy for infringements as the foundation of economic activity (Young 1995).

Neoclassicism and the New Institutionalism

We do not wish to lose the theme of the methodological parallelisms between the judicial process dealing with fringe cases that fall between two established principles and the bargaining situation between individuals in isolated exchange or imperfect markets where a recognized going price is not presupposed. In such cases, the indeterminacy in law corresponds to the area in the contract curve in the well-known Edgeworth Box, where an overlap in subjective interests is analyzed in terms appropriate to both economics and contract law (Jaffé 1974; Lowry 1969). It is surprising that the subdiscipline of law and economics has not explored this important area of common interest more extensively.

In neoclassical economic theory, the traditional assumption of rational economic man has permitted the premise of a rationally coherent market process. An economist might give advice to an individual business on maximizing profits, and this is deemed consistent with the equilibrating maximizing trends of the market process, although it is difficult to explain how the business can be currently functioning if it is not already in fairly close affinity with the optimum efficiency level naturally achieved by the market process. When the lawyer advises his client on how to successfully conform to the law, however, he is analyzing how the courts would rationally determine what the law is. If we hold to the objective theory of law as a "brooding omnipresence in the sky," the lawyer is analyzing a natural rational process toward which rational decision-making judges necessarily gravitate. Nevertheless, judges and market participants may fail to achieve dialectical perfection. The more normative approach to law in the neoclassical tradition is succinctly developed by H. H. Liebhafsky in his "Price Theory as Jurisprudence" ([1976] 1993). Liebhafsky confronts Richard Posner's unequivocal insistence on idealized market principles as the appropriate guideline for judicial resolution of civil disputes. After systematic criticism of the economic assumptions of the Chicago School that Posner represents, Liebhafsky contrasts its position with the economic and jurisprudential theory of John R. Commons and brings out the evolutionary dynamic explicit in Commons's view of the Common Law. For Commons, the tradition of judge-made law in a case-oriented setting maximized the process of empirical adaptation of legal rules to changing economic and social realities (Liebhafsky [1976] 1993, 252). What is not very clearly brought out here, however, is that the economist is striving to formulate a general theory from observed data, abstracting from the individual situations. In the legal process, the judiciary deals with individual cases whose nuances must be clarified in terms of their deviation from the generalized image. A feedback loop then emerges, in which the rulings on the individual cases become the reference base for the generalizations that form the law. This perspective does not exist in economics where a presumption of a proto-mathematical system is held.

The "New Institutionalism" has amended the neoclassical analytic tradition by emphasizing special institutional conditions or circumstances that impair market function. They work out an adjusted rationalization of the deviations from competitive equilibrium, the core principle, dealing with the increasing complexity and uniqueness in special economic and legal situations. The old institutionalists, legal realists, and critical legal studies theorists, by contrast, tend to extrapolate their evaluations from the imbalances in competitive power between the parties and the institutional and historic fabric of the economy. Ronald Coase's now classic article "The Nature of the Firm" (1937) is a cornerstone in the new insitutionalism in that it accepts rational market optimization as an omnipresent force while identifying a market failure—vertical integration—as an institutional product of special transaction costs that inhibit market performance.

A convoluted expression of the New Institutionalism is found in current "rent-seeking" analysis in which deviations from a natural free-market process are attributed to external interventions or aberrations. In this digression from market order, primarily caused by governmentally granted monopolies and legal privileges that give rise to artificial opportunities for excess returns—profits or rents—the economy is perverted into a rent-seeking mode. Under truly competitive conditions, economic rents occur during periods of adjustment, but they are not institutionalized objects of enterprise. When entrepreneurs are tempted to vie for rents, they distort the rational potential of a competitive economy (Buchanan, Tollison, and Tullock 1980). In the meantime, there are radical institutionalists, critical legal studies people, and old and new institutionalists who are agnostic and skeptical, believing that good policy can best be achieved in terms of the specific transaction or problem when appropriately analyzed without the straitjacket of presumed idealized means and ends (Rutherford 1995; Vromen 1995; Altman 1990; Samuels and Schmid 1981). In a much broader sense, views of legal conversation as the essence of the process of consensus building or working agreement in a dynamic modern economy are part of the theoretically agnostic movement.

A rather thought-provoking theoretical inversion has been put forward in a recent volume of collected papers, *The Necessity of Friction*. These essays cover a range of disciplines, including economics. The position is advanced that, as a basic premise for analysis, we should not presume an ideal perfectly rational friction-free process burdened by different levels of friction—transaction costs. Instead, we should accept the reality of friction and analyze its expression in various degrees and ways in the phenomena studied without relying on an empty ideal type (Ackerman 1993).

Adam Smith, Posner, and Law and Economics

One of the more interesting excursions into the use of the history of economic thought as a functional part of contemporary economic discourse is Robin Paul Malloy and Jerry Evensky's *Adam Smith and the Philosophy of Law and Economics*. This work combines an exegesis of the little studied jurisprudential thought of Adam Smith by the author-editors, with three expository essays by others. Against this background, a previously published debate between Malloy and Judge Richard Posner is presented. Evensky completes the effort by abstracting and analyzing the various positions from an economic perspective. This approach is one of the most effective ways of bringing out the different jurisprudential perspectives on law and economics held by Malloy and Posner.

As a self-defined adherent of "classical liberal thought," Malloy finds a congenial commitment in Smith's work to a market-oriented rational process tempered by government interventionism in the interest of a humane and moral society. This would, perhaps, put him in the new institutionalist's camp. Smith did not explain society in terms of natural rationalistic social contract theory, but, instead, relied on "human sympathy" as its cohesive force reserving rational self-interest for commercial processes. Malloy specifically rejects the natural law contractual basis for private property rights that is generally followed by Richard Epstein (1985), another prominent writer in the law and economics field. What characterizes Posner's position is that he is not concerned with original positions or moral premises as is Epstein or Buchanan; rather, he is concerned with the rational force of the market process to maximize utility and human benefits. He finds this process-oriented position promulgated in Smith and recognizes it as a valid core principle in economics and law.

Smith's standard for social behavior in his *Theory of Moral Sentiments* is the "impartial spectator," a first cousin of the "reasonably prudent man" standard imposed on members of society by tort law ([1759] 1976). The recognition of an ideal potential adjustment and rational process is, of course, pure Platonism, and Smith's familiarity with this philosophic tradition is amply demonstrated by his essay on "The History of the Ancient Logics and Metaphysics," which was revised from his inaugural lecture for his chair in moral philosophy at Glasgow University (Smith 1980, 118–20; Lowry 1993). Smith is interesting because of his simultaneous assimilation of the Protagorean subjectivist tradition of human sympathy as the moral basis of society (Lowry 1987, chap. 6).

2. Real Property and Commercial Law as Structures for the Economic Process—Planning and Organization

We have investigated the extent to which the philosophical structure of rational process and order vested itself in jurisprudential procedures and economic theory. We can further examine the manner in which the institutions and requirements of the economic process have been assimilated by the law and legally reinforced economic organizations. Rational deduction with its tradition of formal adversarial argument in the courts and its geometric corollaries has provided a felicitous frame of reference for two-party exchange, as well as the broader perspective for much jurisprudence and macroeconomic thought. At the same time, the practical requirements of the customs and organizational structures of economic life—be it agrarian, commercial, or industrial—have induced creative adjustments in jurisprudence and economic theory. It is to this applied sense of realistic legal and economic process that we now direct our attention in this part of this exploration.

Legal thought has followed two distinct lines of analysis relevant to naturalistically oriented economic theory. One is the emphasis on real property as a rational and natural right, going back to John Locke in economics. The other is an emphasis on rational interaction —as in bargained sale and contract as a source of natural justice or equilibrated fairness. Both lines of thought have currency in contemporary law and economics in reference to entitlements and "takings" questions and in relation to questions of exchange and market processes. Their background and the evolution of their assumptions must be sketched before pursuing discussions of the conceptual foundations of controversial writers in law and economics.

The dichotomy between the traditional agrarian occupation associated with real property and participation in commercial exchange, when viewed in terms of legal and economic history, raises some fundamental problems. These revolve around the significance and context of natural and rational law and rational and natural process arguments that intertwine and bedevil contemporary discussion.

Real Property and Natural Rights: Obsolescent Economics and Jurisprudence

A major challenge to contemporary theory on law and economics is Adam Smith's theory of benevolence, which is in direct contrast with competitive self-interest. Its implications in analyzing real property law, as opposed to commercial law, are far-reaching. One of the most historically unacceptable gambits in contemporary law and economic theory is the tendency to extend the traditional sanctity of private real property to modern concepts of commercial property. We must remember that, originally, "real estate" referred to the royal domain—the realm or kingdom held by the king and parceled out to military vassals with the economic obligation to manage the revenues from these lands and to maintain fortifications and armed forces in support of the Crown. As this system broke down into entailed holdings or tenures, the Common Law built up an elaborate system of detailed rights in land that, by Sir Edward Coke's time in the early 1600s, permitted him to identify the Common Law as a more or less natural law, a historical expression of the natural sapience of the courts and the people of England. In the confrontation between Coke and King Charles I in 1628, the idea of "a government of law" to which the king, himself, was subject achieved a naturalistic endorsement to counter the king's claim to divine right—God's endorsement (Holdsworth 1924, 5:423–93). The importance of the freehold estate and its agricultural surplus in supporting a burgeoning economy during the sixteenth, seventeenth, and eighteenth centuries should not be ignored (Braudel 1982–84).

In freehold agriculture and later, Whig commercial agriculture in Smith's century, production was a permissive process, spurred by individual initiative with the surplus supporting the increasingly urban and commercial society. The money profits accumulated by landowners provided the money capital for commerce and industry. This was the dominant theoretical view in the seventeenth and eighteenth centuries, even into and including Smith's time (McNally 1988; Caton 1985; Smith, *TMS*, 219–20). The freedom to plan and organize one's agricultural pursuits and the evolution of innovative agricultural production, in both crops and livestock breeds, were protected by the boundaries of every man's own land. In an agrarian tradition that evolved out of a semisubsistence agriculture and stable land tenures, few forces other than self-interest and benevolence drove innovation and increased production. Although less than freehold tenures had been swallowed up by enclosures and many peasant prerogatives were being appropriated by larger commercially oriented farmers in the eighteenth century, land ownership was a source of prosperity and self-sufficiency. Land was lost by irresponsible wastrels, drunkards, and gamblers—not through failure to compete successfully with one's neighbors in the marketplace. As Smith saw it in his *Theory of Moral Sentiments*, benevolence and the "invisible hand" were the only pressures on individuals in agriculture to serve the public interest. Since the landlord's needs were simple, his surplus revenues provided the capital funds that supported economic expansion. Each farmer had no hostile competitive concern for his neighbors' level of, or lack of, activity. Envy and desire to acquire alienable land were the only direct competitive forces that would give rise to infringements on neighbors other than raw trespass or theft. This is the primary atmosphere for Smith's picture of the economy in which every man could enter into the race with only simple rules against "jostling" or tripping a competitor. Freedom to plan over one's lifetime and to organize resources over a functional planning area and time period were adequately protected by simple property rights, the continuity of family lines, and farm boundaries. The description of holdings in terms of *premises* illustrates the coalescence of the rationalistic legal tradition and property rights within which men could deduce their own adjustments and conclusions. The framework of deductive logic had become coterminous with the natural rights of Englishmen.

The tradition of the natural rights of Englishmen was reiterated in Blackstone's *Commentaries*, which was contemporary with Adam Smith's *Wealth of Nations* ([1776] 1976) and was oriented to real property and agrarian personal property. The property rights theory, advanced by some in the modern law and economics discussion, is an echo of welfare economics perspectives oriented to an agrarian economy of the sixteenth, seventeenth, and eighteenth centuries that permitted a more casual lifestyle with gentile levels of efficiency.

By contrast, competitive commercial activity involves an implicit zero-sum competition with other participants in the same line of trade or manufacture (Macneil 1974a, 718–19). Every sale a commercial neighbor makes is one that you do not make, which redounds to the benefit of your competitor and vice-versa. Smith understood that the spur to activity in commerce was direct competition. Each competitor was a direct survival threat to self-interested tradesmen, and their service to the public was a direct outgrowth of that self-interest: "It is not from the benevolence of the butcher, the brewer, or the baker, that we expect our dinner, but from their regard to their own interest (Smith [1776] 1976, 26–27). Furthermore, individual benefit must be freely associated with unfettered activity if innovative planning and development is to take place. Merchants can trespass on each others' territory, steal customers, and benefit from driving neighbors into bankruptcy, unlike farmers who sell fungibles in an impersonal and more perfectly competitive market. Sharing scientific information, new product lines, and helping out in peak seasons such as haying or harvest time are not part of commercial competition.

For an agrarian society, laws against theft and trespass plus the public recording and guaranteeing of land titles—one's premises—are sufficient for organization and production planning since these activities take place within the individual holding. When this attitude was applied to commerce in the early modern period, it resulted in state-granted monopolies and in patents in trade and manufacturing. For commerce and production to thrive in a world of expanding opportunities, freedom of entry and entrepreneurship were needed. In addition, fluid allocation of resources and appropriatable markets were necessary to permit the efficient and the innovative to expand. In real property terms, this essentially licenses trespass. A different set of complex rules was required so that competition in the commercial arena could take full advantage of the opportunities provided by the new level of agricultural production that could support a larger percentage of the population off the land in urban pursuits. The benefits of planning, a tenuous process in an ever-changing economic sector, could more easily take place in extended family enterprises and formal aggregations such as partnerships and joint stock companies. In addition, from earlier times, the *commercial contract* with a remedy for its breach had evolved as the basic planning device to provide an organizational time-depth to nonagricultural economic activity. In the last century and a half, it has been supplemented by the immortal limited liability corporation.

Transaction Costs and Benefits of Organization and Planning: The Contract Process versus the Integration Process—the Choices of the Coasean Firm

As a necessary background to this discussion, we must examine the historical distinction between sale and contract. In our Greco-Roman legal tradition, justice between parties on an equal footing is associated with voluntary choice. It began with simple distributions—one of a pair of hunters divided the proceeds of the hunt into two piles, according to his voluntary choice. The other hunter voluntarily chose which pile he wanted. Neither could complain of unfairness since any alleged inequality was *voluntary*. People cannot be presumed to have been voluntarily unjust to themselves (Lowry 1991, 1994; Brams and Taylor 1995). Sale was a voluntary exchange of goods in barter or for money and, for the Greeks, had to be voluntary at the point of execution to be fair. If at any time before the actual exchange, one party ceased to desire the exchange, it would not take place. It would be unjust, from the Greek point of view, to force the exchange or levy damages on the unwilling party (Pringsheim 1950; Lowry 1994). Thus, there was no conceptual justification for an enforceable *contract of sale*, but only an instantaneous passage of title to goods for other goods or for money. If there is an equilibrated market economy with perfect competition, there is no need for commercial contracts to obligate others to perform exchanges in the future since alternative goods and services are always available on the open market at a fair price. Contract theorists have had to justify government intervention to enforce an obligation on an individual who no longer finds it in his or her interest to perform. The most widely accepted rationalization of such patent interference with what was traditionally considered a purely personal moral issue—honoring one's word—is that contract is an allocation of risk: an individualized insurance agreement that covers the risk of price changes (Llewellyn 1930). Of course, this rationalization smacks of an unenforceable gambling contract since the insurable interest is generated by the contract itself. A. T. Kronman has extended this risk-minimizing concept into a Hobbesian frame or reference that focuses on techniques for minimizing the risk of breach of contract (1985). The moral justification of honoring a good-faith promise is a bit thin when it involves cramming a major loss down the unlucky victim's throat, be it done ever so legally.

Perhaps the most insightful discussion of this problem is Ian Macneil's essay, "Restatement of Contracts (Second) and Presentation," in which he puts forward the doctrine of *presentiation*—bringing the future into the present for purposes of structuring an agreement (Macneil 1974a, 1974b). In essence, this is the planning function that Roman law apparently recognized as necessary for commercial organization in a world of imperfect markets and fluid conditions. The embedding of this theoretical premise in the legal rulings is suggested by the principle that damages for breach of contract are not determined by the specific losses suffered by the injured party, but they are measured by the "value of the bargain"—that is, the determinable value of the contract itself. Anticipated speculative profits are not allowed. The Latin maxim "volenti ac consentienti non fit injuria" (Digest 30,4,11; 47,10,1,5) extends the voluntarist justification of sale to contract. It permits vertical integration, or lining up bulk materials for future delivery, equipment for production purposes, and marketing agreements for the future sale of finished products. Thus, the arrangements can be structured in advance, mentally or theoretically, and brought into the present. In essence, this is a credit operation that exists in the imagination of the parties, and it is realized at the time of execution of the various contracts. This is economic planning at the private or microeconomic level. In an imperfect market economy, such a system is necessary to give temporal stability to economic activity. In volatile commodity markets, governments have often organized *futures markets* in order to bring more financial predictability to otherwise capricious future raw materials prices.

In his widely discussed article, "The Nature of the Firm" (1937), as reviewed in his own lectures (Coase 1988), Coase was pointing out that vertical integration would not take place in perfectly functioning markets where firms could buy raw materials and component parts on the market for the same price they could produce them themselves. The explanation for vertical integration, a market deviance, had to be *transaction costs* that led the firm to produce the needed components or raw materials themselves. In other words, there were extra costs associated with market transactions that could be avoided by direct production.

In a very real sense, Coase compared the planning efficiency of two different forms of government facilitation of modern industrial organization—the commercially derived contract and the industrially oriented limited-liability corporation. The tandem evolution of industrial responses to vast economies of scale during the transportation and technological explosion of the nineteenth century and the legal adjustments by courts and legislatures during the same period are proper subjects for future studies in law and economies.

Unhappily, many economists who actively participate in the contemporary discussion have a limited perspective in legal history, and the legal scholars seem overawed by the alleged *hard science* of economics, lacking historical perspective in bringing out the legal aspects of economics. Contract law has evolved, creating enforceable contracts out of even rather vague indications of an intent to make a commitment. If a determinable quantity is indicated, the courts will supply a reasonable price and reasonable terms for the commitment. What is surprising in the discussions associated with the commemorative conference on Coase's seminal 1937 article is that no one took account of the significant evolution of requirements and output contracts by which a mutual agreement to sell and to buy *all* the output of one firm by another is considered definite as to quantity. The same is true of agreements to buy *all* one's requirements from a particular company if that company agrees to sell *all* the buyer requires (see *Royal Brewing Company v. Uncle Sam Oil Co.*, 226 S.W. 656, 1920) This is clearly a move on the part of the courts to extend contract law to flexibly accommodate the need for vertically integrated planning in the dynamic context of the *going concern*. It is the type of organizational process that Paul Joskow (1985) is dealing with in his study of long-term contracts for fuel in electrical generating plants. In associating the "quantity mode" with vertical integration and the "price mode" with contract, the Coasean literature demonstrates a lack of appreciation of this evolution in the contract system (Hart 1988, 124, 126). It should be noted that the judicial grasp of this relational (as opposed to transactional) structure, as expressed in output and requirements contracts, goes back to the turn of the century. The problem seems to be that neoclassical theory assumes that transactions take place at equilibrium price, excluding profits defined as rents or surplus profits. In this context, all the transactions in the market are simple sales or equilibrated exchanges with no surplus profits. Therefore, a large number of the justifications for vertically integrating that are brought up by economists search out special transaction costs and problems associated with technological specificity. Winter recognizes that relationships between firms should be treated as evolving structures and not as simple transactions, but seems unaware of the legal literature on the subject, Macneil in particular (Winter 1988, 177).

Legal theory assumes "mutuality"—both sides benefit—as a requirement for a binding contract. Economic theory deals with mutuality primarily in international trade or in isolated exchange, as in the Edgeworth box (Jaffé 1974). Where both sides anticipate gaining or profiting from the arrangement, most of the policing and information issues evaporate. An example of such a discussion is found in Joskow's article on the coal-fired electric generating industry (1985). Legal theorists have generally accepted, supported by Macneil's work, a "relational theory of contract," which understands most contracts as existing in a milieu of ongoing interactions with anticipations of future mutual advantages that bind the parties together. This line of empirical extrapolation from the realities of business relationships that is followed by the courts contrasts sharply with formal economic perspectives. The new institutionalists in economics are, of course, busily qualifying and modifying traditional economic assumptions of frictionless and costless market processes.

Coase's assumption is that in a perfect market economy, you can buy the requisite inputs for the same price you can produce them yourself.

There would be, therefore, no justification for vertically integrating unless there were additional costs associated with using the market. Writers in the Coase tradition explore problems that grow out of the specificity of design of industrial components, information and control as well as costs of negotiation. These formulations fail to consider the gross differential of remedies available to owners as opposed to those available to contracting parties when problems arise. Contract law provides for money damages equal to the value of the lost bargain. In a commercial economy with developed markets, one can immediately replace undelivered goods from the open or *spot* market at something close to the contract price and then recover damages. The contract, of course, grew out of commerce, not production. In major modern manufacturing with product differentiation, a supplier's breach could be devastating; aside from the delay in replacing the components, damages could exceed the ability of the supplier to pay. With vertical integration, the possibility of a major fiasco is probably limited to the early stages of the production expansion. On the other hand, suppliers with long-term requirements-contracts have adapted the contract to a functional vertical integration. Mutual interests in an ongoing relationship can generate flexibility, renegotiation of burdensome provisions, and cooperation. This phenomenon was raised somewhat in the discussions that arose from Coase's observations of Fisher Body's relation with General Motors before its acquisition. From a dynamic perspective, perhaps the issue is little more than the fact that, in the formative stage, firms have limited capital and can often begin as essentially assemblers of parts supplied by a variety of subcontractors. As success and profitability develop, there is capital to invest in the process and, despite the mythology of formal economic analysis, the suppliers are usually making profits that the corporation would be glad to assimilate. This aspect is captured by the "rent-seeking" formulation used by some writers. More directly, vertical integration can simply be characterized as a legitimate form of expansion that increases profits.

Mutual Transaction Savings and Contract

What is particularly strange in the contemporary discussions of integration is the failure to appreciate the fact that in our interlaced economic fabric, there are many joint products and by-products or even waste materials that can be made use of by other firms. In a dynamic changing economy, many firms with market or cost incentives to expand are producing on the downsloping part of their average total cost curve with marginal costs far below their selling price. If the marketing or distribution of the firm's name brand product is the primary limiting factor in its expansion, a shrewd manager can negotiate supply contracts with non-competing firms that provide components at less than the average cost of production at the scale at which the buyer could operate. Dumping can be profitable as long as the goods are sold at marginal cost plus a profit. A contract to take advantage of an empty backhaul situation being experienced by a local firm making deliveries with its own trucks could be rewarding to both parties at marginal cost plus a small markup, but below average cost—a case of transaction benefits or profits.

When sawmills began to debark their logs in order to produce clean (bark-free) sawdust and chips from slab wood so that thcy could scll this waste to pulp mills, they were faced with the problem of disposing of immense piles of bark. Early entrepreneurs, who developed the bark-mulch business, could get bark by agreeing to haul it away at below cost of hauling! Bark yards with shredding equipment were completely uninterested in going into the sawmill business to vertically integrate their resource base or in starting a chain of garden supply stores in order to market their high-volume, low-value product. Their primary money came from sales by the truckload to large landscaping companies and developers. These latter would be unlikely to be interested in developing a bark business to vertically integrate their requirements because the efficient scale of operations would far exceed their requirements. In other words, an output contract by which the bark firm agreed to buy all and the sawmill agreed to sell all its bark to them, and a requirements contract by which the landscape firm agreed to buy all its requirements and the bark firm agreed to supply all its requirements, would effectively integrate these firms. Clearly, integration by contract is more advantageous than integration by ownership in cases of disparate scales of outputs and requirements. There is every reason to expect that contracts can produce transaction savings as well as transaction costs by deviating from open market operations.

Coase and "The Problem of Social Cost"

The famous 1960 Coase article on social cost promoted a great deal of discussion and helped launch the subdiscipline of law and economics into its current phase. Its sensational Coase Theorem—that in the absence of transaction costs, free negotiations would achieve optimum social welfare regardless of rights allocations—was widely interpreted as an argument against tort liability and government intervention generally. This position has apparently been qualified by Coase and most other economists. Coase has characterized it as a way of framing the problem of transaction costs in a different light than that of vertical integration. In his Nobel Lecture in 1991, Coase said, "The significance to me of the Coase theorem is that it undermines the Pigovian system" (1994, 11). Under the standard economic assumption of a frictionless—zero transaction cost—market, he said, Pigovian regulations to achieve optimum welfare would be unnecessary because of the rational workings of the market. However, his true position is, "If we move from a regime of zero transaction costs to one of positive transaction costs, what becomes immediately clear is the crucial importance of the legal system in this new world" (Coase 1994, 11). Despite this expression of real world legal sophistication, Coase seems to distinguish sharply between regulation and law, in some sense thinking primarily of law as rules for facilitating negotiations.

Most of Coase's examples in "The Problem of Social Cost" involve trespass on agricultural land or public and private nuisance cases. These are infringements on traditional rights of "quiet enjoyment" that protect the microeconomic right to plan individual economic activity at the agrarian level. By limiting his acceptance of law to situations where there are transaction costs, he vitiates the institutional significance of long-term stability in rights appropriate to planning and economies of scale. The ideal of a free market without tort liability as a reference base for analyzing contract law is flawed. Unless there is a legal evaluation of bona fide economic motive on the part of the trespasser or cause of the nuisance, any viable economic activity could be bled to death by trespass or specially generated nuisance with the sole purpose of obtaining a negotiated cash payoff to desist—which essentially is extortion (Lowry 1976).

Tort law needs to be understood as a rather blunt instrument that permits the individual initiation of actions for damages caused by injury to person or property. Such suits come after the fact, and the social policy assumption is that, after a few publicized cases, most businesses and individuals will move toward minimizing such incidents to avoid liability in accordance with the old Greek maxim that "only fools have to learn by experience!" When dealing with rational people, this system is very efficient. When this does not seem to improve general welfare, direct government regulation achieves the desired objective with a minimum transaction cost, and welfare is improved by avoiding injury or damage, though not necessarily defined in purely economic terms. The basic issue is whether the agrarian ideal of individual economic planning within one's own premises is a more important aspect of welfare than the ideal of a perfect rational market. If we had a perfectly equilibrated rent-free economy with everyone living at subsistence, there would be no incentive to "rent-seek" by infringements or threats seeking payoffs. Live and let live legal rights could not be presumed without public enforcement, however. Theft and appropriation could still occur. We are dealing with a tension between an island of individual rights to the protection of the person and property on the one hand and publicly enforced rules requiring accommodation to the general welfare as rationally determined by public processes on the other. This tension and the associated jurisprudential dilemma is well illustrated by the impasse between the "takings" problem and zoning regulations featured in the leading case of *Lucas v. South Carolina Coastal Council* (112 S. Ct. 2886, 1992) (Halper 1995).

For a bit of anecdotal empiricism, I recall attending a state labor meeting out of curiosity when I was a student back in 1946. A delegation of three small, gray men appeared representing the employees of a Fort Worth candy factory. They wanted help in forming a union. There was a machine in their plant that they considered dangerous. They had, however, found the manufacturer's catalog and discovered that safety bars could be purchased for a relatively low price. Although they had never read Coase, representatives of the men who worked around this machine went to the employer and notified him that the employees had decided to "chip in" and buy the safety equipment and asked for permission to install it. This is the epitome of Coase's ideal adjustment in "The Problem of Social Cost" with zero transaction costs and rational negotiations. The boss, however, threw the delegation out of his office, telling them that when he wanted them to tell him how to run his business, he would call them, but in the meantime, they should mind their own! The employees had learned that the primary market consideration was, on the boss's side, the defense of his arbitrary authority—power. This is what rationality meant to him. On the employees' side, the market reality meant unionization and collective bargaining. This was rationality to them, even if it meant risk and uncertainty and perhaps loss of employment. A serious injury and a tort action could have induced the company to install the safety bars, taking care of the problem. OSHA also would have taken care of such a problem in advance of an injury. Of course, that legislation came into effect to avoid the major injury–tort liability route to safety standards and the minimizing of social costs. The ultimate question is whether we are to abstract methodology and policy as deductions from the institutional fabric of our dynamic political economy, on the one hand, or build methodological and policy compensation as amendments to institutional shortcomings—transaction costs—of an idealized friction-free analysis of the market process, on the other.

It is impossible to survey the plethora of articles that this essay of Coase's stimulated. It appeared to provide a sophisticated argument against government intervention in the economy and to indicate that minimizing transaction costs, including tort actions, would permit the market process to perfect the economy without law. Coase, apparently, does not subscribe to this scenario and seems to consider it, now, an attempt to further elucidate the importance of transaction costs. In his Nobel Lecture, in reference to abstract models of negotiation, Coase says, "The process of contracting needs to be studied in a real world setting. We would then learn of the problems that are encountered and how they are overcome, and we would certainly become aware of the richness of the institutional alternatives among which we have to choose" (1994, 12). While Coase sounds very much like an evolutionary institutionalist in such passages and recognizes the importance of specifying rights and rules as a basis for the negotiative process, he does not reflect a grasp of the relational context followed in contract law developed by Macneil. He also is insensitive to the perception of some writers that contract and tort are blurring into a system that provides remedies for breaches of the right to expect certain standards of conduct (Gilmore 1974). The assumption that the assignment of rights and rule making takes care of the legal background for the contracting process is undermined by a recent study of the amorphous and fluid dynamic in the legal process of defining rights (Donnelly 1994).

A basic question regarding the Coase Theorem remains—that is, why did such a jurisprudentially naive formulation of the legal process get taken so seriously by so many members of the legal profession and promote the revival of this subdiscipline in these terms among economists?

Economics as a Modern Legal Philosophy

It is of some interest to note that Pound culminated his book on the philosophy of law by indicating that jurisprudence was ready for a new philosophical generalization. The appeal of market theory from neoclassical economics seems to be keyed to its naturalistic framing of its process in terms of a mathematical *tatonnement* that parallels the legal process of adversarial argument. It was Artistotle's formulation suggesting the mathematical dyad that correlated the legal argumentative process with the analysis of just price in the exchange process. We would not, of course, want to suggest that jurisprudence is currently being repaid after twenty-three hundred years with shopworn merchandise. Nevertheless, the methodological and applied traditions in jurisprudence seem to offer a broader and richer resource base for effective rational discourse and policy implementation than a naturalistically oriented neoclassical economics. Actually, there has been an ongoing interchange between jurisprudence and economic theory over the centuries; rational process, natural law, the sociology of status and interaction, institutionalism and evolution in terms of realism and discourse. Law and political economy have existed as parallel social science disciplines for over two thousand years, and the real challenge is still to cut through the definitional and descriptive formalisms so that both disciplines can benefit from the analytic insights and practical experience of each other. Historical perspective and an emphasis on methodological and applied process are premium keys to this portal.

References

Akerman, N. 1993. *The Necessity of Friction: Nineteen Essays on a Vital Force*. Heidelberg: Physica-Verlag.

Altman, A. 1990. *Critical Legal Studies: A Liberal Critique*. Princeton, N.J.: Princeton University Press.

Brams, Steven, J., and Alan D. Taylor. 1995. Fair Division in Politics. *PS-Political Science and Politics* 28.4:697–703.

Braudel, F. 1982–84. *Civilization and Capitalism, 15th–18th Century*. 3 vols. New York: Harper and Row.

Buchanan, James M., R. D. Tollison, and G. Tullock, eds. 1980. *Toward a Theory of the Rent-Seeking Society*. College Station: Texas A&M University Press.

Caton, H. 1985. The Pre-Industrial Economics of Adam Smith. *Journal of Economic History* 45.4:833–53.

Coase, R. H. 1937. The Nature of the Firm. *Economica* 4:386–405.
———. 1960. The Problem of Social Cost. *Journal of Law and Economics* 3:1–44.
———. 1988. R. H. Coase Lectures. *Journal of Law, Economics and Organization* 4.1:3–48.
———. 1994. The Institutional Structure of Production (1991 Nobel Lecture). In *Essays on Economics and Economists*, Chicago: University of Chicago Press.
Donnelly, S. J. M. 1994. *The Language and Uses of Rights: A Biopsy of American Jurisprudence in the Twentieth Century*. Lanham, Md.: University Presses of America.
Ellickson, R. C. 1989. Bringing Culture and Human Frailty to Rational Actors: A Critique of Classical Law and Economics. *Chicago/Kent Law Review* 65:23–55.
Epstein, R. 1985. *Takings: Private Property and the Power of Eminent Domain*. Cambridge: Harvard University Press.
Gilmore, G. 1974. *The Death of Contract*. Columbus: Ohio State University Press.
Gomez-Camacho, Francisco. 1996. Late Scholastics: Spanish Economic Thought in the Sixteenth and Seventeenth Centuries. Unpublished manuscript. Universidad Pontifica Camillas, Madrid.
Gonce, R. A. 1979. John R. Commons's Legal Economic Theory. In *The Economy as a System of Power*, edited by Warren J. Samuels. New Brunswick, N.J.: Transaction Books.
Halper, Louise A. 1993. Parable of Exchange: Foundations of Social Choice Theory and the Market Formalism of James Buchanan. *Cornell Journal of Law and Public Policy* 2.2:229–78.
———. 1995. Why the Nuisance Knot Can't Undo the Takings Muddle. *Indiana Law Review* 28.2:329–52.
Hart, O. D. 1988. Incomplete Contract and the Theory of the Firm. *Journal of Law, Economics and Organization* 4.1:119–40.
Holdsworth, W. S. 1924. *A History of English Law*. Boston: Little Brown.
Holmes Jr., O. W. [1926] 1953. Letter in *Holmes-Laski Letters*. Edited by Mark D. Howe. Cambridge: Harvard University Press.
Horwitz, M. J. 1992. *The Transformation of American Law 1870–1960: The Crisis of Legal Orthodoxy*. New York: Oxford University Press.
Jaffé, William. 1974. Edgeworth's Contract Curve: Part 2. *HOPE* 6:381–404.
Joskow, Paul L. 1985. Vertical Integration and Long-Term Contracts: The Case of Coal-Burning Electric Generating Plants. *Journal of Law, Economics and Organization* 1.1:33–80.
Kanel, D. 1979. Property and Economic Power as Issues in Institutional Economics. In *The Economy as a System of Power*, edited by Warren J. Samuels. New Brunswick, N.J.: Transaction Books.
Kelley, Donald R. 1990. *The Human Measure: Social Thought in the Western Legal Tradition*. Cambridge, Mass. and London: Harvard University Press.
Kronman, A. T. 1985. Contract Law and the State of Nature. *Journal of Law, Economics and Organization* 1.1:5–32.
Lekachman, R. 1979. Law and Economics. In *The Economy as a System of Power*,

edited by Warren J. Samuels. New Brunswick, N.J.: Transaction Books.

Liebhafsky, H. H. [1976] 1993. Price Theory as Jurisprudence: Law and Economics Chicago Style. In *The Chicago School of Political Economy*. New Brunswick, N.J.: Transaction Books.

———. 1979. Commons and Clark on Law and Economics. In *The Economy as a System of Power*, edited by Warren J. Samuels. New Brunswick, N.J.: Transaction Books.

Llewellyn, Carl. 1930. What Price Contracts. *Yale Law Journal* 40:704.

Lowry, S. Todd. 1969. Aristotle's Mathematical Analysis of Exchange. *HOPE* 1:44–66.

———. 1974a. Aristotle's "Natural Limit" and the Economics of Price Regulation. *Greek, Roman and Byzantine Studies* 15:57–63.

———. 1974b. Lord Mansfield and the Law Merchant: Law and Economics in the Eighteenth Century. *Journal of Economic Issues* 7:605–22.

———. 1976. Bargain and Contract Theory in Law and Economics. *Journal of Economic Issues* 9:1–22. Reprinted in *The Chicago School of Political Economy*, New Brunswick, N.J.: Transaction Books, 1993, 215–36.

———. 1987. *The Archaeology of Economic Ideas: The Classical Greek Tradition*. Durham and London: Duke University Press.

———. 1991. Distributive Economics and the Promethean Meat Division: Myth, Folklore, and Legal Precedent. In *Ancient Economy in Mythology: East and West*, edited by Morris Silver. : Rowman and Littlefield.

———. 1993. A Note on the Ideal of Models: From Plato to Adam Smith. *Brock Review* 2.2: 201–5.

———. 1994. The Market as a Distributive and Allocative System: Its Legal, Ethical, and Analytical Evolution. In *Higgling*, edited by Neil De Marchi and Mary S. Morgan. Durham and London: Duke University Press.

Macneil, I. R. 1974a. The Many Futures of Contract. *Southern California Law Review* 47.3:691–816.

———. 1974b. Restatement of Contracts (Second) and Presentiation. *Virginia Law Review* 60:589–610.

Malloy, Robin P., and Jerry Evensky, eds. 1994. *Adam Smith and the Philosophy of Law and Economics*. Dordrecht: Kluwer Academic.

Mandeville, Bernard. [1924] 1988. *Mandeville's Fable of the Bees*, with a commentary by F. B. Kaye. Indianapolis: Liberty Classics.

McNally, D. 1988. *Political Economy and the Rise of Capitalism: A Reinterpretation*. Berkeley: University of California Press.

Medema, Steven G. 1995. *The Legacy of Ronald Coase in Economic Analysis*. 2 vols. Brookfield, Vt.: Edward Elgar.

Ohrenstein, R. 1996. Economic Thought and Social Justice in the Talmud. Unpublished manuscript, Bayside, New York.

Plescia, J. 1970. *The Oath and Perjury in Ancient Greece*. Tallahassee: University of Florida Press.

Pound, Roscoe. [1922] 1954. *An Introduction to the Philosophy of Law*. New York: Yale University Press.

Pringsheim, Fritz. 1950. *The Greek Law of Sale*. Weimar: Böhlau.

Rutherford, Malcolm. 1994. *Institutions in Economics: The Old and The New Institutionalism*. Cambridge: Cambridge University Press.

Samuels, Warren J. 1993. Law and Economics: Some Early Journal Contributions. In *Economic Thought and Discourse in the Twentieth Century*, edited by Warren J. Samuels, J. Biddle, and T. W. Patchak-Schuster. Brookfield, Vt.: Edward Elgar.

Samuels, Warren J., and A. Allan Schmid. 1981. *Law and Economics: An Institutional Perspective*. Boston: Kluwer-Nijhoff.

Smith, Adam. [1759] 1976. *The Theory of Moral Sentiments*. Glasgow ed. Oxford, Oxford University Press. (*TMS*)

———. [1776] 1976. *The Wealth of Nations*. Oxford University Press.

———. 1980. The History of the Ancient Logics and Metaphysics. In *Essays on Philosophical Subjects*. Glasgow ed. Oxford: Oxford Unversity Press.

Stein, Peter. 1995. Interpretation and Legal Reasoning in Roman Law. *Chicago-Kent Law Review* 70(4):1539–56.

Vromen, Jack J. 1995. *Economic Evolution: An Enquiry into the Foundations of New Institutional Economics*. London: Routledge.

Williamson, Oliver E. 1985. *The Economic Institutions of Capitalism*. New York: Free Press.

Winter, S. G. 1988. On Coase, Competence and the Corporation. *Journal of Law, Economics and Organization* 4.1:163–80.

Young, Jeffrey T. 1995. Natural Jurisprudence and the Theory of Value in Adam Smith. *HOPE* 27.4:755–72.

The Trial of *Homo Economicus*: What Law and Economics Tells Us about the Development of Economic Imperialism

Steven G. Medema

Economic analysis in the last third of the twentieth century has been defined very much by a few key movements, among which must be included that which goes by the title of "economic imperialism"—the application of economic analysis to traditionally noneconomic areas such as political science, law, sociology, and biology. The fundamental distinctive feature of these imperialistic movements is, of course, their traditionally noneconomic nature. From the eighteenth century onward, at least, the subject matter of political economy/economics was the material well-being of individuals and/or nations, culminating in Alfred Marshall's definition of "political economy or economics" as "a study of mankind in the ordinary business of life; it examines that part of individual and social action which is most closely connected with the attainment and with the use of the material requisites of wellbeing" (1920, 1).

This notion of the subject matter of economics was refined by Lionel Robbins already in the 1930s, when he argued that economists do not study "the causes of material welfare," but, rather, the choice process, an insight which led him to conclude that "economics is the science which studies human behaviour as a relationship between ends and scarce means

Presented at the *HOPE* Annual Conference on "New Economics and Its Writing," Duke University, March 29–31, 1996. The author wishes to thank the conference participants and, in particular, Warren J. Samuels, for instructive comments on an earlier draft of the article.

which have alternative uses" (Robbins 1932, 15). Based on this, Robbins rejected the notion that the boundaries between "economics" and "not economics" are set by behavior that is or is not directed toward the enhancement of material welfare. Rather, he argued, economics focuses on the form of behavior "imposed by the influence of scarcity." Thus, "It follows from this . . . that in so far as it offers this aspect, any kind of human behaviour falls within the scope of Economic Generalizations. . . . In so far as [an activity] involves the relinquishment of other desired alternatives, it has its economic aspect. *There are no limitations on the subject-matter of Economic Science save this*" (16; emphasis added). It is Robbins' now-standard, textbook definition of economics that has formed the basis for economic imperialism. Gary Becker, whose work in this vein is without parallel, makes this clear when he describes the method that has motivated his own work: "The combined assumptions of maximizing behavior, market equilibrium, and stable preferences, used relentlessly and unflinchingly, form the heart of the economic approach as I see it" (1976, 5).[1]

The logic of this extension is a simple one: economics is the study of choice, and all of life involves making choices; should not economics, then, apply to all manner of human decisions and thus all areas of human life? If the market for ideas (to say nothing of that for Nobel prizes) is any indication, the answer to this question is surely "yes." (This, of course, is not to say that everyone is buying; after all, what market is there in which some are not put off by the price?) At the positive level, we see the exportation of *homo economicus* to a multiplicity of areas of individual decision making and an assessment of the efficiency of such decisions. On a normative level, we observe, in certain contexts at least, the invocation of an efficiency norm to govern the determination of the constraints under which choices are made.

Of the various imperialistic movements within economics, the field of law and economics ranks (along with public choice) as the most successful, if one measures by the breadth and depth of the market. This having been said, recent work within law and economics has generated results that call into question certain fundamental features of the analysis and perhaps, by extension, economic imperialism generally. In what follows, we shall be particularly concerned with the Coase Theorem,

1. Since the present article deals primarily with law and economics, it is at least worth noting that Richard Posner (1992, 3) works from a similar frame of reference.

which is at the heart of modern law and economics, and with recent evidence suggesting that individuals do not behave as the *homo economicus* characterization would suggest in situations contemplated by the Coase Theorem.[2] Section 1 contains a brief background discussion of law and economics and the Coase Theorem. Section 2 presents the results of some recent experimental and empirical work that casts doubt on the behavioral grounding of the Coase Theorem and the implications thereof. Section 3 offers some thoughts regarding law and economics past and future.

1. The Rights Stuff: Law and Economics and the Coase Theorem

The analysis of the interactions between law and economy has a lengthy history within economics. The work of Adam Smith, Henry Sidgwick, and A. C. Pigou, for example, gave prominent play to the role of the law within a market system, and, of course, the study of the legal-economic process was the bread and butter of Institutionalists such as Robert Lee Hale, Walton Hamilton, and John R. Commons, as well as their Legal Realist contemporaries. The focuses of these analyses were several, including the evaluation of the economic impact (allocational and distributional) of alternative legal rules, the import of the legal structure for the functioning of the economic system, and how economic conditions or forces brought to bear pressures for and resulted in legal change. The demise of Institutionalism and Legal Realism as influential professional forces was accompanied by a substantial diminution of this type of legal-economic analysis, although Chicago antitrust and the work of the Institutionalist remnant kept the flame alive to some degree.

The early 1960s witnessed the publication of two articles that served to simultaneously resurrect and transform legal-economic analysis—Ronald Coase's "The Problem of Social Cost" (1960) and Guido Calabresi's "Some Thoughts on Risk Distribution and the Law of Torts" (1961). Coase's essay was in certain important ways one in the "old" law and economics mode, its purpose being in part to call attention to

2. Some might argue that the problems here are obvious—that people are really not rational maximizers of utility in economic or noneconomic contexts and thus that economic imperialism as an explanatory construct has been doomed from its inception. The position taken here is somewhat different. Individuals tend to respond to price incentives: when the cost of an activity rises, people tend to undertake relatively less of that activity, and conversely. *Homo economicus* offers one way in which to explain or model this. The question is: Is there a better and more accurate way? Within economics, at least, it takes a theory to beat a theory.

the effects of alternative legal-economic policies (broadly defined) on economic performance and the need to analyze the same. Its uniqueness lay in the use of straightforward Marshallian reasoning to analyze the effects of alternative legal rules—in particular, those governing nuisance-generating activities.

The raison d'être of much of modern law and economics comes from the Coase Theorem, which tells us that, if rights are fully defined and transaction costs are zero,[3] the allocation of resources will be efficient and invariant under alternative legal rules. That is, in a world of zero transaction costs, the direction of rights does not matter, only their presence or absence; the structure of law is without effect on the allocation of resources. The Coase Theorem is at once both remarkable and remarkably ordinary. It is remarkable in that it suggests that legal rules really do not matter; it is singularly ordinary in that, since all transactions are ultimately over rights, it simply tells us that the pricing system will function for rights over, for example, nuisance activities, just as it does for rights over, for example, foodstuffs, automobiles, or houses—placing these rights in the hands of those who value them most highly.

Although numerous criticisms have been leveled against the Coase Theorem, it is correct.[4] Of course, that which is logically correct is not necessary realistic, applicable, or sensible. Indeed, were the Coase Theorem generally applicable, the field of law and economics would lose much of its normative import. But for better or worse, we live in a world in which transaction costs are positive, the effect of which is to greatly reduce (and in many cases eliminate) the perceived gains from bargaining over rights that are contemplated by the Coase Theorem. Nonetheless, there are many who argue that the Coase Theorem is more or less applicable to small numbers bargaining situations over legal rights. In fact, Elizabeth Hoffman and Matthew Spitzer contend that their experimental results (which will be discussed later in this chapter) establish "*a presumption in favor of the Coase Theorem*" (emphasis added), by which they mean that "a judge or legislator should start his analysis by

3. The assumptions of fully defined rights and zero transaction costs may be considered redundant under certain interpretations of what is meant by zero transaction costs. See Allen 1991.

4. The exception to this is when consumers are a party to the externality and the marginal utility of income is diminishing, in which case the invariance proposition will not hold, owing to differences that will be observed between the amount one is willing to pay for a right and the amount that one is willing to accept to give up that right. For surveys of the debate over the Coase Theorem, see Cooter 1989; Medema and Zerbe 1997; and Zerbe 1980.

presuming that the parties can and will, in general, exhaust the gains from trade available through private bargaining" and that those who would argue to the contrary "must bear the burden of the proof" (1986, 162).

But even when it is acknowledged that transaction costs are likely to preclude the bargaining arrangements contemplated by the Coase Theorem, the Theorem continues to hold substantial force over legal-economic thinking, for, either explicitly or implicitly, it provides the foundation for the application of the efficiency criterion within the legal decision-making process. While the market-type activity envisioned by the theorem may not be realistically operative, the credo that has emerged is "mimic the market"—that is, assign rights efficiently—so as to mimic the result that would have obtained if the parties could bargain over rights in Coase Theorem–like fashion. Since, in a world of zero transaction costs, parties would voluntarily rearrange rights to place them in their highest-valued uses, the court, in following the efficiency rule, is simply doing what the parties would, but cannot, do.

The foregoing suggests that the basis for the efficiency rule rests on two propositions. The first is that efficiency should be the goal of legal-economic policy—an issue that has been discussed time and again in the literature and will not concern us here.[5] The second proposition is that, in fact, individuals would bargain over rights as the Coase Theorem anticipates if transaction costs were indeed zero. This point has led to the further contention that legal rules should be structured in such a way as to reduce transaction costs, in order to facilitate Coase Theorem–type bargains. These last issues go to the behavior of agents and thus to the underpinnings of law and economics and of economic imperialism generally.

While the Coase Theorem is generally said to turn on the assumption of zero transaction costs (and the meaning given to it), it also embodies the (usually implicit) assumption that agents are rational maximizers who treat rights over, for example, clean air or peace and quiet in a manner identical to rights over standard consumer goods or producer inputs. This raises two immediate questions. First, do consumers and producers behave in the manner contemplated by the rational maximizing model? Second, if they do so, do they also behave in this way when making decisions outside of the traditional consumer good or producer

5. See, for example, the "Symposium on Efficiency as a Legal Concern" (1980) and "A Response to the Efficiency Symposium" (1980).

input context? There is increasing evidence to support the contention that the answer to both of these questions is "no," and, in particular, that individuals do not behave in the manner contemplated by the Coase Theorem. If this is indeed the case, the difficulties raised go to the heart of law and economics—to the explanation of outcomes, to the prediction of the impacts of alternative legal rules, and to the evaluation of outcomes. We thus turn to an examination of a few recent studies that shed light on these issues.

2. Searching for *Homo Economicus* amidst the Legal Thicket

The seemingly endless controversy over the Coase Theorem has led to the undertaking of a number of experimental and empirical studies purporting to "test" the theorem. It should be noted, however, that, as Herbert Hovenkamp has recently pointed out, "conducting empirical tests of the Coase theorem is like conducting empirical tests of the Pythagorean theorem. Given the theorem's assumptions, the results flow out as a matter of logical necessity" (1990, 794). Reflecting this, the results of these "tests" are mixed, some finding substantial support for the efficiency of bargains over rights, and some finding just the opposite—depending on how closely the experimental or empirical conditions correspond to the assumptions of the Coase Theorem.[6] But what will concern us here is not the efficiency issue per se, but what the "tests" reveal about agent behavior in situations to which the Coase Theorem directly or indirectly pertains.

2.1. Experimenting with Coase

Case 1: Coasean World, Lockean Man

Among the various attempts to test the predictions of the Coase Theorem, the experimental tests are perhaps the most interesting, since they offer the potential to mimic as closely as possible the condition of zero transaction costs. The most extensive experimental tests of the theorem are those undertaken by Hoffman and Spitzer (at times with others),[7] all of which involve the same basic experimental framework. There is a range of possible outcomes, each with a different associated payoff. One party

6. In addition to the studies discussed herein, see also those surveyed in Medema and Zerbe 1997.

7. See Hoffman and Spitzer 1982, 1985, 1986 and Coursey, Hoffman, and Spitzer 1987.

(the "controller") is given the "property right" and thus can determine the outcome unilaterally. Consider the following set of possible dollar payoffs (P_A,P_B) in the spirit of Hoffman and Spitzer: (5, 0), (4, 4), and (0, 5). If A is the controller, he will choose (5, 0) unless B induces him to choose a different outcome. The Coase Theorem predicts that (4, 4)—the outcome with the greatest joint payoff ($8)—will be chosen, with the actual distribution of the joint payoff being a function of the negotiation process. It is in B's interest to offer A up to $4 to choose (4, 4) and in A's interest to accept any payment greater than $1.01 to do so.

In well over five hundred experiments with bargaining groups of various sizes conducted within this framework, the parties bargained to the efficient result 92 percent of the time. Given how little the student subjects have at stake in these experiments, even those conducted under conditions of imperfect information suggest very low transaction costs. While this may seem quite unrealistic, these experiments do offer some fairly substantial support for the applicability of the theorem when transaction costs are very low.[8]

Of particular concern here is the fact that, in these experiments, the parties agreed to a nearly equal division of the payoffs (±1 dollar) in the vast majority of the cases. Individual rationality suggests, with respect to this example, that the controller would not settle for less than $5 and could potentially induce the other party to agree to a $7.99–$0.01 split of the $8 payoff, as in, for example, a one-shot game. The fact that so many controllers settle for less than what should be their reservation price suggests either altruism (which contradicts entirely the theory of externalities, Coase Theorem or otherwise)[9] or a potential problem with the experimental environment.

One hypothesis offered to explain this result is that participants in these experiments did not understand the full meaning and import of having a unilateral property right as controllers (Harrison and McKee 1985). Another is that they did not feel a morally justified right to be the controller, since that position was determined on the basis of a coin flip rather than being, in some (e.g., Lockean) sense, earned (Hoffman and Spitzer 1985). Once measures were implemented to control for this—

8. On the rather drastic implications for the extent to which efficient legal bargains are reached in the presence of transaction costs, see the experimental results of Stewart Schwab 1988.

9. If agents are altruistic, the individually rational behavior that is said to generate the externality in the first place would not occur. From a game-theoretic perspective, these equal splits are not within the core.

"educating" subjects or having subjects "earn" the position of controller by winning a preliminary game—the extent of individually rational behavior increased dramatically and without a significant drop-off in the rate at which efficient bargains were made (Harrison and McKee 1985; Hoffman and Spitzer 1985, 1986). Even then, however, 20 to 30 percent of the experiments generated less than individually rational outcomes, suggesting that the subjects behave more like Lockeans than like utilitarians or egalitarians.

These results raise two issues of particular import for the present discussion. The first relates to the social context within which bargains over rights take place. The fact that subjects who had earned the right to be the controller evidenced a greater willingness to seek their own gain than did those who were randomly assigned to the controller's position suggests that social context or situational behavioral norms play a role in determining agent behavior (including the extent to which the behavior would be considered rational) within the bargaining process. What is not immediately clear is whether and how such factors may influence "legal-economic" bargains as opposed to traditionally "economic" bargains. However, the strong possibility that agents may view these contexts differently suggests that there may well be important differences in how agents behave in the different bargaining situations.

Second, the fact that "educating" the subjects in the implications of having the controller right increased the degree to which behavior could be called rational raises the issue of cognitive limitations—for instance, bounded rationality—and their influence on agent behavior. The assumption that agents are familiar with legal rules and respond accordingly (i.e., rationally) is central to the evaluation of the implications of alternative legal rules within law and economics. That the "education" of subjects can have such significant effects in altering their behavior, as in the Harrison and McKee experiments, and, more generally, that cognitive limitations may impair the learning of the law, calls into question the assumption that the behavioral response to legal rules can be determined straightforwardly with the rational actor model. The import of this becomes even more apparent when one considers that studies suggest people are rather ignorant of many noncriminal civil and common laws that pertain to their activities (Ellickson 1989a, 40–41). Of course, this also has implications for Lockean behavior, since perceptions of the extent of rights seem to influence behavior in such circumstances.

Case 2: Altruism

A subsequent set of experiments undertaken by Coursey, Hoffman, and Spitzer (1987) further calls into question the *homo economicus* behavioral characterization. In an attempt to get at the potential influence of an "affront to dignity effect" that may influence externality bargains (by, for example, causing people not to bargain or to be unwilling to assign a value to the externality), Coursey, Hoffman, and Spitzer conducted experiments that introduced a discomforting externality. This was accomplished by introducing the possibility that the "victim" would have to hold one ounce of an unpleasant-tasting liquid in his or her mouth for twenty seconds. These experiments had two possible payoffs: (1) the "polluter" gets $0, and the victim gets $10 and does not have to taste the liquid; (2) the "polluter" gets $20, and the victim gets $10 and docs have to taste the liquid. The latter outcome, where the victim is exposed to the externality is, of course, the efficient one. Out of forty experiments, the efficient outcome was chosen 95 percent of the time. The rather interesting anomaly within these experiments lies in the fact that, when the "polluter" was the controller, fully half of the polluters paid the victim to taste the liquid (paying an average of $4.36), even though the polluter had the right to force the victim to do so without any compensation.

The immediate issue raised by this result is that of altruism and its influence on bargaining behavior in this context. At first glance, one might argue that this seemingly altruistic behavior is without great import, since its only effect is distributional—efficiency being obtained 100 percent of the time when the "polluters" are the controllers. However, if we assume that the distributional implications of law are an important ingredient in legal decision making or in the evaluation of the potential outcomes of alternative legal rules, it becomes important to understand how the potential for altruistic behavior might manifest itself in various contexts. For example, is such behavior equally evident in bargaining over the price of, say, a rug at a bazaar or over the price of an automobile? That is, to what extent does behavior vary with the context of the bargain, and how does behavior in the legal context differ, if at all, from that in more overtly economic contexts?

More important, however, these experimental results do not establish that the altruistic behavior evidenced is strictly distributional in its implications. The experimental framework employed by Coursey, Hoffman, and Spitzer is all-or-nothing: the subject either tastes the foul liquid or does not. Suppose, instead, that the externality takes the form of a continuum of possible externality levels, such as with pollution. How might altruism manifest itself here? Altruism, after all, is simply a form of forbearance. The "polluter" is willing to forgo a portion of his potential gain for the sake of the victim. In these experiments, this entailed the payment of unowed compensation to the victim, but, again, the experiments were all-or-nothing. Might it not be the case that, with a continuous externality, the "polluter" might choose, instead, simply to emit less of the externality? If so, the altruistic behavior pointed to by these experiments would have allocative (or efficiency) as well as distributional effects, which again calls into question the ability of the standard model to correctly evaluate the effects of alternative legal rules.

Case 3: The Stability of Tastes and Preferences

One of the major limitations of the Hoffman and Spitzer experiments is that they fail to get at the Coase Theorem's invariance proposition—that the parties will bargain to *the same* efficient result regardless of to whom rights are initially assigned. That is, in these experiments there is a unique efficient result, so that efficiency and invariance go hand in hand. This does not allow for the possibility that, for example, divergences between the amount that one is willing to pay (WTP) to acquire a right and the amount that one is willing to accept (WTA) to give up that right may cause individuals to bargain to *different* efficient results, depending on to which party the right is initially assigned. Might effects such as the normative sanction for rights, an affront to dignity, or wealth effects cause a divergence between WTA and WTP? While the evidence regarding the existence of a divergence between WTA and WTP is not uniform,[10] it seems to weigh in favor of the existence of a nontrivial divergence, one that is too large to be explained solely in terms of wealth effects. In particular, recent experimental treatments of this issue support the contention that WTA may be substantially greater than WTP, often more than twice as great (Hoffman and Spitzer 1993, 69–85).

While this literature is too vast to survey here, one set of experiments, undertaken by Daniel Kahneman, Jack Knetsch, and Richard Thaler (1990), probes this issue in the context of the Coase Theorem and, in a number of different types of experiments, finds significant "endowment effects." Using items such as mugs, pens, binoculars, and chocolate bars, they find that individuals, when given the opportunity to exchange

10. See the survey by Hoffman and Spitzer (1993) and the references cited therein.

these items for cash, exhibit a strong reluctance to part with entitlements and thus that, contrary to standard assumption of economic theory, preferences are apparently not independent of entitlements. The value that the subjects place on these objects "appears to increase substantially as soon as the individual is given the object" (Kahneman, Knetsch, and Thaler 1990, 1342), and the resulting disparity between WTA and WTP does not dissipate in repeated trials (i.e., with market experience). They suggest that this endowment effect is most likely to occur for items that are not easily replaceable, which makes the endowment effect particularly important for the Coase Theorem–type bargains over rights, since things like a nice view, clean air, and water are not easily replaced, and it thus can be expected that people will refuse to sell such goods even at prices somewhat greater than their reservation price for buying them.

Two implications of these WTA versus WTP experiments are particularly important. The most obvious is that the presence of endowment effects contradicts the assumption of stable preferences (see, for example, the quotation from Becker, above). While preference stability predicts an invariant allocation of resources under alternative rights assignments, the results discussed here provide strong evidence against invariance in the outcomes of bargains even when transaction costs are zero. Second, endowment effects reduce the gains from trade, as compared with a world in which preferences are independent of endowments. Since fewer mutually advantageous exchanges are possible, the volume of trade is lower than it otherwise would be (Kahneman, Knetsch, and Thaler 1990, 1344). Given the size of the potential disparity between WTA and WTP, one can conceive of situations where each party's WTA is greater than the other party's WTP, so that no trade would occur, whereas if WTA were equal to WTP, we would see bargains consummated. Experiments run to test this implication in a Coase Theorem context revealed substantial undertrading relative to the theorem's predictions (1339–41). Even when transaction costs are negligible, then, there does not seem to be much room for confidence in the generation of an invariant outcome when consumers are party to an externality.

These implications, in turn, have a further implication—calling into question what it means to assign rights efficiently (or "mimic the market") when transaction costs are sufficiently high to preclude bargaining. If, because of endowment effects, the efficient outcome when A is given the right is X, and the efficient outcome when B is given the right is Y, and the divergence between X and Y is nontrivial, what does it mean to assign rights efficiently or develop efficient legal rules? This question has yet to be addressed.

2.2. Beyond the Shadow of the Law

Case 4: Order without Law (I)—Love Thy Neighbor
A recent empirical study undertaken by Robert Ellickson (1991) examines, among other things, the effects of open- versus closed-range laws on cattle-trespass disputes in Shasta County, California. Under open-range laws, cattlemen are not usually responsible for accidental trespass damage, whereas they are strictly liable under closed-range laws. Ellickson finds that cattlemen and their neighbors do in fact cooperate to resolve their disputes regardless of who is liable, as the Coase Theorem suggests. However, the evidence also suggests that it is not Coase Theorem–type mechanisms at work here; rather, individuals seem to rely on community norms to determine their behavior. For example, while the theorem predicts that the cattleman would install a fence if he were liable (closed range), and that the neighboring farmer would do so if he were liable (open range), it is almost always the cattleman who installs the fence because both cattlemen and their neighbors believe the cattleman is morally obligated to do so since his cattle cause the damage. As such, the parties do not bargain "in the shadow of the law," but beyond it; community norms seem to have much more force than the legal rule in place. Ellickson suggests that this may be due to the fact that relations among the neighbors are both complex and continuing, because of which the transaction costs associated with acquiring information and litigating disputes are high, and reliance on norms offers a lower-cost way of resolving these disputes.[11]

Ellickson also finds that the citizens of Shasta County seem to be very ignorant of certain important aspects of relevant law and ignore those aspects of the law that conflict with their view of the world. For example, ranchers tend to believe that vehicle-livestock collisions are governed by strict liability, so that the passage of closed-range ordinances increases the rancher's liability for damages in these collisions. In fact, however, these vehicle-livestock collisions are governed by the law of negligence in both open- and closed-range situations, and the farmer is as likely to be found

11. Ellickson (1989a, 1991) also suggests that this norm-based behavior points to the need to revise certain of the behavioral concepts underlying law and economics.

liable in one situation as in the other (Ellickson 1991, ch. 5). The existence of social norms that seem to drive the perception of rights suggests that there exist cognitive barriers to dissonant information (Ellickson 1989a, 42–43), which again calls into question the manner in which individuals respond to legal rules or to changes therein.

Two other empirical studies offer similar evidence for the role of situational norms in Coase Theorem–type situations. In a study that has interesting commonalities with that of Ellickson, Nick Hanley and Charles Sumner (1995) examine an externality situation owing to the roaming of red deer in the Scottish Highlands, which causes damage to growing trees and, in the process, imposes substantial costs on the owners of these forests, the value of the timber from which is diminished. In addition, the wandering deer may destroy growing crops on farmland, and, when they stray onto sheep grazing land, reduce the forage for sheep, thus imposing costs on both farmers and sheep ranchers. The beneficiaries of the red deer population are estate owners, who derive substantial income and estate value from the presence of red deer on their estates.

Given the level of damage, the small number of parties, the ease of quantifying damage to forests, and the relative ease with which estate owners could reduce the size of their herds, the situation seems to reflect an inefficiently high deer population and a fertile ground for the working of Coase Theorem–type mechanisms. Even so, there is no evidence of any instances of Coasean bargaining between owners of deer estates and neighboring landowners. What one does observe, however, are Deer Management Groups, which neighboring landowners have established "to coordinate deer management across neighboring estates . . . and forest/farmland, in order to reduce the level of the externality." The advantage of such groups is that they "effectively [internalize] the externality across members of the group," thereby avoiding the third-party effects that can result with bilateral bargaining (Hanley and Sumner 1995, 93). It is interesting to note the parallel between the rise of the cooperative Deer Management Groups and the behavior of neighbors revealed in Ellickson's study of cattle ranching in Shasta County. While the law offers a low-cost option (free government culling) for dealing with red deer damage, groups of neighboring landowners in essence ignore the law and work out a solution among themselves, perhaps because the transaction costs associated with the cooperative efforts of the Deer Management Groups are lower than those that would attend bilateral negotiations of the Coasean variety (Hanley and Sumner 1995, 93), or, following Ellickson, because of the interest in maintaining harmonious relations among neighbors.

Perhaps the most unique empirical test of the Coase Theorem is John Donohue's (1989) analysis of the Illinois employment experiment (Woodbury and Spiegelman 1987), which attempted to determine whether the payment of bonuses to unemployed workers for securing employment, or to employers for hiring unemployed workers, would reduce the duration of unemployment and the costs associated with the unemployment compensation system. While the experiment was conducted to ascertain how such bonuses might affect the duration of unemployment, its application to the Coase Theorem is straightforward. The efficiency hypothesis predicts that mutually advantageous bargains will be struck under either scheme, and all workers and employers who satisfy the eligibility requirements will collect bonuses. The allocative invariance proposition suggests that members of the worker payment group (WPG) will find jobs and collect bonuses at the same rate as members of the employer payment group (EPG). The invariant distribution hypothesis predicts that members of the WPG and EPG groups will have the same aggregate compensation (wage plus bonus). The WPG workers would be expected to have lower wages than EPG workers, reflecting a bargaining away of a share of their bonus, as compared to EPG workers' higher wages as employers bargained away a share of their bonus.

Donohue's inquiry into the results of the Illinois experiment reveals that they contradict the predictions of the Coase Theorem on all counts. To begin with, the number of bonuses paid to WPG workers was about five times that paid to EPG employers. Furthermore, many workers and employers who met the requirements for bonuses failed to submit a voucher to receive their bonus—particularly employers. Given this, says Donohue, "the conclusion that a number of individuals and employers acted inefficiently is hard to rebut" (1989, 573). The experimental results also revealed that members of the WPG had a significantly greater improvement in obtaining employment, relative to the control group, than did members of the EPG, which, along with the differential bonus collection rates among the groups, violates the allocative invariance prediction of the theorem (569–77). Finally, there was no significant difference in wages across the WPG and EPG hirees, so that aggregate (wages plus bonus) compensation was higher for WPG workers than for EPG workers, in violation of the invariant distribution prediction of the theorem. That is, it appears that workers did not bargain with employers over the wage or the bonus as a result of this program (586–90).

Donohue (1989, 591–601) contends that transaction costs are extremely low here, and thus that the theorem fails in a case quite favorable to its success, but his conclusion has been challenged by Ellickson (1989b) and James Lindgren (1990), both of whom contend that Donohue greatly underestimates the effect of transaction costs within this experiment. Collecting this so-called free money actually involves a substantial number of steps (and even more for employers than for workers), the aggregate effect of which is to make the process rather costly, *relative to the size of the bonus*. The relative size of these transaction costs can thus explain (and, indeed, would lead one to predict) both the low bonus-collection rates and the differential bonus-collection rates between WPG and EPG subjects.[12] Moreover, the presence of stigma and institutional rigidity effects[13] would lead one to predict minimal bargaining over wages and bonuses (in an amount different from the control group), a result supported by the Illinois experiment. In fact, Ellickson finds the results of the Illinois experiment very consistent with his own study of Shasta County: people often tend to rely on norms rather than on "legal rules" to govern their behavior, particularly when the stakes are low and there is an expectation of a continuing relationship, as among neighbors in Shasta County and between employers and employees in the Illinois experiment (Ellickson 1989b, 627–28).

Case 5: Order without Law (II)—Of Confucius and Contracts

One of the important underlying features of the Coase Theorem is the idea that rights must be well defined and fully enforceable at law in order for bargains over rights to be consummated in the manner envisioned by the Coase Theorem. The converse of this is that, when rights do not exist or are not enforceable at law, the potential for problems such as

12. See Lindgren 1990, 583 and Ellickson 1989b, 625. Of course, if transaction costs were zero, the entire premise of the experiment would disappear, since job search is a positive transaction cost phenomenon (Lindgren 1990, 578).

13. The stigma effects would come from the worker identifying himself with the program and trying to bargain (in effect, over the EPG bonus) to secure a higher wage or in offering (because of the WPG bonus) to work for a lower wage, and institutional rigidities would inhibit employers from engaging in such bargaining in order to avoid treating these new employees differently from existing employees.

opportunistic behavior will greatly reduce the incentive to undertake, and thus the making of, such bargains. This difficulty, of course, goes beyond the types of legal disputes to which the Coase Theorem is usually applied, to include bargains over rights generally through the contracting process. One of the implications of this is that, in an area without a well-developed system of contract law, the rise of a smooth system of contracting and exchange will be precluded.

As Janet Landa (e.g., 1981, 1994) has shown, however, this prediction does not hold true—that is, transactions without law do not uniformly break down, and a case study in the success of such contracting can be found among the Chinese middlemen of Southeast Asia. These traders use the Confucian code of ethics to classify potential trading partners into various categories based on social distance: kin, class, village, dialect or province, and nation. The Confucian code specifies that the degree of obligation of one person to another varies with social distance, falling as one moves farther away from the self. Given these Confucian norms, the most reliable group with which to trade will be one's kinsmen, and the least reliable non-Chinese. Making the necessary classification of potential trading partners is relatively easy and can usually be accomplished by noting his dialect, surname, and place of origin. The result of this process, Landa finds, is the formation of ethnically homogeneous middleman groups (EHMGs), which share a like code of Confucian ethics that promotes mutual trust among traders and imposes informal social sanctions, such as ostracism from the group, on those who fail to meet their contractual obligations.[14]

It should be clear that the point to be taken from this is not that law does not matter. Indeed, one can point to innumerable examples of situations where unspecified rights or the absence of a legal enforcement mechanism does indeed lead to the breakdown of transactions (or impedes the development of such), along the lines implied by neoclassical economic theory or even standard transaction-cost economics. But, as Landa's work illustrates, the choice process takes place within a larger framework of social relations—informal institutions—the explanation for which necessitates the incorporation of, for example, sociology, anthropology, and political science (in Landa's case) to explain agent behavior and the rise or role of informal institutions.

14. Landa finds similar phenomena among other social groups in a variety of cultural contexts. See Landa 1994, 1996.

One feature common to several of these empirical studies—Ellickson's, Landa's, and Donohue's in particular—is the presence of nonnegligible transaction costs. The problems raised by transaction costs are amenable to analysis within the standard rational choice framework, where they would be treated in a manner identical to the treatment of costs generally and through such subjected to the forces of optimization. Indeed, this is how transaction costs have traditionally been treated within law and economics, as reflected, for example, in the dictum that agents will bargain over rights as long as expected gains exceed expected costs, where the latter include the costs of transacting.

While we have observed in the foregoing that agents do not necessarily behave according to the dictates of rational choice theory when transaction costs are very low, it is useful to put this to one side for a moment to consider the question of how agents respond when transaction costs are nonnegligible. The studies of Ellickson, Landa, and Donohue, especially, suggest that agents fall back on other factors, such as norms, to govern their actions when transaction costs, and especially information costs, are high. The counter that falling back on these norms constitutes a rational response to the presence of transaction costs misses the point in that, while such may indeed be the case (or very well may not), rational choice theory provides us with little insight into the problem—into, that is, why people do what they do. Rational choice theory may provide an ex post justification for reliance on norms to govern individual relations or decision making, but in and of itself it does not, a priori, enlighten us as to how agents will behave.

This is not to say that high transaction costs are the sole rationale for the existence of or reliance on norms, as witnessed by the Lockean behavior exhibited by subjects in the Hoffman and Spitzer experiments, where transaction costs were very low (and a continuing relationship was not expected). However, the evidence does seem to suggest a greater propensity to rely on norms or rules of thumb to govern decision making when transaction costs are high—for bounded rationality reasons or otherwise. The explanation for and prediction of such behavior would seem to necessitate the bringing in of insights from other disciplines, as Ellickson and Landa have done.

3. Looking Back and Looking Ahead

How does the historian of economic thought look at the field of law and economics and economic imperialism generally? It is still far too early to pass any sort of final judgment on either, as neither law and economics nor the so-called imperialist project has run its course or reached its final form. Nonetheless, sufficient time has passed, and evolution taken place, for one to offer some perspective on the past, and, perhaps, into the future.

It was noted at the beginning of this discussion that law and economics began in this century as but one facet of a general or multidisciplinary social science approach to law during the Legal Realist period—an age when law came to be seen as instrumental in nature and the interrelations between legal and economic processes came to be increasingly recognized. But post-1960 law and economics took on a very different form. The field arose as a unidirectional phenomenon, applying economics to law and not the other way around, and as the *economic* analysis of law, rather than as part of a general social-scientific approach to legal thinking. In both of these senses, post-1960 law and economics arose as an imperialistic movement, purporting, in the hands of some at least, to provide *the* key to legal reasoning.

Many economists have looked askance at the imperialist project, and perhaps the vast majority of scholars in law and other disciplines upon which economists trained their sights regarded these forays with suspicion, contempt, or disdain, the theories proffered as wrong, and the normative prescriptions repugnant. But the field of law and economics, at least, and I would argue, economic imperialism generally, is beginning to mellow as it approaches middle age. Law and economics rocketed to prominence because, in the hands of its most able exponents, the field seemed to offer substantial insights into the legal arena at a time when legal thinking was in search of moorings and economists were armed with rather new, sophisticated weaponry for analyzing individual choices. And, following the Beckerian dictum, this weaponry was "relentlessly and unflinchingly" applied.

Recently, however, a number of law and economics scholars have begun to search for a more behaviorally grounded law and economics. Why? Two reasons can be suggested. First, the application of the rational actor model within law and economics has long been under attack by many within the legal community—including by individuals sympathetic to the law and economics project—on the grounds that it is an inaccurate depiction of behavior within the legal realm. The fact that so many law and economics scholars today have at least one foot in the legal community (that is, are both legal scholars and economists, and thus multidisciplinary, rather than simply economists doing law) may make them more open to the validity of this criticism and to the search for a more accurate or well-rounded depiction of agent behavior, particularly in light of evidence such as that described in this essay. Second, recent scholarship within economics—by, for example, Richard Thaler and Robert Frank, and the application of ideas of Herbert Simon and Daniel Kahneman and Amos Tversky—has cast doubt on the extent to which one can fruitfully apply the rational actor model and has begun to offer new and insightful ways to think about and model individual behavior. The openness of many in the law and economics community to the insights provided by other fields may make them more open to these insights and their application.

As Alfred Marshall noted in his *Principles*, "the whole range of man's actions in society is too wide and too various to be explained by a single intellectual effort" (1920, 636)—economics or otherwise. Reflecting a similar sentiment, Ronald Coase (1977) predicted a rather short life for the economic imperialism movement, mainly because economists were exporting utility theory, which he considered to be of dubious value outside of economics (and even within it), and because economists lacked the specialized knowledge to make major, continuing contributions to these other disciplines and thus would eventually be driven out. These predictions have not been entirely borne out by the course of events. Yet, economists have by no means taken over these disciplines, either. What has transpired, however, is the incorporation of certain important insights from economics into the standard work in these other disciplines—which is as it should be, since economics has something useful to say (although likely in more tempered form that some imperialists may believe) to these other disciplines. More important, from the perspective of economics, economists have begun to bring back insights from certain of these other disciplines into their economic analysis. At present, this is much more along the lines of a trickle than a tidal wave, but at least it has some promise.

This having been said, it would be wrong to think that law and economics is coming full circle, back to its early-twentieth-century form. Indeed, it would be unfortunate if it did so, since post-1960 law and economics has done a great deal to enrich our understanding of legal-economic processes. Great insights often come from pushing an idea (even an incorrect one) to the limit to see what happens; then, when the dust settles, you see what you've got and proceed accordingly. In the process of doing this, the field of law and economics seems to be moving back toward its roots in its incorporation of the insights of other social sciences, a movement that holds the promise of a richer law and economics. As Marshall noted, "Specialists who never look beyond their own domain are apt to see things out of true proportion" (1920, 636). Law, after all, like so many things, is too important to be left solely to the economists.

References

Allen, Douglas W. 1991. What Are Transaction Costs? *Research in Law and Economics* 14:1–18.

Becker, Gary S. 1976. *The Economic Approach to Human Behavior*. Chicago: University of Chicago Press.

Calabresi, Guido. 1961. Some Thoughts on Risk Distribution and the Law of Torts. *Yale Law Journal* 70:499–553.

Coase, Ronald H. 1960. The Problem of Social Cost. *Journal of Law and Economics* 3 (October): 1–44.

———. 1977. Economics and Contiguous Disciplines. In *The Organization and Retrieval of Economic Knowledge*, edited by Mark Perlman. Boulder, Colo.: Westview Press.

Cooter, Robert D. 1989. The Coase Theorem. In *The New Palgrave: Allocation, Information, and Markets*, edited by John Eatwell, Murray Milgate, and Peter Newman. New York: Norton.

Coursey, Don L., Elizabeth Hoffman, and Matthew L. Spitzer. 1987. Fear and Loathing in the Coase Theorem: Experimental Tests Involving Physical Discomfort. *Journal of Legal Studies* 16 (January): 217–48.

Donohue, John J., III. 1989. Diverting the Coasean River: Incentive Schemes to Reduce Unemployment Spells. *Yale Law Journal* 99 (December): 549–609.

Ellickson, Robert C. 1989a. Bringing Culture and Human Frailty to Rational Actors: A Critique of Classical Law and Economics. *Chicago-Kent Law Review* 65.1:23–55.

———. 1989b. The Case for Coase and against Coaseanism. *Yale Law Journal* 99 (December): 623–87.

———. 1991. *Order without Law: How Neighbors Settle Disputes*. Cambridge: Harvard University Press.

Hanley, Nick, and Charles Sumner. 1995. Bargaining over Common Property Resources: Applying the Coase Theorem to Red Deer in the Scottish Highlands. *Journal of Environmental Management* 43 (January): 87–95.

Harrison, Glenn W., and Michael McKee. 1985. Experimental Evaluation of the Coase Theorem. *Journal of Law and Economics* 28 (October): 653–70.

Hoffman, Elizabeth, and Matthew L. Spitzer. 1982. The Coase Theorem: Some Ex-

perimental Tests. *Journal of Law and Economics* 25 (April): 73–98.
———. 1985. Entitlements, Rights and Fairness: An Experimental Examination of Subjects' Concepts of Distributive Justice. *Journal of Legal Studies* 14 (June): 259–97.
———. 1986. Experimental Tests of the Coase Theorem with Large Bargaining Groups. *Journal of Legal Studies* 15 (January): 149–71.
———. 1993. Willingness to Pay vs. Willingness to Accept: Legal and Economic Implications. *Washington University Law Quarterly* 71 (spring): 59–114.
Hovenkamp, Herbert. 1990. Marginal Utility and the Coase Theorem. *Cornell Law Review* 75 (May): 783–810.
Kahneman, Daniel, Jack L. Knetsch, and Richard H. Thaler. 1990. Experimental Effects of the Endowment Effect and the Coase Theorem. *Journal of Political Economy* 98 (December): 1325–48.
Landa, Janet T. 1981. A Theory of the Ethnically Homogeneous Middleman Group: An Institutional Alternative to Contract Law. *Journal of Legal Studies* 10 (June): 34–62.
———. 1994. *Trust, Ethnicity, and Identity: Beyond the New Institutional Economics of Ethnic Trading Networks, Contract Law, and Gift-Exchange*. Ann Arbor: University of Michigan Press.
———. 1996. Doing the Economics of Trust and Informal Institutions. In *Foundations of Research in Economics: How Do Economists Do Economics?* edited by Steven G. Medema and Warren J. Samuels. Aldershot: Edward Elgar.
Lindgren, James. 1990. "Ol' Man River . . . He Keeps Rollin' Along": A Reply to Donohue's Diverting the Coasean River. *Georgetown Law Journal* 78 (February): 577–91.
Marshall, Alfred. 1920. *Principles of Economics*, 8th ed. London: Macmillan.
Medema, Steven G. 1995. The Coase Theorem. Working Paper, no. 9510. University of Colorado at Denver, Center for Research on Economic and Social Policy.
Medema, Steven G. and Richard O. Zerbe Jr. 1997. The Coase Theorem. In *The Encyclopedia of Law and Economics*, edited by Boudewijn Bouckaert and Gerrit De Geest. Aldershot: Edward Elgar.
Posner, Richard A. 1992. *Economic Analysis of Law*, 4th ed. Boston: Little, Brown.
Response to the Efficiency Symposium. 1980. *Hofstra Law Review* 8 (summer).
Robbins, Lionel. 1932. *An Essay on the Nature and Significance of Economic Science*. London: Macmillan.
Schwab, Stewart. 1988. A Coasean Experiment on Contract Presumptions. *Journal of Legal Studies* 17 (June): 237–68.
Symposium on Efficiency as a Legal Concern. 1980. *Hofstra Law Review* 8 (spring).
Woodbury, Stephen A., and Robert G. Spiegelman. 1987. Bonuses to Workers and Employers to Reduce Unemployment: Randomized Trials in Illinois. *American Economic Review* 77 (September): 513–30.
Zerbe, Richard O., Jr. 1980. The Problem of Social Cost in Retrospect. *Research in Law and Economics* 2:83–102.

Putting a Different Spin on QALYs: Beyond a Sociological Critique

Joshua Cohen

In their *Health and Efficiency: A Sociology of Health Economics*, Malcolm Ashmore, Michael Mulkay, and Trevor Pinch (AMP) devote several chapters to the concept of quality-adjusted life years (QALYs). The QALY approach defines the value of a person's life in terms of the number of years that a person can expect to live multiplied by that person's level of well-being (his or her quality-of-life adjustment factor) during those years. Levels of well-being can be measured by asking respondents to rate health states in relation to two arbitrarily defined "anchor points." For instance, death can be assigned the value zero and perfect health the value one. If a person faces the prospect of living in a wheelchair for ten years, and that person feels that life in a wheelchair has half the value of life in perfect health, the number of QALYs is five. QALYs can be subsequently used in cost-utility analyses as a means of determining the cost-effectiveness of alternative medical treatments, for instance.[1] In turn, these cost-utility analyses may serve as a means of prioritizing medical treatments; priority of a treatment is determined on the basis of its comparative cost-per-QALY ratio (Williams 1985).

AMP's point of departure is a sociological study of health economics as a subdiscipline within economics. They are severely critical of both the QALY concept and its (potential) application in the British National Health

I would like to thank Mary Morgan for her constructive comments on a preliminary draft of this article. I would also like to thank John Davis, the discussant of my paper at the 1996 *HOPE* conference, for his comments and suggestions.

1. Note that QALYs are not used in cost-benefit analyses. Cost-utility analyses differ from cost-benefit studies in that utilities are not expressed in monetary terms, whereas benefits are.

Service. AMP are sociologists who, during the 1980s, worked together at the University of York in Britain. Their choice of health economics as an object of sociological study seems a logical one, given the fact that their department was located adjacent to the University of York Center for Health Economics. This center was and is considered the focal point for health economic research in Britain. It was the breeding ground for early QALY research in Britain, which began in the 1970s. It has contributed to the founding of two top-quality health economic journals—the *Journal of Health Economics* and *Health Economics*.

AMP have frequently been involved in public debates with researchers from the York Center for Health Economics. Many of these debates revolved around the so-called QALY league table—a table of cost-per-QALY figures drafted in 1986 by the York Center's director, Alan Williams. This controversial table prioritized medical treatments according to comparative cost-per-QALY ratios. The table provoked an outcry from the medical community in Britain and the United States. It was particularly worrisome to medical ethicists that medical treatments would be prioritized according to economic criteria. AMP became somewhat involved in the ethical debate, but they focused most of their attention on sociological aspects.

AMP's critique is appealing mainly because it, unlike the majority of studies on QALYs, sharply distinguishes the issues of defining and measuring QALYs from distributing QALYs. I also have "qualms about QALYs" (per Smith 1987), but unlike Smith's distributional concerns, my qualms are primarily related to conceptual and measurement matters. It seems of utmost importance to know *what* is going to be distributed *before* tackling distributional issues. If it turns out that QALYs are unmeasurable, or conceptually flawed to begin with, then there would seem to be no use distributing QALYs. Consequently, equity concerns at this point would be irrelevant.

I also agree with AMP that QALYs are "socially constructed." It seems useful to study QALYs from a sociological perspective—that is, to investigate who developed QALYs, which political and perhaps ideological interests were at stake, and how QALYs were put together. However, AMP's story misrepresents the QALYs approach in a number of ways. Crucially, it misrepresents the story behind the measurement of QALYs. It does this by falsely suggesting that the QALY approach *imposes* quantification of qualitative judgments. In my view, the QALY approach does not impose quantification; it *explores* the *possibility* that qualitative judgments can be numerically represented—much the same as the psychophysical approach to measuring sensations in psychology explores the possibility that qualitative judgments of stimuli can be numerically represented. What is needed to amplify AMP's study is a historical contextualization of QALYs that places QALYs firmly within the context of clinical, psychological, and economic quality of life measurements. The issues surrounding QALYs then become associated primarily with psychology and psychological measurement.

Section 1 of this chapter begins with a brief summary of the main points in AMP's sociological critique. What is missing in this critique is an adequate appreciation of QALYs' historical roots. This deficiency translates into a number of misconceptions and inadequately grounded claims. In order to remedy this, I set out in section 2 a historical outline of recent quality-of-life measurement, placing QALYs within this interdisciplinary tradition. In section 3, I argue for a psychophysical interpretation of the QALY approach. Here, the longer term historical connections between the QALY method and the psychophysicist program are investigated. Section 4 assesses the claims put forward by AMP with regard to the (im)possibility of measurement of quality of life. Finally, section 5 explores certain conceptual distinctions between belief, desire, and choice. Here, I describe the problem of intentionality, in particular, the problem of measuring intentional variables. I conclude with an evaluation of the role that measurement, using the psychologist's notion of experience utility, plays in relation to framing decision scenarios, and bootstrapping the expected utility hypothesis relative to expected utility theory.

1. Synopsis of AMP's Critique

AMP's book is about the possibly pernicious effects of "economics imperialism" in the area of health care. One of the main themes of the book is the allegation that QALYs constitute a peculiar artifact of the "economist's culture" and concomitantly a way of "colonizing the mind" of decision makers in the health care sector. AMP suggest that the fact that health economists even attempt to *measure* quality of life owes to their inherent culture of quantification. This "culture of numbers" is severely criticized for doing the impossible: measuring what is unmeasurable. Furthermore, because the health economists' instruments (their ways of measuring QALYs) reflect *their* value structure, the measurement process distorts "real" preferences and therefore renders the outcomes of QALY studies dubious. It is further argued that the QALY concept is a health economist's invention that, when employed in cost-utility analysis, reduces highly complex matters of health and health resource allocation to ostensibly simple calculations. The fear is that the numerical expressions of benefits will lead a life of their own (see also Self 1975, 91–93). This "simplification" of a complex problem is deceptive, AMP argue, for it remains to be seen whether the assumptions made in the process of simplification are valid.

In summarizing AMP's main arguments, I have oversimplified AMP's critique of QALYs, perhaps even to the point of caricaturizing it. Now I hope to rectify this caricature, at least partially, by discussing AMP's specific criticisms of measurement procedures such as magnitude estimation. This said, it remains the case that AMP's study is virtually a-historical. As such, *it* creates a caricature of QALYs. It is this image of QALYs that I hope to rectify first.

In light of the broad history of health-related quality-of-life measures and the history of QALYs in particular (see section 2), AMP's allegations and claims regarding the health economist's supposed hegemony with respect to quality-of-life measurement, seem exaggerated to say the least. The QALY concept is anything but a sole artifact of the (health) economist's culture. In fact, QALYs are an artifact of a number of disciplines, including the economist's. Even if an economist coined the term, its meaning is derived from an interdisciplinary culture of psychologists, clinicians, and economists. The suggestion is blatantly false that health economists are single-handedly "colonizing the mind" of those who work in the health sector and those who have an interest in that sector's efficiency. *Clinicians*, during the 1940s and 1950s, interested in improving both the cost and clinical efficiency of alternative medical regimens, introduced the idea that morbidity and mortality are two subdimensions that ought to be combined on a unidimensional scale (Klarman, O'Francis, and Rosenthal 1968; Bush, Fanshel, and Chen 1972; Weinstein and Stason 1977). And well before the establishment of health economics as a subdiscipline, politicians and hospital administrators addressed the problem of cost inefficiency in the health care sector, albeit mostly in ad hoc fashion (Ginzberg 1987).

It might be the case that part of the reason AMP attribute so much of the change in thinking about the management of the health care sector to health economists is that they have accepted the health economist's rhetoric on QALYs. Health economists have a tendency to act as if their ideas with respect to health state measurement and health sector reform are uniquely original and must be passed on to others who are as yet oblivious to the problem. Gavin Mooney for instance, claims that health economists need to take on the role of "educating others—be they doctors, nurses, administrators, politicians, patients or the public generally . . . to try to change a way of thinking" (1992, 6).[2] He clearly sees the health economist as a missionary of sorts—someone who will reveal the inner secrets of the problems in health care management. Mooney is unaware, or perhaps ignorant, of the fact that health care managers and providers have for some time been exploring many ways of improving both the clinical and economic efficiency of hosptial practice. To say that "what is currently done in health services by way of output measurement is really pretty dreadful" (48–49) completely ignores the vast clinical literature on health state measurement which has been published since the 1940s (see Bowling 1991; Spilker 1991).

"Managerialism" as Michael Bury (1994) calls it, a system of monitoring costs and benefits in the health care sector, is not something that crept out of the economist's culture only to invade the minds of noneconomists who were somehow ignorant of the problem. "Managerialism" in health practice probably started out in the general practitioner's office hundreds of years ago (Glasser 1991). Monitoring the effects of treatment was (and is) a key to the success of any doctor's practice. Here, the two most important dimensions were (and are) mortality (number of life-years) and morbidity (quality of these life-years). The practice of monitoring seems to have become fully *systematized* during the 1940s and 1950s. Fortunately, several prominent health economists such as Anthony J. Culyer have acknowledged that "much of the genuine innovation [in health measurement] . . . has come from outside the ranks of the economics profession, from operations researchers, psychologists, epidemiologists, and clinical researchers" (1981, 8). C. Gudex also admits that the "impetus behind the original development of such concepts as the QALY came more from two other groups—the members of the medical profession and of health service management" (1990, 218).

2. Mooney is one of several health economists who AMP cite as having successfully convinced the British medical community of the need to use QALY analysis. AMP also refer to P. Drummond, A. Maynard, and A. Williams as having been pivotal figures in the QALY debate. Using textual analysis, AMP carefully examine how these health economists attempted to persuade the British medical community to accept QALYs as a means of prioritizing health care treatments. Oddly, they then leave the impression that health economists were successful in their efforts. However, what AMP seem to have overlooked is that the British medical community, like its counterpart in the United States, is still currently deeply divided over prioritizing health care.

AMP's attacks on the value-ladenness of the QALY analysis appear to also have been given impetus by health economists' rhetoric on this issue. Health economists tend to argue that preferences concerning health states have no specific substantive attributes such as pleasure or satisfaction. These preferences refer to nothing but what the respondent desires, which could literally be anything. In a discussion of the issue of what QALYS measure, Culyer distinguishes between three separate utility concepts: two—pleasure and happiness—have "substantive" attributes; the other kind of utility is strictly formal. This latter is merely a "means . . . of ranking preferences or choices" (Culyer 1990, 16). Citing Alchian's famous paper on utility, Culyer puts his weight behind the idea of a formal utility with no implications other than the possibility that "we can assign numbers to entities or conditions which a person can strive to realize" (17). According to Culyer, formal utility has allowed for "extensive exploration of 'measurement'" (17), and it has "clarified important meanings (e.g., ordinal, interval and ratio scales), . . . yielded up experimental techniques like the [category] rating scale, the standard gamble, and the time trade-off method for the empirical study of the values [including health state values] that people have" (17). In light of the definition of QALYS and the measurement methods employed in QALY research (see sections 2 and 3), it seems extraordinary to defend, as Culyer does, a purely formal version of utility without any reference to substantive attributes. The language of QALYS is couched in terms of *quality of life* assessment. Moreover, it emphasizes the role of actually experiencing certain mental states of consciousness that relate to sensations of *well-being* (see Veit and Ware 1982; Kane and Froberg 1989; Busschbach 1994).

It also appears doubtful whether QALY analysis can attain the ideal of observer value-neutrality. First, the selection of parameters included in the quality-of-life component already constitutes a value judgment on the part of QALY analysts. Thus, the QALY approach has to surrender the idea of strict value neutrality even at the stage of designing its questionnaires. During the next stage, the point at which QALY analysts evaluate answers to the questionnaires, the QALY approach is even more susceptible to a breakdown in value-neutrality. In order to fulfill the requirements for any *interpersonal* comparison of preferences, one needs for each individual a complete ranking of alternatives, and one needs to establish for each pair of individuals, *i* and *j*, that "it is just as good to be an individual with *i*'s preferences in circumstances A as to be an individual with *j*'s preferences in circumstances B" (Scanlon 1991, 29). Let us call this statement "X." The problem now is how to establish that statements such as X are true. It would appear that the observer as a third person has to make a value judgment in order to determine whether *i* and *j* are equally *satisfied.* QALY proponents often suggest that this particular problem of value judgments can be overcome by simply stating that all QALYs are given equal weight, regardless of who gets them (see Torrance 1976). As a result, interpersonal comparisons are rendered possible by fiat. However, even the statement that a QALY is the same for everybody constitutes a value judgment.

2. Quality of Life Measurement in Recent Historical Perspective

QALYs can be considered a unique type of health-related quality-of-life (HRQL) measure. HRQLs were developed in clinical practice long before health economics became a subdiscipline in economics. One of the first well-known and much-used indices was the Karnofsky performance index devised in 1948. This index is a clinical effectiveness indicator that measures patients' physical functioning following medical treatment for cancer. It has enjoyed a modicum of success in clinical trials as a reliable measuring instrument of patients' physical functioning. Despite the initial success, it was recognized early on that this indicator left out an important element in the overall well-being of patients: their psychological well-being. Although, generally speaking, psychological well-being tended to correlate well with physiological well-being, the exceptions to this tendency were too numerous to ignore. Consequently, starting in the late 1950s, the focus of clinicians involved in HRQL research shifted toward the inclusion of psychological measures of well-being. It should be noted that these morbidity measures had not been ignored by clinicians before the 1950s. However, unlike mortality measures, pre-1950 measures of morbidity had been comparatively ad hoc and lacked systematic validation.

Operations researchers and psychologists joined clinicians during the 1960s and 1970s in developing sophisticated measures of health states and quality of life, coupled with techniques for generating these measures. Work on health state measurement at that time was genuinely interdisciplinary, with operations researchers, clinicians, and psychologists collaborating on several pathbreaking papers in the field of health state and quality-of-life measurement (Bush, Fanshel, and Chen 1972; Rosser and Watts 1972).

The impetus for developing QALYs came directly from clinical experience during the 1960s and 1970s using HRQLs (see, e.g., Rosser and Watts 1972; Rosser, Kind, and Williams 1982; Gudex 1990). The essence and innovative feature of QALYs—namely, combining morbidity and mortality measures in a *unidimensional* scale—paralleled the development of combined physiological-psychological measures just mentioned. By the late 1950s, in clinical research, it was recognized that survival duration was not a sufficient indicator of clinical effectiveness, just as physiological well-being was not a sufficient indicator of overall well-being. Some systematic account had to be taken of the *quality* of life led following treatment. In a cost-effectiveness study by economists Klarman, O'Francis, and Rosenthal (1968), morbidity, seen in terms of a qualitative assessment of physical and mental functioning, and mortality were integrated for the first time in a *systematic* fashion. As far as I know, Bush, Fanshel, and Chen (1972) were the first to use the term "quality-adjusted life year." Their quality-adjusted life year was the product of "function weights," "duration in health states," and the "probability of successful medical intervention." The method of integrating morbidity and mortality slowly gained formal recognition in HRQL research during the 1970s. Perhaps the final stamp of approval concerning the validity and feasibility of this integration came in a now famous essay by J. Pliskin, D. Shephard, and M. Weinstein (1980) entitled "Utility Functions for Life Years and Health Status."

Initially, during the late 1970s and early 1980s, QALY studies were carried out within a multidisciplinary framework. QALY analyses were conducted in a clinical setting with health economists, psychologists, and clinicians working alongside each other. Since the mid 1980s, the interdisciplinary character of QALY analyses seems to have abated. This has coincided with the institutionalization of health economics as a subdiscipline. Health economists have created several fora for specialized discussions on health economics, including the *Journal of Health Economics* and *Health Economics*. Although these fora do not exclude clinical or other noneconomic input, they tend to confine discussions to the domain of "economic" problems that concern the rational allocation of scarce resources.

Since the mid 1980s, there has been an explosive development of quality-of-life measures in the clinical literature. Computer searches in the various social and medical science indexes indicate that since 1986, however, QALYs have scarcely been used by clinicians, while QALYs remain popular with health economists. I suppose that this has to do with the divergent objectives that clinicians and health economists have. On the one hand, health economists are naturally focused on quality-of-life measures that can be readily used in calculating *economic* efficiency. For this purpose, single-figure QALYs fare well: "The [QALY approach] generates a single measure that reflects both the quantity and quality of life" (Weeks 1996, 24). Economic efficiency is usually defined in terms of minimizing cost-utility ratios. On the other hand, clinicians, psychologists, and sociologists working on HRQLs tend to concentrate on measures that gauge *clinical* efficiency (see Cleary and Wilson 1995; Weeks 1996). Clinical efficiency is defined in terms of the most effective means of treatment—those yielding the greatest benefit with a minimum of side effects. For the purpose of improving clinical efficiency, other indices not necessarily reducible to a single figure, such as the Sickness Impact Profile, Nottingham Health Profile, and Quality of Well-Being Index, seem more appropriate.

3. Psychophysical Connections: The Longer History

It is evident that since the late 1960s HRQL researchers have increasingly viewed the mental and physical components that comprise quality of life as interdependent. Attempts at measuring quality of life have correspondingly focused on the physical-mental interdependence. In this respect, HRQL researchers resemble nineteenth-century psychophysicists, who set out to formalize the relationship between physical stimuli and mental sensations on the basis of behavioral experiments. Human subjects were confronted with a variety of physical stimuli (e.g., brightness, loudness). Researchers explored the possibility that experiment participants could respond to the stimuli numerically—that is, give their numerical estimates of the sensations evoked. The sensation could be *indirectly* measured through measuring the amount of stimulus necessary to give rise to "just noticeable differences" in sensation intensity.

3.1. Fechnerian Psychophysics

Inspired by Bernouilli's early-eighteenth-century analysis of the relation between mental and physical magnitudes. Gustav Fechner sought to show empirically that mental sensations *corresponded* in a mathematically exact sense to the physical attributes impinging on a person (see Boring 1929, 275). Fechner acknowledged his "debts" to both Bernouilli and Laplace in his introduction to *Elemente der Psychophysik* (1860). Bernouilli had held that mental and physical magnitudes are related to each other in such a way that the "mental fortune" (the perceived value of some amount of wealth) always depends on its ratio to the "total fortune" (total amount of wealth) of its possessor. Formally, Bernouilli posited that the increment of utility (dU) was equal to the ratio of the increment of wealth to total wealth (dW/W) times constant C: $dU = C(dW/W)$. Bentham, without referring to Bernouilli, similarly held that any increase in mental pleasure derived from an increase in wealth would depend on the original amount of wealth possessed, and would increase at a decreasing rate the more wealth one would acquire. Fechner equated in more general terms the increment of sensation (dS) to the ratio of the increment of stimulus to total stimulus (dR/R) times a constant K: $dS = K(dR/R)$.

One of Fechner's methods for determining just noticeable differences in sensation intensity (dS) anticipated indifference curve analysis both in psychology during the 1920s and in economics during the 1930s. The *differential limen* method involves two stimuli, one of which acts as a standard stimulus of comparison and remains constant during the experiment. The other is altered until the perceived difference in sensation resulting from the stimuli has disappeared. The differential limen is then a statistical quantity representing the theoretical point between what is a just noticeable difference and what is just not noticeable.

In the 1870s, Joseph Delboeuf carried out experiments that supported the Fechnerian view that sensations are quantifiable magnitudes. In contrast to Fechner, however, Delboeuf developed the concept of the "sense-distance," which was analogous to the "just noticeable difference" but different in that "sense distances" are *not* considered constant over the range of a scale of sensation. In other words, just noticeable incremental differences may vary. Delboeuf held that sensations are separated by *variable* distances that can be compared by using the categories of judgment "greater," "equal," and "less." Suppose there are three sensations A, B, and C. Delboeuf assumed that it is always possible to determine whether the distance AB is greater than, equal to, or less than the distance BC. Under certain circumstances AB may actually be equal to BC. If it is then found that the stimulus necessary to produce sensation B is the geometric mean of the stimuli for A and C, then it has been shown that S (sense distance AB) = $k \log R$ (Fechner's law).

S. Stevens suggested that psychophysics was "saddled with an unfortunate childhood" (1961, 226–27). Fechner's "dogma" concerning the supposed logarithmic relation between sensation and stimulus, and his postulate of constant divisible units of sensation, tainted the image of psychophysics, at least temporarily, according to Stevens. What experimental psychologists should have done, in Stevens's view, was to take up the mid-nineteenth-century psychophysicist Plateau's suggestion that sensations increase as a power function of stimulus intensity, not as a logarithm of stimulus intensity. Not surprisingly, this is what Stevens did in his early (1930s) psychophysical research. Staging a comeback, psychophysics in the 1930s turned to inventing more sophisticated procedures, such as category rating and magnitude estimation, for measuring sensory response.

3.2. Magnitude Estimation and QALYs

To calculate the quality-of-life adjustment factor, a number of techniques can be used, including the category rating technique originally conceived by the psychologist L. Thurstone in 1929, the standard gamble technique originally set out by John von Neumann and Oskar Morgenstern in 1947, and Stevens's magnitude estimation developed during the 1930s. Stevens's technique was the preferred method at the outset of QALY research. The origins of the magnitude estimation technique can be traced back to Plateau who developed a method for finding "equal-appearing intervals." His method involved asking respondents to select a stimulus which appeared midway between two given stimuli. For example, respondents would be presented with a black and a white piece of paper and given several pieces of paper with varying hues of gray. Subsequently they would be asked to tell which piece of gray paper appears midway between the color black and white. Stevens's general method of magnitude estimation involved relating a *reference* stimulus to a set of other stimuli. For example, in examining people's perception of length, an experimenter might present a line of a given length and ask the respondent to call that line a number, say, 10. Subsequently, the respondent is presented with a second line and is asked: What number would you give this second line if the first line was given a 10? The point of the procedure is to have the respondent number subsequent lines in proportion to the reference stimulus (Stevens 1959, 38).

Rosser, Kind, and Williams conducted a much-cited QALY study using magnitude estimation (1982). They classified states of illness in terms of eight levels of physical disability and four levels of mental distress, yielding thirty-two possible combinations of distress and disability. These combinations were called "health states." For example, no mental distress and no physical disability is one possible health state, while a severe physical disability coupled with severe mental distress is another. AMP focus on the seemingly simplistic way health states are classified in this study. They argue that this must be a reflection of the researchers' value structure. This criticism is perhaps legitimate, though rather uninteresting. First of all, it is not a QALY-specific criticism. A similar story can be told about virtually any measurement endeavor, as is well attested in the history of experimental psychology. Second, the really interesting question is left unanswered: namely, to what *degree* does the health state classification reflect the researchers' value structure? It is not questioned even by the authors of the original study that the health state classification scheme as initially designed reflected to some degree the researchers' goals and values. Williams, one of the coauthors, admitted that the initial classification needed some elaboration to qualify as an adequate means of describing health states. However, AMP's suggestion that the study *solely* reflected the researchers' perspectives is wrong. The health state classification was designed in *coordination* with doctors, nurses, patients, and hospital administrators at several hospitals in Britain. Clinical input was deemed essential in order to fine-tune the health state classification scheme and make it acceptable for use in the National Health Service.

Once health states were classified, a single health state, "perfect" health, was designated as a reference state and given the unit value. Five other "marker" states were ordinally ranked in order of severity by the respondents, who in this study included doctors, patients, nurses, and hospital administrators. Subsequently, respondents made judgments concerning the relative degrees of severity of the various marker states. So, for instance, regarding two states, respondents were asked, "How many times more ill is a person in state two as compared with state one?" (Kind, Godfrey, and Gudex 1990, 60). Respondents were told to bear in mind that the ratios they estimated would in part determine the distribution of health resources in the National Health Service.

There are some rather obvious conceptual problems attached to methods like magnitude estimation. For one thing, a respondent might not be able to translate his or her subjective responses to stimuli into numbers (Stevens 1959, 54). It can be asked whether a respondent can meaningfully answer questions like "How many times more ill is a person in state two as compared with state one?" with numbers that reflect genuine preferences. The *hypothetical* nature of the measurement procedure is also problematical, and has been criticized (AMP 1989; Megone 1990).

3.3. QALYs, Psychophysics, and Utility

Comparison between the QALY approach and the psychophysicist program reveals a number of interesting similarities. On a general level, both are concerned with transcending the Cartesian mental-physical dualism. They both seek ways of establishing, in a precise manner, the relationship between stimuli and sensations. Both use magnitude estimation and category rating to elicit valuations of sensations. Category rating was originally developed by Thurstone during the 1920s and 1930s to measure social attitudes. An example of category rating applied to health state measurement is George Torrance's (1976) "feeling thermometer" technique. Respondents place health states on a line extending from zero to 100 (zero represents the least desirable health state, 100 the most desirable). Health states of varying degrees of severity are placed onto the "thermometer" by the respondent in such a way that the relative distance between the markers representing the health states corresponds to the respondent's feelings about the relative differences in desirability.

QALY analysis further derives its methodology from a Benthamite utilitarian perspective on utility. Jeremy Bentham had maintained that feelings were comprised of seven dimensions, among which *intensity* and *duration* were the two key dimensions to be measured. Likewise, the QALY approach treats intensity (the quality-of-life adjustment factor) and duration (life expectancy) as the two dimensions to be measured and combined. Moreover, QALY analysis makes implicit use of Bentham's principle of utility, which suggests that objects like health states contain utility in varying degrees in accordance with the evaluator's beliefs and desires. This implies that, in order for a person to impute "value" to a health state description, the description has to contain a capacity to trigger certain positive or negative feelings in the evaluator's mind. Subsequently, through a set of mental operations ("transformation" and "response" functions; see Veit and Ware 1982, 235–37), the evaluator attributes "value" to the health state description. The "value" thus attributed is often called *experience* utility by psychologists. According to Daniel Kahneman and C. Varey, experience utility is analogous to the entity that Bentham described as a hedonic quality of experience (1991, 128).

4. Measuring Preferences

AMP's arguments against measurability of quality of life seem reasonable at first glance. It seems reasonable, for instance, to be skeptical as to whether "the economist [has] . . . any genuine yardstick for measuring objectively a diversity of factors [such as the dimensions involved in health state measurement]" (Self 1975, 9). It also seems intuitively correct to argue, as AMP do, that quality of life is not on a par with length and weight, as far as measurability is concerned. In this regard, it is plausible to suggest that the dimensions that comprise quality of life are so varied as to be incommensurable. However, despite all the misgivings one might have about quantifying and comparing quality of life intra- or interpersonally, it seems premature at best and unreasonable at worst to write off measurement out of hand, as AMP do.

4.1. Commensurability

With respect to *intra*personal comparability of values, AMP invoke the incommensurability argument. This argument asserts that if an alternative A is better than another alternative B on some dimensions, while being worse than B on other dimensions, this implies that there is no way of telling which alternative is better at both the intra- and interpersonal levels. However, there is an alternative, "intentional" view,[3] which suggests that it is plausible to think that the dimensions involved, however different, are normally given *weights* in relation to underlying mental states of consciousness such as beliefs and desires. If, given two alternatives A and B, a person is freely able to make up her mind as to which alternative

3. My source of inspiration for this "intentional" view is D. Dennett's *Intentional Stance* (1987).

she prefers; it is presumed that she acts rationally,[4] so it would seem reasonable to suggest that she mentally *weighs* the *reasons* she has for or against *preferring* the alternatives. This process of weighing reasons for preferring would appear to take place against the backdrop of her beliefs and desires as mental states of consciousness.[5] These preferences are not necessarily fixed; they could evolve as a result of the weighing process. Indeed, reasons for preferring alternatives might become salient in the course of weighing. Setting up the binary choice of A or B might elicit reasons for or against preferring the alternatives, reasons which might not be conscious to the weigher without having the binary choice set up.

It should be noted that the foregoing does not imply that reasons for preferring are invariably reducible to some homogeneous mental quality such as pleasure (Sandoe and Kappel 1994, 172). What is being suggested here is an *experiential* model of utility and preference as opposed to the more conventional preference-satisfaction model. An experiential model measures the degree to which the various ingredients that may contribute to a person's well-being yield actual mental states of consciousness which include pleasure and pain but do not preclude other qualities.

Situating this account in the QALY context, suppose that a person is offered alternatives A and B. A is the health state described as being slightly disabled physically (e.g., unable to run or walk long distances) while having no mental distress. B is described as being slightly mentally distressed (e.g., paranoia induced by drug treatment) while in excellent physical shape. The experiential model suggests that when making a choice between these quite diverse alternatives, it seems plausible to assert that the reasons a person has (for preferring or not preferring A and B are weighed in relation to that person's mental states (beliefs and desires). It is not denied here that in some cases the alternatives are so disparate (or so unknown) that a person cannot decide which alternative she prefers (a genuine case of incommensurability based on incompleteness; see Putnam 1995). Indeed, QALY studies have shown just this. They have demonstrated some of the problems uniquely connected to incompleteness (see Busschbach 1994, chs. 3 and 4).

4. Rational action is taken here to mean acting with reason based on reflective consideration of the alternatives and the circumstances in which the alternatives are evaluated. This does not necessarily mean that rational action is action in pursuit of self-interest. Nor does it presuppose conscious "mathematical" reasoning.

5. Here, preferring is the act of mind leading to the ultimate choice made. As is discussed in section 5, a preference can nevertheless be distinct from a choice.

4.2. Measurability

If the case for commensurability of alternatives based on weighing reasons for preferring is accepted, then an important precondition of measurement is met. Perhaps AMP would go so far as to accept this. If so, their critique would now concentrate on the alleged *distortive* effects of quantification. Specifically, they assert that QALYs measure the *health economist's* conception of what constitutes health-related quality of life, not the "ordinary conception of [health-related] quality of life" (106). Furthermore, it is alleged that measuring qualitative judgments necessarily presupposes the idea that people actually number their preferences in their minds. To counter the first of these spurious claims, I have already shown that QALYs are by no means uniquely influenced by the health economist's views on health-related quality of life. The second claim misses the point of measurement in the social sciences entirely. The point of measurement in this "human" context is to investigate how it might be *possible* to numerically *represent* certain preference orderings (see Krantz, Luce, Suppes, and Tversky 1971). This certainly does not presuppose any numerically sophisticated reasoning on the part of ordinary people, nor does it presuppose that measurement is possible in the human context. For this to be true, first it has to demonstrate that preference orderings are representable in such a way that measuring them makes sense. Second, measurement will have to show whether or not these representations do in fact map onto reality.

According to a consensus view of measurement theorists, measurement is assigning numbers to events or objects according to consistent rules of assignment. Different kinds of measurement suit different kinds of scales; for instance, nominal and ordinal measurements lead to nominal and ordinal scales, respectively. When restricted to rank orderings, measurement does not permit propositions or hypotheses that are appropriate for interval scales; that is, it cannot be said how *much* harder an object is on the scale compared to another object. Nevertheless, ordinal rankings do constitute measurement (Stevens 1959, 24–25). On an interval scale, the numbers ascribed to stimuli not only indicate ordinal rankings but also suggest that the intervals between the numbers are the same. Temperature is measured this way. The zero point and unit of measurement are arbitrarily fixed, while adding units of temperature is a meaningful operation. On a ratio scale, it is meaningful to use "*X* times" comparisons—twice as much pleasure, three times as heavy, ten times as long. On this scale, only the unit of measurement is arbitrarily assigned, while there exists an actual zero point on the scale. Magnitude estimation is a way of establishing a ratio scale of a subjective magnitude like quality of life (see the example discussed in section 3.2).

It seems intuitively reasonable to suppose that *degrees* of preference exist—that it is possible not only to ordinally rank preferences but also to rank the *intensity* of preferences. The statement "I prefer A more than B" is ordinal. The statement "I prefer A *much* more than B, and I prefer B a *little* more than C" is still ordinal but is leading toward becoming cardinal. An economist, W. Armstrong (1939), in a time when talk of cardinal measurement was taboo in the profession, was prepared to jump the hurdle from ordinal to cardinal ranking of utility. If utility can be quantified to the point of rank orderings—that is, we can assert of two alternatives that one is greater than the other—it can be further explored how far apart the rank orderings are. Armstrong argues that what can be inferred from observation are degrees of preference. By introspection, one can observe that alternative A is preferred to B more strongly than A to C. Moreover, one can think of a preference diminishing to a point of indifference where the interval AB is equal to the interval AC. Here, B is said to have a measurable position between A and C in terms of the relation between A and C (465). So, introspectively, Armstrong provides a way of thinking about the possibility of interval scale utility. More rigorously, Morgenstern and von Neumann's theory of expected utility (1947) provides a way of *representing* preference orderings axiomatically so that numerical representations of utility can be constructed.

In the QALY context, it is important to find out whether there exist empirical operations that can be used to determine greater or less than relationships or, alternatively, equality-of-intervals relationships with respect to quality-of-life preferences. One way of approaching this problem is to represent preference orderings as having a structure that conforms to the von Neumann–Morgenstern axioms. Using, among others, the completeness and transitivity axioms, von Neumann and Morgenstern derived a technique for numerically measuring preference orderings: the standard gamble technique. This technique has been frequently used in QALY research. It is typically used as follows. The respondent is confronted with a pair of choices. One choice is remaining in a current, less than perfect, health state; the other involves a probability (p) of being immediately restored to perfect health and some probability ($1 - p$) of dying immediately. The respondent is asked to vary p until he or she is indifferent between the choices. The respondent's "utility" for the certain health state is given by the probability of perfect health in the gamble at which point of indifference is reached.

5. Distinguishing between Preference and Choice

AMP's critique bases itself on the notion that quantification of quality of life is either to be rejected outright, or, if measurement is hesitantly accepted, doubts are raised concerning its relevance due to its supposed distortive effects on "real" preferences. Here, it is essential to take account of AMP's *conceptual* distinction between preference and choice. AMP point out this distinction but do not pursue its implications at the empirical level, beyond the claim that a wedge may be driven between preference and choice owing to the distortive effects of QALY analysis.

5.1. Preference, Choice, and Framing

Conceptually, choice is best seen as the actual *picking* of an alternative. Choice manifests itself at the end of a process of deciding on various alternatives. Preference is taken to underlie choice, but it is not necessarily equal to choice.[6] If all preferences were identical to ultimate choices, then empirical studies would have little or no trouble identifying preferences on the basis of choices. However, choices may be forced on respondents despite their preferences, in which case preference and choice diverge. Furthermore, if we take John Harsanyi's view, people may exhibit "manifest" preferences, which would not be their "true" preferences if they were "fully informed" and reasoned with utmost care with a "state of mind most conducive to rational choice" (1982, 55).

It is important, then, to maintain a theoretical framework of how people value objects and events and how they eventually choose which objects to pick, which acknowledges such distinctions. Traditionally, health state measurement research has made exactly the distinctions mentioned here (see Kane and Froberg 1989). The researcher pursues a model of human behavior that stipulates how stimuli produce sensations, which, in turn, are transformed into overt responses or choices (Veit and Ware 1982, 234–36). The sensations in this model are called "utils," taken to be pref-

6. This is not the conventional way economists view preference and choice. The conventional preference-satisfaction view does not distinguish between preference and choice, nor does it attribute anything substantive to preference.

erences *underlying* choice. Information contained in the questionnaire items may affect both the preferences for and the ultimate responses to these items. An important goal in social science research is "to understand the environment well enough to be able to manipulate outcomes" (233). If it is understood what affects people's perceptions of quality of life and their preferences regarding quality of life, it may then be known which environmental changes would result in higher quality of life judgments. For this purpose, "it is necessary to use measurement techniques that allow tests of hypotheses that are . . . *causal* in nature" (234; emphasis added). One such hypothesis might be that putting health states in a positive light may affect the respondents' preferences toward health states and, in turn, their choices (see McNeil, Pauker, Sox, and Tversky 1982). If, as a result of designing the questionnaire items in a positive light, health states are valued higher than before, then this suggests the importance of so-called *framing* effects on the respondents' *perception* of health state descriptions.

Thus, the inclusion of a conceptual distinction between preference and choice seems to make good sense, given the dependence of health state valuation on the *framing* of the questionnaire items in a QALY study. To illustrate this, consider the Rosser, Kind, and Williams study already mentioned. That manipulation of preferences through framing is both a real possibility and that it can have significant implications is beyond doubt. From all sides of the academic spectrum, manipulation has been discussed. Philosopher T. Scanlon points out that "preferences are notoriously sensitive to the background of information and experience within which they are formed" (1991, 29). Psychologists Daniel Kahneman and Amos Tversky (1979) show how researchers can and do (consciously and unconsciously) manipulate the outcomes of experiments. A preeminent psychologist inspired by the psychophysics program, Stevens, also mentioned the possibility of experimentally "conditioning" respondents to answer in particular ways (1959, 39). Health economists G. Loomes and L. MacKenzie suggest that framing questions can produce "utility evaluation effects" (1990, 90).

Framing may even be aimed at *direct manipulation* of ultimate *choice*. An illustrative example of how this works was conveyed to me by a Dutch psychologist working with QALYs at the Erasmus University hospital in Rotterdam. He admitted that in his research he sometimes tried to directly manipulate the interviewees' evaluation of medical risk. He gave me an example that involved eliciting preferences using the standard gamble technique which included risk appraisal. Apparently, including a risk component introduces a complication to the procedure of measuring quality of life that some respondents cannot (or perhaps are not willing to) think through and work out. It is thought that interviewees sometimes overestimate the risks involved in medical treatment, even when the "objective" risks are known to them. The psychologist told of his telling interviewees to think twice about not exaggerating the risk involved in medical treatment—that is, to pare down their subjective assessment of risk.

Framing may involve more subtle forms of manipulation, however. In the Rosser, Kind, and Williams study, respondents were asked to bear in mind that their answers to the questionnaires would influence the ways in which National Health Service resources were spent. Putting the question this way may have resulted in a different set of responses from framing the question differently. For example, the questionnaire might not have included a clause related to health resource distribution. It is plausible that by introducing an external factor such as distribution, responses might be more reflective of distributional concerns than underlying "real" preferences. Framing may also involve formatting the questions slightly differently. In a recent article, J. Hux and Daniel Naylor (1995) demonstrate that the interpretation of equivalent expressions of (medical) therapeutic benefit in terms of risk reduction depends on the format of the expressions—whether they are denoted in absolute or relative terms. When risk reduction (risk attached to a specific medical condition) as a result of therapy is presented in relative terms, respondents show more favorable valuations of the therapeutic benefits of risk reduction than if risk reduction is presented in absolute terms.

5.2. Intentionality

The stipulation of the dimensions disability and distress entails that a respondent's choices among health states are made with *these* parameters in mind. Preferences may depend on attitudes toward these parameters. However, preferences may well be different if other parameters had been stipulated. So, an interesting question is, do the categories mentioned on the questionnaire match the respondents' categories? This is called the *correspondence* problem by AMP (105). One way to improve correspondence is to elaborate the health state classification scheme to incorporate more and better defined dimensions in accordance with clinical results that identify such dimensions. If categories correspond, if respondents can relate to the categories in the questionnaire, then the researcher may be justified in believing that when she can get respondents to perform exercises like magnitude estimation, she can elicit their "true" preferences, which are inferred from their choices. But, is this correct? Has she not left out a number of important considerations? Take the possibility that preferences may be tainted by prejudice about what it is like to be in certain health states? This prejudice could be coming from the interviewer, but it may also be reflected in society's way of thinking about illness and health. This is a possibility suggested by C. Megone (1990). It would then seem imperative that QALY researchers try out as many sensible parameters in the questionnaires as possible. This would mean giving as much leeway to the respondents as is feasible—that is, allowing them to cite relevant parameters without outside interference.

Consider also the possibility that when the researcher attributes preferences to respondents, she may be appealing to her *own* notions of how good or bad the alternatives are. As D. Davidson puts it: "The propositions I must use to interpret the attitudes of another are defined by roles they play in my thoughts and feelings and behavior; therefore in interpretation they must play appropriately similar roles" (Davidson quoted in Scanlon 1991, 35). Immediately the question arises, are there shared reference points (i.e., the interviewer and respondent are in agreement as to what their beliefs and preferences are) which make it sensible to think that the researcher is attributing to people the *right* set of mental states on the basis of responses to a QALY questionnaire?

At this point, *intentionality* enters the discussion. When an interviewer asks a respondent about his preferences, the replies she gets stand in need of interpretation in light of both the interviewer's own set of beliefs and preferences, and her beliefs with respect to the respondent's beliefs and preferences. Intentionality turns on the "folk psychology" notion that (rational) actions are *caused* by beliefs and desires. The act of choosing is an intentional act; it constitutes picking means that are *believed* to be effective in promoting certain ends which are *desired*. According to this view, the ability to measure causal beliefs and desires depends on observation of behavior (behavior taken in a much broader sense than is usually the case in economics, hence not limited to choice behavior in the market but including verbal reports, gestures, etc.). However, inferences from choice behavior can only be made if either preferences or beliefs are known. For instance, someone's preferences can be inferred from his choice behavior if his beliefs are known. Here, beliefs and desires are taken to be *real*, intervening mental states (mediating reason and action) with causal roles to play in producing behavior. A major problem related to measuring intentional mental states is how to separate out choices, preferences, and beliefs as discrete entities. Is it possible to measure these independent of each other and independent of our own presuppositions about what these entities should be? In other words, when measuring someone's preferences on the basis of his choice behavior, how do we get evidence of a person's beliefs that is *independent* of his actual choice behavior? Daniel Dennett (1987) suggests that a person's beliefs in one situation can be approximately inferred from his choice behavior in other situations given his *other* beliefs and desires. But, of course, this leads to an infinite regress, for these other beliefs and desires are apparently only inferable from that person's choice behavior in yet another situation given other beliefs and desires. A. Rosenberg believes for this reason that however useful intentional variables are as a first approximation to human behavior they will never "divide nature at the joints" (1992, 235).

But is Rosenberg's characterization of intentionality correct? I do not think so. A careful reading of Dennett (1987) reveals that although intentionality ascribes causal roles to beliefs and desires, it does not portray them as being necessarily discrete physical entities. Intentionality, as originally expounded by Dennett, is a *holistic* approach to human behavior. Beliefs, desires, and choices are not to be carved up discretely, but are to be viewed as "whole systems," with beliefs and desires not being "attributable in isolation" (58). Intentionality deals with the "prediction and explanation from belief-desire *profiles* of the actions of whole systems" (58; emphasis added). These systems are "envisaged as a close kin of . . . decision theory and game theory" (57–58). As such, intentional system theory is a point of departure which quite naturally paves the way toward cognitively understanding the real roles that belief-desire profiles play as causal duos. Rosenberg's inclination to be microphysicalist about intentional variables seems to lead him astray from the actual account of intentionality.

5.3. Intentionality and Bootstrapping

It seems that expected utility theory depicts behavior normatively. Viewed this way, beliefs and desires in an expected utility framework are "ought" entities. Beliefs taken as subjective probabilities *ought not* to deviate from objective probabilities. Likewise, choices *ought* to reflect preferences. It is in this respect that von Neumann and Morgenstern take up an *intentional stance* toward the entities they postulate without committing themselves one way or another as to the "real" nature of these entities. This can be illustrated by examining the role *probability* plays in the codetermination of preferences. By introducing probability and the concomitant possibility of risk attached to an option, von Neumann and Morgenstern suggest that these variables codetermine choice. The axiomatic structure of their theory, together with the idealized assumptions concerning the equality of both belief and objective probability and preference and choice, allow von Neumann and Morgenstern to represent uniquely *measurable* outcome *possibilities.* What this does not convey, however, is how *actual* sets of beliefs, desires, and choices interrelate. This is where bootstrapping comes in.

Clark Glymour argues that hypotheses are always confirmed with respect to a theory by a piece of evidence provided that, using the theory, it can be deduced from the bit of evidence an instance of the hypothesis, and the deduction does not guarantee such an instance (1980, 127). Theory, according to Glymour, can be simply a set of (interconnected) postulates, one of which is the hypothesis to be confirmed or possibly disconfirmed. Empirical data can provide a bootstrap confirmation for the hypothesis *relative* to the other postulates (the rest of the theory). For example, suppose someone's utility function is hypothesized as having a particular form, such as a specific function of prices and quantities of two bundles of goods.[7] Suppose further that this utility function is a part of a typical microeconomic set of equations, a theory, that can be used to determine that person's behavior. An experiment is carried out on the person, giving her different budgets and observing her choices when she faces different prices. The data, her choice behavior, *may* provide a "bootstrap confirmation" of a certain hypothesis (e.g., she acts *as if* she is setting her marginal utilities equal to zero) relative to the theory, set of equations including the Lagrangian, utility function, budget constraint, and so on. Since the data might have disconfirmed the hypothesized utility function, Glymour's bootstrap strategy is falsifiable.

The bootstrap strategy can also be applied with respect to von Neumann and Morgenstern's expected utility theory. In this case, expected utility theory may be viewed as a set of postulates. Let us suppose that the

7. This example is adapted from Hausman 1992, 39–41.

postulates are the standard ones put forward by von Neumann and Morgenstern. For example, given three prospects u, v, and w, more of what a prospect offers is preferred to less, given that the prospect is desired, preferences are transitive, preferences are state-independent (in other words, prospects in one state of nature should not be affected by prospects in a different state of nature), and preferences are continuous over the entire range of possible probability values (that is, probabilities and utilities may be traded off for all possible probability and utility values). This list of postulates is not exhaustive, but for purposes of exposition it should be sufficient. The last postulate is an important one to examine. It is, in effect, the expected utility hypothesis. It hypothesizes that the expected utility of a sure prospect is the mathematical expectation of the sum of probabilities times utilities of the uncertain prospect. To illustrate, suppose the following scenario is put to a respondent: There is a prospect A and a prospect B. Prospect A is the certainty prospect, the prospect of having current less than perfect health for y years. B is the prospect of having perfect health for y years following an operation with, however, a p percentage *risk* of dying during treatment. In an experiment using the standard gamble technique, data regarding the valuation of current and perfect health states may be generated by varying p until the respondent is indifferent between options A and B. At the point of indifference the following equation will hold: $(1 - p)u + (p)v = w$, where u is the "value" of perfect health to the respondent; v, the "value" of death; and w, the value of current less than perfect health. Obtaining p values that induce indifference bootstrap confirms the expected utility hypothesis relative to the other postulates included in expected utility theory. There are possibilities of disconfirmation. If preferences are intransitive or discontinuous, or if more is not preferred to less, then no p values will induce indifference. Hence, the equation will not hold. Or, if B were to be presented as the prospect of perfect health for y years following an operation with a p percentage of *success* instead of a p percentage of *failure*, the p value at the point of indifference may well be different from the p value obtained initially.

The bootstrapping strategy is invariably used in health state measurement practice. In general terms, a psychological model involving health state descriptions as stimuli provides an explanation of behavior in terms of hypothesized utility, transformation, and response functions. Responses are generated using a number of elicitation techniques. These responses are taken to reflect respondents' sensations. The hypothesized functions can be instantiated, like the utility functions, through bits of confirming evidence relative to the model. Psychological bootstrapping is neatly summarized by Veit and Ware as follows: if "data support the predictions of the model, subjective stimulus . . . and response . . . values can be derived from the model" (1982, 238).

5.4. How Measuring Experience Utility Can Actually Bolster AMP's Critique

If the manner in which questionnaire items (descriptions of health states) are presented makes a difference in people's perceptions of health states, then this suggests that preferences are manipulable and subject to change. Conventional QALY research, however, relies heavily on the assumption that respondents' preferences remain stable over time. Intuitively, it appears reasonable to question this assumption. AMP rightly criticize health economists for often *simply* assuming stability of health state preferences. As a person's life changes (e.g., as a result of medical intervention), so can a person's set of preferences. It is well known that people cope with illness by adapting to changed circumstances, effectively rendering original health state preference values obsolete.

The questions that now arise are how one accounts for these changes in a QALY model and whether the changes are measurable. Psychologists have suggested that what determines a person's well-being are *experienced* preferences at present, not expected preferences or preferences elicited in the past (Kahneman and Varey 1991). Therefore, it is imperative that preferences are measured at different points in time to account for changes as a result of possible adaptation or coping effects. As the experience of being in a health state sinks in and becomes internalized in the patient's mind, his notion of quality of life may change. This idea turns on the notion that *experience* utility depends on changes in the perception of quality of life in relation to a reference state of what is considered by the evaluator to be normal functioning. Over time, these reference states can shift. It is interesting to note that clinicians have actually used QALYs as an evaluator of *changes* of preferences in an analogous way. Measurements are not limited to one-off expected values; they are performed at various critical junctures to determine if preferences indeed shift (Gelber, Glasziou, and Simes 1990).

It is clear, then, that measurement can actually help undermine a number of overly simplistic assumptions made in QALY analysis. Stability of preferences is an obvious example. Likewise, measurement using varying parameters may falsify the assumption that preference and choice are equal. In addition, measurement can assist in sharpening the conceptual distinction between preference and choice as the discussion on framing points out.

6. Concluding Remarks

Sociologists might think that I am trying to disqualify their approach to studying the scientific practice of QALYs by objectifying measurement and deemphasizing the socially constructed nature of QALYs. This article, however, is not an attempt to disqualify the sociological perspective, nor does it objectify measurement. The sociological critique of QALYs is not by any means moot. It suggests the questionable character of a number of crucial assumptions such as stability, quantification, and correspondence. Furthermore, it points to the underlying political and sometimes ideological interests at stake in QALY research. Despite this, it does not furnish adequate foundations for its attack on both the assumptions and the alleged socially constructed nature of the QALY concept. It unfolds an interesting story without providing hints as to how the problems attached to the story may be resolved.

It seems that this critique lacks demonstrative convincibility *because* it eschews measurement that could paradoxically help bolster its case. Understanding the sociology of the QALY model requires not only a sociological account of the QALY concept but also a historical consideration of how the concept evolved, an account of the psychological model used to underpin the concept, and an account of the role that measurement plays in the QALY approach. Here, it is essential to understand how measurement, intentionality, and bootstrapping interrelate. Consider interpreting a respondent's reply to a QALY questionnaire that simply asks which health state the respondent would choose, A or B. Suppose a respondent writes down that he would choose health state A over health state B. Now, an investigator wants to infer from this response behavior the respondent's beliefs and desires. How can the investigator justify inferring from this behavior that the respondent actually *prefers* A to B, and that he *believes* that A will leave him better off than B, without resorting to the *intentional* presuppositions (1) respondents do what they prefer, given their beliefs, and (2) the respondent and investigator share certain basic reference points with respect to their beliefs and preferences? In practice, investigators seem to do just this. They infer beliefs and desires taking an intentional stance toward human behavior which includes reference to their own beliefs and desires and past beliefs and desires of the respondent they are interviewing. Measuring actual behavior can act to *bootstrap* confirm or disconfirm the original intentional hypotheses put forward.

It seems that part of the problem with AMP's critique is that they have accepted an account of QALYs (the standard health economist's version) which is itself deficient. The standard health economist's view is that QALY research is cut off from psychology by virtue of its only evaluating choice or response behavior (no probing of the mind involved). This claim does not correspond to the actual practice of QALY research, however, which is very much concerned with mental states by virtue of its elicitation methods.

References

Armstrong, W. 1939. Determinateness of the Utility Function. *Economic Journal* 45:453–67.

Ashmore, Malcolm, Michael Mulkay, and Trevor Pinch. 1989. *Health and Efficiency: A Sociology of Health Economics*. Milton Keynes: Open University Press.

Bentham, Jeremy [1899] 1970. *An Introduction to the Principles of Morals and Legislation*. London: Burns and Hart.

Boring, E. 1929. *A History of Experimental Psychology*. New York: Appleton.

Bowling, A. 1991. *Measuring Health*. Milton Keynes: Open University Press.

Bury, Michael 1994. Quality of Life: Why Now? A Sociological View. In *Concepts and Measurement of Quality of Life in Health Care*, edited by L. Nordenfelt. Dordrecht: Kluwer.

Bush, J., S. Fanshel, and M. Chen. 1972. Analysis of a Tuberculin Testing Program Using a Health Status Index. *Socio-Economic Planning* 6:49–68.

Busschbach, J. 1994. *De Validiteit van QALYs*. Arnhem: Gouda Quint.

Cleary, P., and I. Wilson. 1995. Linking Clinical Variables with Health-Related Quality of Life. *Journal of the American Medical Association* 273:59–65.

Culyer, Anthony J. 1981. Health, Economics and Health Economics. In *Health, Economics and Health Economics*, edited by J. van der Gaag and M. Perlman. Amsterdam: North-Holland.

———. 1990. Commodities, Characteristics of Commodities, Characteristics of People, Utilities, and the Quality of Life. In *Quality of Life: Perspectives and Policies*, edited by S. Baldwin, C. Godfrey, and C. Propper. London: Routledge.

Delboeuf, Joseph 1883. Examen critique de la loi psychophysique: Sa base et sa signification. Paris Bailliere.

Dennett, Daniel 1987. *Intentional Stance*. Cambridge, Mass.: MIT Press.

Fechner, Gustav 1860. *Elemente der Psychophysik*. Leipzig: Breitkopf and Hartel.

Gelber, R., P. Glasziou, and R. Simes. 1990. Quality Adjusted Survival Analysis. *Statistics and Medicine* 9:1259–76.

Ginzberg, E., ed. 1987. *Medicine and Society: Clinical Decisions and Societal Values*. Boulder, Colo.: Westview Press.

Glasser, M. 1991. *Physician-Patient Relationships: An Annotated Bibliography*. New York: Garland.

Glymour, Clark 1980. *Theory and Evidence*. Princeton, N.J.: Princeton University Press.

Gudex, C. 1990. The QALY: How Can It Be Used? In *Quality of Life: Perspectives and Policies*, edited by S. Baldwin, C. Godfrey, and C. Propper. London: Routledge.

Harsanyi, John 1982. Morality and the Theory of Rational Behavior. In *Utilitarianism and Beyond*, edited by A. Sen and B. Williams. Cambridge: Cambridge University Press.

Hausman, D. 1992. *The Separate and Inexact Science of Economics*. Cambridge: Cambridge University Press.

Hux, J., and Daniel Naylor. 1995. In the Eye of the Beholder. *Archives of Internal Medicine* 155:2277–80.

Kahneman, Daniel, and Amos Tversky. 1979. Prospect Theory: An Analysis of Decision under Risk. *Econometrica* 47(2):263–91.

Kahneman, Daniel, and C. Varey. 1991. Notes on the Psychology of Utility. In *Interpersonal Comparisons of Well-Being*, edited by J. Elster and J. Roemer. Cambridge: Cambridge University Press.

Kane, R., and D. Froberg. 1989. Methodology for Measuring Health-State Preferences. *Journal of Clinical Epidemiology* 42:345–54.

Kind, P., C. Godfrey, and C. Gudex. 1990. What Are QALYs? In *Quality of Life: Perspectives and Policies*, edited by S. Baldwin, C. Godfrey, and C. Propper. London: Routledge.

Klarman, H., J. O'Francis, and G. Rosenthal. 1968. Cost-Effectiveness Analysis Applied to the Treatment of Chronic Renal Disease. *Medical Care* 6:48–54.

Krantz, D., R. Luce, P. Suppes, and A. Tversky. 1971. *Foundations of Measurement*. New York: Academic Press.

Loomes, G., and L. MacKenzie. 1990. Scope and Limitations of QALY Measures. In *Quality of Life: Perspectives and Policies*, edited by S. Baldwin, C. Godfrey, and C. Propper. London: Routledge.

McNeil, B., S. Pauker, H. Sox, and A. Tversky. 1982. On the Elicitation of Preferences for Alternative Therapies. *New England Journal of Medicine* 306:1259–62.

Megone, C. 1990. Starting from Aristotle. In *Quality of Life: Perspectives and Policies*, edited by S. Baldwin, C. Godfrey, and C. Propper. London: Routledge.

Mooney, Gavin 1992. *Economics, Medicine and Health Care*. Brighton, Conn.: Harvester Wheatsheaf.

Pliskin, J., D. Shephard, and M. Weinstein. 1980. Utility Functions for Life Years and Health Status. *Operations Research* 28:206–24.

Putnam, H. 1995. On the Rationality of Preferences. Unpublished manuscript, Harvard University.

Rosenberg, A. 1992. *Mathematical Politics or Science of Diminishing Returns*. Chicago: University of Chicago Press.

Rosser, R., and V. Watts. 1972. The Measurement of Hospital Output. *International Journal of Epidemiology* 1:361–68.

Rosser, R., P. Kind, and A. Williams. 1982. The Value of the Quality of Life: Some Psychometric Evidence. In *The Value of Life and Safety*, edited by M. Jones-Lee. Amsterdam: North-Holland.

Sandoe, S., and S. Kappel. 1994. Changing Preferences. In *Concepts and Measurement of Quality of Life in Health Care*, edited by L. Nordenfelt. Dordrecht: Kluwer.

Scanlon, T. 1991. Moral Basis for Interpersonal Comparisons. In *Interpersonal Comparisons of Well-Being*, edited by J. Elster and J. Roemer. Cambridge: Cambridge University Press.

Self, P. 1975. *Econocrats and the Policy Process*. London: Macmillan.

Smith, A. 1987. Qualms about QALYs. *Lancet* i:1134–36.

Spilker, B., ed. 1991. *Quality of Life Assessments in Clinical Trials*. New York: Raven Press.

Stevens, S. 1959. Measurement, Psychophysics and Utility. In *Measurement, Definitions and Theories*, edited by C. West Churchman and P. Ratoosh. New York: Wiley.

———. 1961. Psychophysics and the Sensory Function. *American Scientist* 49:221–41.

Stigler, G. 1965. *Essays in the History of Economics*. Chicago: University of Chicago Press.

Thurstone, L. 1929. *The Measurement of Attitude*. Chicago: University of Chicago Press.

Torrance, George 1976. Social Preferences for Health States: An Empirical Evaluation of Three Measurement Techniques. *Socio-Economic Planning Science* 10:129–36.

Veit, C., and J. Ware. 1982. Measuring Health and Health-Care Outcomes: Issues and Recommendations. In *Values and Long-Term Care*, edited by R. L. Kane and R. A. Kane. Lexington, Mass.: Lexington Books.

von Neumann, John, and Oskar Morgenstern. 1947. *Theory of Games and Economic Behavior*. Princeton, N.J.: Princeton University Press.

Weeks, J. 1996. Taking Quality of Life into Account in Health Economic Analyses. *Journal of the National Cancer Institute* 20:23–28.

Weinstein, M., and W. Stason. 1977. Foundations of Cost Effectiveness Analysis for Health and Medical Practice. *New England Journal of Medicine* 296:716–21.

Williams, A. 1985. Economics of Coronary Artury Bypass Grafting. *British Medical Journal* 291:326–29.

A History of an Intellectual Arbitrage: The Evolution of Financial Economics

Paul Harrison

It seems evident that "recent" developments (or innovations) in economics have been taking place much more in terms of "what" gets studied rather than in "how" it gets studied. I mean that the tools of economic analysis are changing at a lesser rate than where they are being applied. As evidence for this purported trend, I submit the anecdotal observation of growth in the applied "fields" of economics. Not only are there "new" fields such as experimental, health, and environmental (natural resources), but there has been a rejuvenation of others, such as urban and law and economics. Perhaps the most significant illustration has been the sharp rise in research activity within some fields, in particular labor and finance.

Because of the increasing importance of the applied fields within economics, I think it is appropriate to consider the evolution of these fields and their interaction with economics "proper" (that is, primarily with the micro "core," but also with econometric and macroeconomic theory). To do this, I will turn my attention to the analysis of a particular case—the

For useful comments, questions and discussion I thank the participants of the 1996 *HOPE* conference, as well as the Kress Seminar in the History of Economic Thought. In addition, I thank Eric Ralph, Roger Backhouse, and Neil De Marchi for their detailed comments and criticism, which were very helpful in revising this article. Remaining shortcomings are, of course, my own.

field of finance, particularly "financial economics" since I do not focus on the business and organizational aspect of finance.

This article examines how the fledgling field of finance became part of the empire of economics. This was an almost accidental annexation, which quite literally sparked a revolution in the practice of finance. The story involves two themes and to some extent concentrates tightly on them to the exclusion of an, admittedly important, broader social context. The primary theme is the role of arbitrage. Arbitrage was the notion that allowed economics to revolutionize finance and which simultaneously brought finance into the fold of economics. The idea of arbitrage went a long way in producing implications for financial markets. It also went a long way in "legitimizing" finance as a field of economics; here was the epitome of market efficiency. The subtheme is how research is done—with a focus on inductive versus deductive investigation. The incursion of economics into finance spawned innovations in the field of finance but was also accompanied by a rigid deductive approach (framework). I argue that this deductive dominance has created a tension between theory and observation and has inhibited subsequent innovation in the field.

The story's outcome for orthodox economics is one of success, but with some serious questions raised at the end along the lines of "where do we go from here". My analysis illuminates the attractiveness of the neoclassical paradigm in that it is simple and powerful. Recent increases in the use of heterodox theory and method pall when compared to the tremendous growth in application of the standard core. These applications have been more than self-indulgent. I would argue that the application of economics has provided an important alternative understanding of its "fields." However, I also want to make the case that this success is the success of intellectual arbitrage, and it cannot last because its own success eliminates the reasons for that success, erasing the opportunity. The pace of innovation in finance, for instance, seems to have slowed and the new sparks now come more from the tinder of inductive observation than from deductive "core" theorizing.

Such an exercise seems particularly relevant in the context of this volume. Not only is finance itself relatively new as a field of economics, but also I want to think about how the old and the new interact, how the field and its interaction with core theory affects economics as a discipline, and perhaps most important, what we can learn about how economics gets done. My story of an intellectual arbitrage suggests that the expansion of economics (sometimes called the "colonization") to "new" fields is profitable for economists. But there may be diminishing returns to this arbitrage, which should play an important role in how economists respond to anomaly. Similarly, newness in economics is often arbitrage, too—an idea borrowed from somewhere else and sold retail. We should be quick and critical in looking past fanciness to determine if there is value added in the new idea or method.

1. The Arbitrage Opportunity

For a long time, the study of financial markets was not done by economists. This changed rather suddenly around 1960. I want to explore why this reversal occurred and present two arguments. First, I argue that the application of economics to financial markets presented a scholarly "arbitrage opportunity." Significant implications could be derived from application of essential "core" economics. Second, I argue that financial markets were "converted" in the eyes of economists from a "casino" to the idealized market.

One can guess that in the 1950s (and earlier) speculative markets were not deemed sufficiently academic. (Presumably even after 1965 a significant but decreasing number of economists still held [hold] this opinion.) Perhaps the experiences of Keynes and Fisher, both of whom participated actively in the market, were enough to ward off other economists. Fisher was well known to have lost his fortune in the 1929 crash. Keynes wrote that "the management of stock exchange investments of any kind is a low pursuit . . . from which it is a good thing for most members of our Society to be free" ([1939] 1983, 66). That it was indeed considered a "low" pursuit has been evidenced by its continued linkage over the ages (including today) with gambling, greed, idleness, bankruptcy, cheating, and manipulation.

Not only was the stock market inappropriate academic fodder, it must also have seemed a place where the logic of economic theory could add little value. After all, what use would be science applied to the realm of chance and opinion and the crash of 1929— the very antithesis of science? Keynes, for instance, made a famous statement likening the market to a casino.

We must also note that the stock market was not as important then as today. Not as much business equity was being sold, not as many government bonds were being auctioned, and fewer consumer savings were "in the market." Most individuals did not even own stocks, and there were legal restrictions on the percentage (50 percent) of personal trusts and estates that could be invested in stocks.

The desired point is simply that economists did not do research on financial markets, which is not completely to say that no research was done on them. Nonacademic "how-to" books of investing, written by practitioners, were plentiful. Academic insights were sparser. Louis Bachelier ([1900] 1964) wrote an unknown and unheralded (until 1960) dissertation in mathematics on stock market prices that turned out to be a precursor to much of modern finance—his advisor felt the topic inappropriate.

There was a trickle of empirical research on the subject. Alfred Cowles (1933) and Cowles and H. Jones (1937) presented evidence that stock market forecasters were worse than random forecasts. Holbrook Working (1934) and Maurice Kendall (1953) confronted financial market prices that appeared to have completely random changes. These articles were considered heresy by financial practitioners—and by many academics, too.

Theoretical research had also been undertaken. An early important work was *The Theory of Investment Value* (1937), a dissertation by John Burr Williams (a Harvard graduate student), which presents the idea that a stock's value should be based on its discounted future dividends. This was the bible of investing, at least until the 1960s. I know from my own research (Harrison 1994) that the idea of using future dividends to determine the value of a stock existed at least since the early eighteenth century. It is doubtful that this was considered a radical idea in 1937 and probably explains why it was easily adopted by practitioners. Most other economists paid no attention.

Unheralded theoretical research, which would eventually have an impact, was also completed around 1955 by Harry Markowitz. Markowitz, a graduate student at the University of Chicago, had the insight that stocks should not be picked solely on future dividends because one should be interested in risk as well as return. Markowitz concluded that this was a resource allocation problem since an investor must choose between two desirables: high return and low risk. He developed a theory of "portfolio selection," which was published in the *Journal of Finance* in 1952. His larger theory, which included optimal portfolio selection as well as the benefits of diversification, was completed as his dissertation in 1955 and published as a book in 1959.

Markowitz's article and theory did not make a splash. It was not used by academics or on Wall Street and was hardly cited until the 1960s. He would eventually share the Nobel prize in economics in 1990. Economics in 1990 had changed since his dissertation defense in 1955, when Milton Friedman said to him, "Harry, I don't see anything wrong with the math here, but I have a problem. This isn't a dissertation in economics, and we can't give you a Ph.D. in economics for a dissertation that's not economics. It's not math, it's not economics, it's not even business administration" (as quoted in Bernstein 1992, 60).[1]

Finance as a field *did* exist. The American Finance Association had been separate from the American Economic Association since 1940, and the *Journal of Finance* was published since 1945. As an example of what the field was like in the 1950s, consider the report of Bernstein:

> Most of the articles the Journal published had to do with Federal Reserve policy, the impact of money on prices and business activity, taxation, and issues related to corporate finance, insurance, and accounting. The few articles that appeared under the rubric "Investments" dealt with topics like liquidity, dividend policy, and pension funding. In issues up to 1959, I was unable to find more than five articles that could be classified as theoretical rather than descriptive. The rest contain plenty of numbers but no mathematics. No other article in the issue that carried Markowitz's paper contains a single equation. (1992, 42)

Things were about to change. The theoretical work that Markowitz had started would be picked up first by James Tobin and then by one of Markowitz's graduate students, William Sharpe.[2] Tobin, following up his views on Keynes's "liquidity preference" theory, hypothesized that savers would diversify between risky and risk-free assets. He added a risk-free asset to the Markowitz model. The result is known as the "separation theorem." Briefly, it identifies one optimal portfolio of risky assets, which will be the same for everyone. Individuals need only choose,

1. Bernstein's 1992 book, *Capital Ideas: The Improbable Origins of Modern Wall Street*, is the only history I know of that covers the development of the same ideas as in this article. However, I want to concentrate much more on "why" than on "what" happened. Bernstein's compilation includes much information from his private correspondence and interviews with the individuals involved. I will frequently quote from these as they give insight into what the researcher was thinking. Of course, we must keep in mind that mostly these are recollections and so might be shaded.

2. Despite Friedman's grilling, Markowitz was awarded his Ph.D. and took a job at the RAND Corporation. Sharpe was a graduate student at UCLA under Jack Hirshleifer, and it was Hirshleifer who arranged for Sharpe to do his dissertation under Markowitz.

based on their risk-aversion, the amount to be invested in that risky portfolio and the amount to be invested in a risk-free portfolio. Tobin's essay was published in 1958 (and would be cited in his Nobel prize award in economics in 1981) with a footnote distinguishing between his article and Makowitz's forthcoming book: "Markowitz's main interest is prescription of rules of rational behavior for investors; the main concern of this paper is the implications for economic theory . . . that can be derived from assuming that investors do in fact follow such rules" (66).

Even the simplified portfolio model of Tobin was impractical to use, had any practitioners desired to do so. There were too many calculations required (the covariances of each stock with every other one), the accuracy of the estimates even if calculated would be suspect, and the cost of computing the calculations was too high. In a 1966 article, for instance, William Baumol reported that a simplified version of the Tobin/Markowitz model would cost between $150 and $350 for a single run. But it was not intended to be practical—it was a theoretical strand pursued by academic economists interested in theoretical results. That it had implications for actual market behavior and set the stage for a unified theory of asset prices would be important for the economic digestion of finance.

2. The Arbitrage Exploited

Three major finance papers by economists between 1958 and 1965 introduced the neoclassical "core" theory into the field of finance with important results. Tobin's simplification of Markowitz was further simplified into the Capital Asset Pricing Model (CAPM) by Sharpe in two stages. First, in 1961, he developed the "single-factor" model, which was an idea of Markowitz's passed down to his graduate student. The point of the single-factor model was that it became necessary only to determine how each stock covaried with the market index rather than with every other stock. This development reduced computing time from 33 minutes to 30 seconds, and suddenly optimal portfolio determination was within the reach of practitioners. As computing power would increase in the 1970s, the practice of finance would be transformed by Sharpe's calculations of "beta."

The CAPM (1964) was the crowning achievement of the Markowitz research strand for two reasons. It introduced a theory of market equilibrium for the stock market, and it determined that the "market portfolio" is the "single risky portfolio" of both Sharpe's and Tobin's earlier articles.[3]

The empirical strand of research due to the early observers of speculative prices came to economic fruition the next year. The implication of random prices was unsettling to many economists. For instance, Kendall's assertion of random prices at the presentation of his 1953 paper to the Royal Statistical Society was allegedly met by some vehement disbelief. The disquiet was resolved with the formation of the Efficient Markets Hypothesis (EMH), which was "proved" by Paul Samuelson (1965) and Benoit Mandelbrot (1966). Both showed that if prices actually are "correctly" forecasted, then the resulting market price *should* behave randomly because it will be subject only to the remaining unforecastable (random) part.[4]

From private correspondence with Samuelson, Bernstein paints the following picture:

> Samuelson was enthralled by Houthakker's description of pandemonium provoked by Kendall's statement that the behavior of speculative prices looked as though the Demon of Chance had drawn a series of random numbers. He took heart at the way the economists and statisticians had reacted to Kendall as an upstart invader of their turf and an enemy agnostic. Delighted, Samuelson said to himself: "Work the other side of the street! The nonpredictability of future prices from past and present prices is the sign, not of failure for economic law, but the triumph of economic law after competition had done its best." (1992, 117).

I think it is interesting to note that despite the inductive roots of the EMH in the early observation of speculative prices, it was the economic "proof" that made sense for the economists. Samuelson in discussing his own finding described his reaction as one of "initial shock—and then, upon reflection, that it is obvious [but] it was not a finding of fact. It is a purely deductive, theoretical piece" (as quoted in Bernstein 1992, 123). Now the prices that had been so unexplainable had a "scientific" explanation—the market actually was "properly" behaved. Eugene

3. Both of these ideas were being simultaneously and independently developed by a professor at Harvard (John Lintner).

4. I have pointed out elsewhere (Harrison 1993) that Working (1949) put forth the first exposition of this theory without formalizing it. Some have also given credit to Bachelier ([1900] 1964), although that work seems to be more of a description than a theory.

Fama, an empirically oriented researcher at the University of Chicago, translated Samuelson's (et al.) proof into the EMH and became its main proponent (see Fama 1970). He presented further statistical evidence, assembled the arguments, and disseminated it to the field—and to the practitioners.

The third piece actually predates the first two. It is the Modigliani-Miller theorem, which appeared in Franco Modigliani and Merton Miller (1958) and Miller and Modigliani (1961). Although there would be many modifications to it, their most fundamental contribution is known as the MM theorem, which states that the value of a firm is independent of how its financing is divided between debt and equity. However, while it is clearly finance, it is not explicitly about financial markets. I see the other two articles as being much more important to mainstreaming finance to economists. But all three of the essays share a common theme, which I take up in the next section.

3. Arbitrage via Arbitrage

So, beginning essentially in the 1960s, economists started to examine financial markets. Just a slow trickle at first, but James Tobin, Paul Samuelson, Paul Cootner, William Baumol, Jack Hirshleifer, and Franco Modigliani make up a distinguished list. Even more important than individuals "crossing over" were the theoretical developments; however, I do not want to tell this as a story of "great" individuals taming an uncharted field. They may have been pioneers, but the story is about how and why their theory took hold. The neoclassical "core," it turned out, had useful things to say about speculative markets. There was an opportunity for intellectual arbitrage. The research initiated a significant shift in how financial markets and the field of finance are viewed by both practitioners and economists.

First is the equilibrium theory of the CAPM. The essence of the argument is essentially that the risk-adjusted return must be the same for every stock. If it was not, then investors would buy (or sell) the offending stock until supply and demand changed to bring its return into line. This equilibrium argument is powerful and compelling. But, it is basically only the enforcement of the law of one price through arbitrage.

Second is the equilibrium theory of the EMH. The essence of that argument is that "information" introduces an arbitrage opportunity that will be erased. Stock market prices therefore will be sufficient statistics, reflecting all of the available ("known") information. This can be viewed as arbitrage in the market for information, implying that stock prices accurately reflect the anticipation of fundamental values.

From the standpoint of an academic economist, financial markets had been converted from the most tangled underbrush to the pristine ideal of textbooks. Here were perfect markets—a market where the power of arbitrage was supreme; where thousands of individuals with millions of dollars in incentives were pursuing information and pouncing on arbitrage opportunities. The traded good was almost as generic as a widget; there was a plethora of publicly available information; there was easy entry and exit; and trading was relatively costless and free from other frictions. The theoretical implication of such perfectly functioning markets was that they were efficient. The invisible hand would enforce not only the "right" price but also the "right" allocation of resources. The casino could be trusted. What more inviting place for economists to venture?

Thus the words of M. F. M. Osborne would soon become the norm: "The stock market is a gigantic decision-making phenomenon. It deserves scientific attention from those who would like to understand how decision making occurs, naturally, and in the large. As an economic phenomenon, we believe the market can reproduce in a few weeks a scaled version of supply-demand relations that would take many years to complete in a different setting" (1962, 245).

The successful application of economic theory in finance must be attributed to the notion of arbitrage. Not only could something "scientific" be said about speculative market prices, but also the economics theory seemed able to explain reality. This made finance all the more palatable to economists. Arbitrage was the theoretical force behind each of the major economics innovations in finance.[5]

The Modigliani-Miller theorem, for instance, relies on an arbitrage argument to prove its point. Briefly, assets with the same expected payoffs and the same riskiness of those payoffs must have the same value. Consider the firm as an asset. Its business and its payoffs are identical,

5. In a survey of finance professors in 1981 of what they considered to be the "significant contributions to finance literature," Philip Cooley and J. Louis Heck (1981) reported the following results for the top seven contributions (in order): Modigliani and Miller (1958) (voted for by 85 percent), Markowitz (1952) (83 percent), Sharpe (1964) (69 percent), Fama (1970) (47 percent), Miller and Modigliani (1961) (45 percent), Black and Scholes (1973) (42 percent), and Tobin (1958) (37 percent).

regardless of its financing and therefore so must be its value. That this has to be true is enforced by arbitrage.

In private correspondence with Bernstein, Miller declared that the arbitrage proof made "their conclusion unassailable":

> This arbitrage proof was the decisive distinction between our approach and those of our pedecessors, David Durand and John Burr Williams. They thought [the theorem] might or might not hold; but we showed it had to hold in the kind of perfect capital markets that economists had long made central to their analysis. . . . If it did not hold, the capital markets would be grossly and consistently violating one of the most venerable tenets of economics, to wit, the Law of One Price. (1992, 173)

It is interesting to note how Modigliani and Miller rely on "perfect capital markets." For them, this was the deductive underpinning on which to build their theory—a simple theory with strong (and nonintuitive) implications. It points out the importance of the EMH in this literature because the EMH supports the assumption of proper capital markets. Thus the EMH, besides making "order" out of the chaotic market also justifies the use of core assumptions and so makes the Modigliani and Miller results, as well as the arbitrage argument in the CAPM, stronger.

Another example is the later Black-Scholes options pricing formula, which was derived in 1971 (although not published until Black and Scholes 1973). Their essential contribution in pricing contingent claims (an endeavor at which Samuelson notably failed) was in how to take the aspect of time into account when considering asset prices. The key to solving the puzzle turned out to be an arbitrage argument. Because a stock and a bond could be combined to mimic exactly the payouts of an option, the price of the option must be the same as the price of that "replicating portfolio," or there would be an arbitrage opportunity.

The Black-Scholes formula, as with the CAPM, was abstract enough to be grounded in equilibrium (arbitrage-enforced) theory while it was specific enough to be directly applicable to real investment practices. The use of the Black-Scholes formula and the CAPM in actual investing must be attributed to the fact that they were simple to use and were intuitive. But, of course, what made them simple to use was that the pricing implication flows directly from the assumptions, of which the arbitrage one is crucial.

While it seems that the introduction of price equilibrium through arbitrage brought finance permanently into the fold of economics, it does not seem that the academic conversion was complete. Recognition for the field was gradual. At the end of the 1960s and the beginning of the 1970s, professors just began to be hired for "finance" and courses just started to be offered on "investments." While financial markets have become part of the larger discipline of economics, their academic home is still mostly relegated to business schools, which, although they offer higher salaries, still have the stigma of not quite being "true" economics. This is despite the fact that articles in finance frequent the leading journals and that "corporate finance," "financial economics," and "investments" courses are among the most popular with undergraduates.

Regardless of whether economics was profoundly changed, finance certainly was. The implications of economic theory for the practice of finance were utterly new and could not be ignored. Eventually calculating "betas," using the "Black-Scholes formula," diversifying, and investing in the "market index" became the norms on Wall Street where previously these tactics had been nonexistent. Furthermore, the field had become an academic discipline with a theoretical base. Much subsequent innovation came from the university and not the brokerage house.

In fact, finance has become the "proving ground" for new price theory and econometric technique. This puts the field at the forefront of the technical envelope, as measured by the use of mathematics and computers. Because of the availability of large quantities of data, because of the desirable properties of stock prices, and because of the monetary rewards to a "successful" innovation, it is still the most ideal "real world" market. But this has created some kind of a feedback effect, where innovations in finance have found their way back to the "rest" of economics. In particular, this is true for statistical and computer techniques.

4. Efficient Markets and Economists

Such a complete incursion of neoclassical theory into what was essentially an economic theoryless vacuum could not occur more than once. It would seem inevitable that the arbitrage opportunity that economists had in the field of finance was erased. Certainly, that did not end the field—it is no doubt stronger now than ever. But it has changed the nature of subsequent research and subsequent innovation. After all, now the "right" theory was in place, so that the subsequent research has become more and more focused on refinements—fine-tuning, testing, tweaking, and the same thing plus epsilon. It would be a disservice to minimize the importance of more recent developments such as the Arbitrage Pricing Theory (APT), the use of "real options" in decisions of investment under uncertainty, and synthetic portfolio insurance, among others. However, even these "innovations" have to a large extent followed directly from one of the previously discussed theories. But my point is not to establish the genealogy of later theory; rather, I want to suggest an argument of diminishing returns. Eventually, the optimal place to search for refinements must become the failings of the theory, not the theory itself.

The underlying assumptions, ultimately, were not completely desirable, and the real world, upon closer inspection, did not correspond perfectly with the predictions (implications) of the models. Given the huge value added at first in applying the theory, this was a forgivable discrepancy. But as the marginal utility of applying the theory declined, eventually greater expected value came from attacking the theory.

All of the cases presented here have already had their theoretical basis attacked for a variety of reasons. Richard Roll (1977) argues that the CAPM is not testable and therefore not useful. Robert Shiller (1981) finds that stock prices seem to vary too much to behave according to the EMH. The Modigliani-Miller theory had the honor of being so "unrealistic" that it was criticized from day one. The Black-Scholes formula relies on the normal curve of error to describe stock returns—which is patently false.

In response, there has been an upsurge in inductive research and efforts to learn from the data. Disaffection with the orthodoxy often results in a tendency toward inductive theorizing. Peter Earl (1983) refers to this as "reluctant positivism"—the desire to be more "realistic" whenever possible. An entire subfield of finance—"empirical finance"—has grown up essentially around data analysis. These empiricists have been the leaders in documenting the failures of the EMH and of the CAPM.[6]

Defenders of the orthodox theory are often put in the awkward position of ignoring reality. When disagreements arise between the "core" theory and observational facts, these economists frequently opt to support the theory. Certain observations, they feel, imply such "ridiculous" theory that it is more desirable to maintain the faulty "core." Neil De Marchi

6. The ongoing defense of the EMH corresponds closely to Lakatos's description of the protection of the background presumptions that make up the unquestioned "hard core" of what he calls a "scientific research program."

(1995) documents Samuelson's zealous refusal to accede to price changes being random or having nonfinite variance. Samuelson, for instance, describes the pure random walk for speculative prices as "ridiculous . . . absurdities" (as quoted in Bernstein 1992, 116, from private correspondence between the two).

Such efforts often mire quickly in tautology. Fischer Black, for instance, argues that "we might define an efficient market as one in which price is within a factor of 2 of value. . . . The factor of 2 is arbitrary, of course. Intuitively, though, it seems reasonable to me. . . . By this definition, I think almost all markets are efficient almost all of the time. 'Almost all' means at least 90%" (1986, 533). Or some begin down the slippery slope, as in Sanford Grossman and Joseph Stiglitz, who state: "We propose here a model in which there is an equilibrium degree of disequilibrium" (1980, 393).

The view of speculative markets as the best real-world example of efficient markets is likely to remain. However, it has been somewhat of a curse to economics. Numerous violations, paradoxes, and anomalies in the perfect behavior of stock market prices have drawn into question not only the assumptions of how the market works but also, at times, the very "rational" and "optimizing" behavior of individuals. Some observers have cited "bubbles," "fads," "over-reactions," "mania," "panic," "crowd psychology," and "noise traders" as prevalent in financial markets.

Furthermore, the arbitrage argument taken to its logical extremes implies that the "market index" cannot be outperformed. Yet money management and investment advice is an ever-growing field. Another extreme implication of arbitrage is the Paul Milgrom and Nancy Stokey (1982) no-trade result. While enchantingly elegant to economic theorists, it is clearly violated millions of times each day.[7]

No market can be completely perfect in that information is not symmetric, expectations are not identical, and arbitrage is not instantaneous. Thus we have an interesting (ongoing) tension between reality and the abstract theoretical ideal. In economics, this tension is not unique to finance, and it may well be an inevitable by-product of modeling. We may, in fact, be observing the life cycle of an intellectual arbitrage.

7. It might be interesting to consider a story, similar to this history of finance, that describes the Gary Becker revolution in labor economics. His application of the neoclassical "core" could also be seen as an arbitrage opportunity exploited, a process that made economic order of what was thought beyond systematic economic analysis—perhaps also eventually inducing backlash over the usefulness of an overly stylized theoretical world.

The neoclassical ideal, from its deductive roots, is introduced to finance with success—success in that the implications derived from the ideal are viewed as important. However, once the ideal is in place it is treated as the "truth." Eventually, some discomfit grows with its ability to explain reality. While there is clearly a desire to reconcile the theory with real-world observation, this effort is sometimes strained. In the context of finance, despite the inductive activity, I do not see any way that the underpinnings of the ideal will be challenged, although some of their implications might be. I think arbitrage *is* the fundamental truth—both theoretically and empirically. But we certainly cannot rule out the "discovery" of new uses or implications of the no arbitrage condition. And perhaps other intellectual arbitrages are already under way that will change finance, such as the application of neural networks or the use of experiments.

In concluding, I want to point out that while my discussion has given a prominent place to arbitrage, this should not be conflated with progress. Arbitrage is a process, not a progress. Which is not to say that under some criteria the evolution of finance has not been "getting better," but this might ultimately be subjective. I hope to have made the case for why the community of economists liked this change. That the community of practitioners also adopted this change seems evident; why they did is perhaps more practical than ideological—to make money.

So, in my view, intellectual arbitrage is an engine for innovation. Thus finance being arbitraged by neoclassical economic theory is not a story of the "better" muscling in on the "weaker." Although the neoclassical core does have more academic cachet, I see what transpired as in some sense marginal utility based. I do not want to overemphasize this metaphor. But there can be payoffs to doing something differently. Economics makes inroads into political science and sociology, while mathematics, engineering, and statistics, as well as psychology, rhetoric, feminism, and literary criticism, make corresponding inroads into economics.

Likewise, arbitrage in the market is a process that may result in tendencies toward a steady-state equilibrium, but arbitrage does not have to be inexorably linked with efficiency (it may be a necessary condition but not a sufficient condition). In a dynamic world, of course, we may only be able to make statements about tendencies. Regardless, in this case, it would be risky to suggest that the presented evolution was the inevitable one. We might, for instance, even speculate on how financial theory would look if the approach of Working or Mandelbrot had become dominant. Hopefully, however, this evolution is a revealing one.

References

Bachelier, Louis. [1900] 1964. Theory of Speculation. In *The Random Character of Stock Market Prices*, edited by Paul H. Cootner. Cambridge: MIT Press.

Baumol, William J. 1966. Mathematical Analysis of Portfolio Selection. *Financial Analysts Journal* (September–October): 95–99.

Bernstein, Peter L. 1992. *Capital Ideas: The Improbable Origins of Modern Wall Street*. New York: Free Press.

Black, Fischer. 1986. Noise. *Journal of Finance* 41:529–43.

Black, Fischer, and Myron S. Scholes. 1973. The Pricing of Options and Corporate Liabilities. *Journal of Political Economy* 81:399–418.

Cooley, Philip L., and J. Louis Heck. 1981. Significant Contributions to Finance Literature. *Financial Management* (10th anniversary issue): 23–33.

Cowles, Alfred, III. 1933. Can Stock Market Forecasters Forecast? *Econometrica* 1:309–24.

Cowles, Alfred, III, and H. Jones. 1937. Some Posteriori Probabilities in Stock Market Action. *Econometrica* 5:280–94.

De Marchi, Neil. 1995. Comment on Niehans. Unpublished manuscript, Duke University.

Earl, Peter. 1983. A Behavioral Theory of Economists' Behavior. In *Why Economics Is Not Yet a Science*, edited by Alfred S. Eichner. Armonk, N.Y.: M. E. Sharpe.

Fama, Eugene. 1970. Efficient Capital Markets: A Review of Theory and Empirical Work. *Journal of Finance* 25:383–417.

Grossman, Sanford, and Joseph Stiglitz. 1980. On the Impossibility of Informationally Efficient Markets. *American Economic Review* 70:393–408.

Harrison, Paul. 1993. A Methodological Critique of Market Efficiency. Unpublished manuscript, Duke University.

———. 1994. The More Things Change, the More They Stay the Same: Analysis of the Past 200 Years of Stock Market Evolution. Ph.D. diss., Duke University.

Kendall, Maurice G. 1953. The Analysis of Time Series. Part I: Prices. *Journal of the Royal Statistical Society* 96:11–25.

Keynes, John Maynard. [1939] 1983. Memorandum for the Estates Committee. Kings College, Cambridge, May 8. In vol. 12 of *The Collected Writings of John Maynard Keynes*, edited by Donald Moggridge. New York: Cambridge University Press.

Mandelbrot, Benoit. 1966. Forecasts of Future Prices, Unbiased Markets and "Martingale" Models. *Journal of Business* 39:242–55.

Markowitz, Harry M. 1952. Portfolio Selection. *Journal of Finance* 7:77–91.

———. 1959. *Portfolio Selection: Efficient Diversification of Investments*. New York: Wiley.

Milgom, Paul, and Nancy Stokey. 1982. Information, Trade and Common Knowledge. *Journal of Economic Theory* 26:17–27.

Miller, Merton H., and Franco Modigliani. 1961. Dividend Policy, Growth, and the Valuation of Shares. *Journal of Business* 34:411–33.

Modigliani, Franco, and Merton H. Miller. 1958. The Cost of Capital, Corporation Finance, and the Theory of Investment. *American Economic Review* 48:655–69.

Osborne, M. F. M. 1962. Periodic Structure in the Brownian Movement of Stock Prices. *Operations Research* 10:245–79.

Roll, Richard. 1977. A Critique of the Asset Pricing Theory's Tests. Part I: On Past and Potential Testability of the Theory. *Journal of Financial Economics* 4:129–76.

Samuelson, Paul A. 1965. Proof that Properly Anticipated Prices Fluctuate Randomly. *Industrial Management Review* 6:41–49.

Sharpe, William F. 1964. Capital Asset Prices: A Theory of Market Equilibrium under Conditions of Risk. *Journal of Finance* 19:425–42.

Shiller, Robert. 1981. Do Stock Prices Move Too Much to Be Justified by Subsequent Changes in Dividends? *American Economic Review* 71:421–36.

Tobin, James. 1958. Liquidity Preference as Behavior toward Risk. *Review of Economic Studies* 67:65–86.

Williams, John Burr. 1938. *The Theory of Investment Value*. Cambridge: Harvard University Press.

Working, Holbrook. 1934. A Random-Difference Series for Use in the Analysis of Time Series. *Journal of the American Statistical Association* 29:11–24.

Part 3

Social-Contextual Perspectives on How Economists Reason

Methodological Stance and Consumption Theory: A Lesson in Feminist Methodology

Mary L. Hirschfeld

Feminist analysis has come late to economics—the field of feminist economics having taken shape just within the last ten years. While feminist economics is still in its infancy, its practitioners intend their work to move far beyond simply adding women and women's issues to mainstream economic theory.[1] Many feminists have argued that neoclassical economics is profoundly shaped by masculine biases in both its content and its method.[2] As these criticisms of modern-day economics take shape, it becomes clear that the large project of tracing out the influence of gender on the history of economic thought yawns before us (Seiz 1993).

Work in feminist history of thought has begun (Pujol 1992), but there is as yet no work in economics analogous to the penetrating work done by feminists in the history of other fields like biology. Evelyn Fox Keller (1985; 1995), for example, has developed rich insights into the history of biology using the concept of gender in combination with the methods advocated by Andrew Pickering (1995). Similar work in economics should be rewarding.

Feminist discussion of the masculine influence on methodological and theoretical choices often leads to insights and critiques raised elsewhere by nonfeminists. For example, feminist economists have criticized neo-

1. Throughout I use the terms *mainstream* and *neoclassical* interchangeably. My usage is probably easier to define in terms of those I don't include: Austrians, Institutionalists, Marxists, and Post-Keynesians.

2. Nelson 1996, the essays in Nelson and Ferger 1993, and Harding 1995 are leading examples of these critiques.

classical economists for overvaluing simple models of human behavior. Feminists would urge models of human behavior which include connections between individuals, the impact of social norms on behavior, and a richer dynamic framework. Such models would be less likely to rely on the static equilibrium concepts of rational mechanics and would be more likely to resemble the complex models Philip Mirowski (elsewhere in this volume) dubs "cyborg science." Indeed, as Mirowski notes, feminist theorists from other fields have (not coincidentally) had an important impact on the development of cyborg science.

This article does not provide the type of thick analysis of the impact of gender on the history of economic thought that needs to be done. However, it does offer an example of how masculine methodological forms have precluded study of economic behavior that might prove fruitful under different methodological frameworks. The methodological stance favored by an overwhelming majority of economists analytically separates the economist and (in most cases) the "policy maker" from the economy. The economist studies the economy with the aim of providing advice to the policy maker, who then sets policy to control or manipulate the economy to achieve desired ends. I refer to this stance as the control stance. The control stance undergirds the field of welfare economics, and it is present in any consideration of the welfare implications of a given economic model.

Both the norm of consumer sovereignty (the principle that the preferences expressed by individuals best reflects their true utility functions) and the assumption of rational consumer behavior are central to welfare economics. Without either principle, the project of welfare economics of assessing economic policies becomes extremely complicated, if not outright impossible. Admitting complex consumer behavior threatens the project of welfare economics. That threat could be part of the general resistance economists have expressed toward genuinely studying consumer behavior.[3]

An alternative methodological stance, which I call the conversational or democratic stance, would provide much stronger motivation to inquire into how consumers actually behave. In the conversational stance, the individuals who constitute the economy are not passive objects of study. Instead, they are viewed as the intended audience for economic

3. Efforts to study consumer behavior for the purposes of improving our description of the economy do go forward, but they constitute a small area of economic research.

theorists. Findings about the economy are shared with individuals within the economy who can use that knowledge in shaping their own lives or as they participate in the political process to shape their society.

Theoretical and empirical work on actual consumer behavior is of much more value when it is considered from the conversational stance. Such work, which complicates the project of a single policy maker would, in contrast, be of great value to individuals within the economy, who could then use that information to improve their own decision making. While such information may not be useful in determining an optimal economic system, it could enhance economic welfare directly by improving consumer "technology."

In the discussion that follows, I expand on the concept of the control versus the conversational stance and link it to feminist theory. I then turn to a more detailed discussion of how the control stance resists empirical study of actual consumer behavior. Finally, I discuss the work of two economists, Hazel Kyrk and Tibor Scitovsky, who do inquire into consumer behavior in some depth, a choice facilitated by their use of the conversational rather than the control stance.

1. Feminist Theory and Methodological Stance

Although feminist economics promises to generate profound additions to and changes in the content of economic theory, here I focus on feminist discussion of economic method. Julie Nelson (1996) has argued that the methodology favored by mainstream economists is biased because it reflects a preference for qualities associated with masculinity and a disdain for qualities associated with femininity. As Nelson observes, the following methodological values tend to be gendered:

Masculine	Feminine
rigorous	intuitive
precise	vague
objective	subjective
scientific	nonscientific
detached	committed
mathematical	verbal
formal	informal
general	particular

Economists prefer masculine values, and they tend to think of the masculine values in their positive connotations and feminine values in their negative connotations. But there are negative connotations that could be attached to the masculine values: for example, too much detachment could lead to irrelevance. Similarly, there are positive connotations that could be attached to the feminine values: the dismissive term *intuitive* could be replaced by the term *insightful*, for instance. Paying attention to these gender values could help economists develop a methodology that draws on the positive side of both masculine and feminine values. A sustained investigation of a more inclusive methodology is offered by Donald McCloskey (1985), who then connects his[4] methodological work to the issue of gender in his 1993 essay. Neither Nelson nor McCloskey advocates an end to the formal models used by neoclassical economists, however; they simply call for more room for other approaches. It is important to note here that the neoclassical preferences for masculine qualities will be held by anyone, male or female, who has adapted to the culture of the economics profession.

The Control Stance and the Conversational Stance

The premium on masculine bias discussed by Nelson can be seen in the stance most economists take toward their subject matter. In the commonly used control stance, the economist perceives herself as analytically separate from the economy. She addresses her finding toward other economists and potential policy makers who are, like herself, analytically outside of the economy. While some of her work is directed to understanding how the economy works, much of her work aims at elucidating sound economic policy.[5] The policy maker, with the advice of the economist, seeks to manipulate the behavior of individuals within the economy to attain desired social ends.

The economist/policy maker does not, at least consciously, try to control the economy to meet her own ends.[6] The implicit aim is to maximize social welfare, however social welfare may be defined. However

4. The insistence of our language on distinguishing gender becomes problematic from time to time, doesn't it?

5. According to Daniel Hausman (1984), the goal of controlling the economy is often used as a justification of the instrumental approach to economics. Milton Friedman (1953) provides an example of an instrumental approach to science.

6. See Samuels 1988.

benevolent the aims of the economist/policy maker might be, there is a hierarchical relationship contained in the control stance. Individuals within the economy are the passive subject matter to be manipulated by those "outside" the system.

The control stance can be contrasted with an approach toward the economy that I call the conversational, or democratic, stance. In the conversational stance, the economist recognizes that he, too, is part of the economy. He has a feeling of connection with his subject, and his intended audience is the individuals within the economy. One of the goals of his work is to provide knowledge about the economy to individuals for use in their own lives. For example, individuals with insight into the factors that drive consumer behavior might be able to use that insight to make better choices. Individuals with knowledge about how the economy works might be able to navigate a more successful path through the economy. The idea that economic knowledge might be used to inform individual behavior is the distinguishing feature of the conversational stance. As we shall see in the following discussion, that stance points toward areas of research that are less promising when they are perceived from the control stance.

Economists in the conversational stance can also discuss policy questions. The individuals in the economy who are the intended audience are also potential participants in the social decision-making process, so knowledge about policy issues can inform both their public and their private choices. Here the distinction between the conversational stance and the control stance is quite subtle. Most economists in the control stance likely also believe that their work on economic policy is to become part of a public discussion of what policies we, as a society, should choose.

However, an economist who has elsewhere adopted the conversational stance tends to approach policy questions from a less centralized perspective. He generally relinquishes the goal of giving a *comprehensive* evaluation of the social system. This follows from the fact that the economist in a conversational stance is not analytically outside of the economy. From within the economy there is less purchase from which to ascertain what a global optimum would look like. Economists in the control stance locate themselves outside the economy and are thus more inclined to believe that they can identify global optima. It is ironic that control stance economists who advocate market economies on the grounds that no centralized planner would have sufficient information to coordinate economic activity simultaneously believe that they or a designated policy maker could, at least in theory, have sufficient information to determine a globally optimal set of policies.[7]

If Mirowski is correct that cyborg science is the way of the future, then we can expect to see models that are more reflective of the conversational stance. According to Stuart Kauffman of the Santa Fe Institute, we live in a world poised between chaos and order. He writes, "in such a poised world, we must give up the pretense of long-term prediction. We cannot know the true consequences of our own best actions. All we players can do is be locally wise, not globally wise" (1995, 29).

The control stance embodies the masculine values of detachment and control or domination. Feminists writing about science have linked the emphasis on detachment to masculinity, using both historical analysis (Merchant 1980; Bordo 1987; Easlea 1980) and psychology (Dinnerstein 1976; Chodorow 1978). Likewise, feminists have linked the control or domination goal of scientists to qualities traditionally associated with masculinity. Fox Keller quotes Francis Bacon on the promise of scientific inquiry: "I am come in very truth leading to you Nature with all her children to bind her to your service and make her your slave" (1985, 39),[8] wherein the link between domination (or control) is clear.[9] It is worth noting that the control stance is analogous to the stereotypical role of the father in the Western nuclear family—he comes home from work (is separate from the family) and as head of the household is in charge of making decisions for the family.

In contrast, the conversational stance involves the more feminine qualities of connection and identification. Feminists have written about connection as an alternative way of learning about the world (Belenky, Clinchy, Goldberger, and Tarule 1986). The most commonly cited instance of this methodological connectedness being fruitfully applied in the natural sciences is Barbara McClintock, who attributed her discoveries in genetics to her "feeling for the organism" (Fox Keller 1983). Feminists have not yet (to my knowledge) contrasted the masculine emphasis on controlling one's subject matter with a counterpart feminine emphasis. I believe that thinking of the scientist's role as being a provider

7. As I argue below, the belief that sufficient information could be attained by the policy maker is sustained by systematically assuming away complex human behavior and complex human values.

8. Of course, most economists don't want to make the economy their slaves.

9. This quote is by no means isolated. See Easlea 1980 for numerous passages written at the beginning of the scientific revolution which explicitly promote science as a tool for domination, and which extol domination as a masculine virtue.

of information for the individuals within the social system the scientist is studying can serve as that feminine counterpart.[10]

There are two final points to make about methodological stance. First, most feminist economists also practice from the control stance—policy evaluation is as important in feminist economic work as its is in mainstream economics. Indeed, this essay is essentially written from a control stance. The conversational stance is a feminist concept only in the sense that it is identified as a stance that embodies feminine values. Second, as I advocate the usefulness of the conversational stance, I do not intend to argue for it as a replacement for the control stance. A central function of social science is to evaluate and judge society.[11] Rather, I see the conversational stance as a useful complement to the control stance.

2. Welfare Economics and the Control Stance

I turn now to a concrete example of how the conversational stance opens up the range of questions an economist can usefully explore. Here I lay out the basics of the neoclassical model, highlighting the relationship between consumer theory and welfare economics. As we shall see, whether one is inclined toward laissez-faire or pro-government type policies, violations of neoclassical consumer theory pose large problems for an economist using the control stance.

Neoclassical Consumption Theory and Welfare Economics

In neoclassical theory, individuals are assumed to maximize given utility functions subject to whatever constraints they face. The elements of the utility function can be broadly defined to include a wide range of factors, including the well-being or utility of others. The only restriction placed on utility functions is that they be rational. Rationality requires that the individual can make a rank ordering of all states in the world (including the possibility of being indifferent between two choices), and that such rank orderings are transitive (if A is preferred to B, and B is preferred to

10. Institutionalists do maintain this stance, at least as an option. J. Ron Stanfield (1983) calls it the cultural relevance function of the scientist, though he still subordinates it to the policy relevance function. In his sympathetic treatment of institutionalists, Allan Gruchy (1947) criticizes Thorstein Veblen for being insufficiently interested in policy questions. The feminine counterpart is probably limited to the social scientists. It's difficult to imagine how natural scientists could communicate their findings to the objects of their study!

11. As Samuels 1988 argues, social science has a necessarily normative content.

C, then A is preferred to C). The result of the consumer's maximization process is a set of market demands.

The model of consumer behavior is thus used to "explain" market demand, but it has another important role in economic theory—it lies at the heart of all normative judgments economists make about the economy, most especially in the field of welfare economics. Jerome Rothenberg (1968) presents the concept of consumer sovereignty as one of the important elements of welfare economics. He distinguishes the descriptive aspect of the term, which refers to the fact that in a market system, production is geared toward meeting those demands, from the normative aspect. In the normative aspect, the performance of the economy is judged by how well it meets consumer demands. The normative principle of consumer sovereignty entails two assumptions: it assumes that what individuals want is really in their best interest, and it assumes that individuals are capable of translating those wants into the appropriate market demands (that is, consumers are rational).

Rothenberg distinguishes consumer sovereignty from the principle of freedom of choice, which is the norm that individuals should be allowed to choose freely, regardless of whether or not "we" think their choices are wise. Welfare economics then adds on a normative principle of how to assess the impact of policies that impact more than one individual. The most common principle used is Pareto optimality. A policy is Pareto optimal if it makes at least one individual better off as it leaves no other individual worse off.

The consumer sovereignty norm lies at the heart of welfare economics, which is the basis of the policy evaluations economists make. One of the cornerstones of economic theory is the effort to prove that, under the assumptions of perfect competition, free markets maximize economic welfare. Much of the business of economics is engaged in determining the extent to which market imperfections (violations of the assumptions of perfect competition) reduce economic welfare, as well as the degree to which such welfare reductions can be corrected by the state. Another source of questions for economists centers on the degree to which government interventions into the economy for other purposes (e.g., taxation) reduces economic welfare. In all of these questions, the efficiency of the economy is evaluated according to how well the economy meets consumer demand.[12]

12. See Penz 1986 for a discussion of how the norm of consumer sovereignty lies at the heart of macroeconomic theory as well.

Dealing with Complex Consumption Behavior from the Control Stance

For as long as economists have propounded their model of consumer behavior, they have been greeted with a large body of criticism that questions the reasonableness of their model. Critics have questioned whether we can truly take preferences as given in a world where social norms affect behavior (Veblen 1899); where individuals act out of habit or impulse; or where individuals can adapt their preferences to fit their circumstances (Hahnel and Albert 1990).[13] If preferences are not given, or if consumers are not rational in their decision making, the claim that an economic system which meets the consumer preferences which are revealed by consumer choice maximizes social welfare becomes difficult, if not impossible, to sustain.

Economists in the control stance who acknowledge these problems have two options. The first, which has been pursued by Austrian economists, is to abandon all claims that the economic system maximizes economic welfare. Instead, they base their advocacy of the market system on the normative principle of freedom of choice. Consider, for example, William Hutt (1936), who is widely thought to have coined the term *consumer sovereignty*. In that work, Hutt used the term in the descriptive sense of Rothenberg. Unlike mainstream economists, however, Hutt advocated consumer sovereignty as a normative standard by appealing to the principle of freedom of choice, rather than to the postulate that there is a necessary relationship between consumers' market preferences and their welfare. Indeed, Hutt is very eloquent on the numerous ways in which consumers' market demands are *not* necessarily in their own best interest.[14]

Despite his recognition of the complexities of consumer behavior, Hutt does not advocate further research into them. His survey of the problems is focused on sustaining the argument that, in virtually all instances of consumer "irrationality," more harm would be done by limiting freedom of choice than by allowing consumers to make whatever mistakes to which they were prone. Hutt argues that there are no absolute criteria available for judging the value of consumer preferences. Without such criteria, evaluating policy responses becomes next to impossible and the

13. See Lane 1991 for a thorough discussion of the limits of the neoclassical model of consumer behavior.

14. See chapters 16, 17, and 18 in Hutt 1936.

best option is to uphold the value of freedom of choice.[15] Having concluded that consumer irrationality is not a compelling reason to intervene in the market, Hutt moves on to other issues. His control stance prevents him from seeing any other reason to further study consumer behavior.

The second option available to economists in the control stance who recognize the complexities of consumer behavior is to try to determine what sort of economic system or set of policies would best deal with those complications. There is a large and (not coincidentally) complex literature that takes this approach. One of the principle problems confronted in the literature is determining which criteria should be used to evaluate the efficiency of the market if market demands are not taken as expressive of human welfare. Penz's (1986) attempt at finding an ideal version of the sovereignty principle is an example of this type of effort.[16] A different dilemma occurs in many situations where preferences are endogenous. In those cases, a public policy deemed optimal at one point in time might change preferences in such a way that the policy would no longer be deemed optimal after it was implemented (Cowen 1993). Should policy makers know what true preferences they are trying to meet, they are confronted with the problem of determining what they are. There's no measure of preferences nearly as easy to use as the market demand measurement they would replace. Finally, even if the standard is determined, and the informational problems are overcome, the type of policy that would be dictated conflicts with the normative principle of free choice—rendering it unlikely to be a politically viable option (Rothenberg 1968).

I do not mean to suggest that there is no valuable work exploring the impact more complex assumptions about human behavior have on welfare economics. Hahnel and Albert (1990) provide a good survey of such work and offer their own welfare framework, which incorporates a version of endogenous preferences. However, Hahnel and Albert explicitly rule out other types of complexity (myopic preference formation, for example) on the grounds that such behavior is unsuitable for the project of welfare economics. Indeed, they argue that whether or not the behavioral assumptions they adopt are reflective of actual human behavior is irrelevant for welfare economics. That may be. However, it clearly misses the point that study of consumer behavior might be of importance for consumers.

15. These are exactly the types of problems that confront mainstream economists who do try to formulate policy recommendations in the face of complex consumer behavior, as we shall see.

16. See Rothenberg 1991 for a criticism of Penz.

Overall, economists in the control stance face an unappealing choice should they recognize the complexities of consumer behavior. On the one hand, they can maintain consumer sovereignty and justify it on the normative grounds of freedom of choice, losing the value of the claim that they have anything to say about consumer well-being.[17] On the other hand, they can try to find some other standard by which to evaluate the economy, but in that case they most likely have to give up any hope of developing a model that is general enough to be easily applied to a wide variety of situations. It is little wonder that the majority cling to the neoclassical model of consumer behavior. However, were economists to make use of the conversational stance, they would find studying consumer behavior more fruitful, as the work of Hazel Kyrk (1923) shows.

3. Kyrk's *Theory of Consumption* and the Conversational Stance

Hazel Kyrk spent the bulk of her career as a professor at the University of Chicago with a joint appointment in the departments of economics and home economics. Kyrk earned her Ph.D. at the University of Chicago, and her dissertation, *A Theory of Consumption*, won the Hart, Schaffner and Marx Prize in 1921 and was published in 1923. That work is considered seminal in the field of consumer economics in the discipline of home economics (Magrabi, Chung, Cha, and Yang 1991). In *A Theory of Consumption*, Kyrk discusses the consumer's interaction with the market, critiques marginal utility theory, and sets out her own theory of consumption, which is meant to be an apparatus to understand the formation of consumer desires. Her theory is meant to be a comprehensive framework to capture many of the complexities of consumer behavior. Yet, she avoids the tangles to which the mainstream literature is prone. Her easy engagement with the complex questions raised by consumer behavior stems from her use of the conversational stance.

A Summary of Kyrk's theory

Kyrk critiques the mainstream economics of her day on two counts.[18] First, she argues that they have been insufficiently interested in investigating the consumption half of the economy. Kyrk attributes this deemphasis of consumption to an overly narrow definition of what con-

17. Rothenberg 1991 takes this option without acknowledging this cost.

18. See Hirschfeld 1994 for a more complete discussion of Kyrk's work and how it fits in to the history of economic thought.

sumption is:

> To what extent the attitude with which the majority of economists have taken toward consumption as a field for economic inquiry is due to their narrow interpretation of the term, and to their failure to see all the modes of activity involved, is an interesting question. When writers upon economics make the statement that matters within the field of consumption are of no concern to the economist as such, how are they defining consumption and economics? What is the main economic problem, it is pertinent to inquire, and what are these activities which have no bearing upon it? If the economic problem is wholly the problem of turning out commodities in large and ever-increasing volume and consumption is merely a passive process of utilization, the economist may well feel that he has only a limited interest in the way it is carried on. (1923, 14)[19]

She later points out that consumption is also the half of the economy assigned to women, but she does not suggest that there is any connection.

Kyrk's second critique of mainstream economics centers on the marginal utility theory of consumption. She covers the standard critiques of marginal utility theory that were made at the time: preferences are not individually formed—they have a strong social component; the rational thinking assumed by marginal utility theory gives no scope for the existence of impulses, habits, prejudices, and other "irrational" behavioral patterns; hedonism is not the main motivator in human behavior. For Kyrk, the matter is quite straightforward: modern sociology and psychology describe a human nature so vastly removed from the human nature assumed by marginal utility theorists that the two views "cannot stand together." It makes no sense to proceed as though psychologists had learned nothing since the early 1800s. Kyrk does acknowledge that marginal utility theory might be a good basis for price theory, but for consumption theory (and its related question of how well the market economy fosters human welfare) the marginal utility theory is wholly inadequate.

Kyrk goes on to comment on the origin of the "error" made by marginal utility theorists about human nature:

> Of course, the assumption that men follow "self-interest" based upon the observation of the business man's calculation of profit and loss,

19. Unless otherwise noted, all page citations are from Kyrk 1923.

> cannot be transferred to a field not controlled by pecuniary standards. Here, as has frequently been pointed out, the economists made their mistake. . . . They ascribed to human nature what the institutional organization was really responsible for. Self-interest and calculation may be satisfactory clues to the business man's conduct, but they cannot be carried over to the interpretation of consumers' choices. Business activity is an incomplete activity in which money is an end, but in the consumer's activity money is only a means for carrying out a wide variety of purposes. . . . The consumer, of course, may deliberate and compare alternative courses of action, but the thing involved is not a difference in quantity, but a difference in resulting situations which may be quite different in kind. . . . Further, what he wants and how he comes to want it remain an unsolved problem. (144)

She is pointing out that the consumer has no guide like profits to say that spending money on a dress, for example, would yield more "utility" than money spent on a lecture series. The benefits of the two expenditures may be too disparate to compare. Kyrk later draws on Mitchell 1937 to argue that whereas an incompetent firm may be driven out of business, an incompetent consumer faces no similar penalty. In sum, maximizing behavior may be a good assumption for a firm, but a poor assumption for a household.

Kyrk spends several chapters situating the consumer in the economy and discussing the descriptive aspects of consumer sovereignty. She investigates the issues that impact the consumer in interactions with the economy. Kyrk discusses the distribution of income, the impact of industrialization on consumer choices and consumer lifestyle, and the problems a consumer faces in the marketplace when confronted with advertising, monopoly power, and information problems.[20]

The last half of the book is devoted to Kyrk's theory of how consumer preferences are formed. Drawing on philosophy, psychology, and sociology, she formulates a theory of how wants are formed. From philosophy (citing Dewey most frequently), Kyrk argues that humans are born with innate tendencies and desires, which then interact with the environment. Humans perceive the world through the lens of their innate and acquired desires, and objects in the environment are perceived as more or less useful for meeting those desires. Value arises through the interaction of the individual and the environment. Obviously, the types of values that

20. Kyrk 1950 is well worth reading on this subject.

emerge will have a wide variety of expressions as the environment and history of a group varies.

Humans organize their multifarious economic values into one coherent set of values, which Kyrk calls a "standard of living." The standard of living is the set of goods and activities that an individual designates as "essential" or desirable. From an individual's point of view, the standard of living is as binding a constraint as is price and income. There are social costs to not conforming to the standard of living. A drop in standard of living necessitated by a drop in income is viewed as painful, not just because there are fewer goods (a lot of vacations entail "roughing it" and are viewed as pleasurable exactly because one is less encumbered by goods) but because it involves a loss of social status. A person experiences a rise in income as a decrease in concern about maintaining the essential elements of her or his standard of living, along with an increase in "discretionary" income. A sustained rise in income will allow the person to adopt a higher standard of living and the rise in social status that comes with it. A loss in income is more painful than a gain in income is pleasurable.

Individuals inherit their standards of living from the society in which they are raised. By the time one reaches adulthood, one does not have much real freedom of choice after all, since one's desires have been imposed on one. To reiterate, these standards of living are perceived by the individual as an exogenous constraint as binding and as beyond the individual's control as the income and price constraints she faces in the market.

The social standard is the product of the economic possibilities that confront a group and the cultural legacy the group has inherited. Three basic principles underlie cultural choices. First, some goods are selected for their "organic utility" for an individual life; this would be nutrition, shelter, and so on. Second, some elements of a standard of living are selected for "conventional necessity" or their prestige value,[21] and Kyrk believes such systems of prestige may be necessary for group survival. Third, elements that represent the group's concept of welfare are included; these might cover the arts, religious practice, and so on. Various goods will include some or all of these characteristics. Thus, goods are really "bundles of utilities."

The standard of living evolves as individuals with some economic surplus (income above that required to maintain the essentials of their standard of living) may experiment with new goods and services. The

21. Here Kyrk draws on Veblen's idea of consumption as an emulative process.

successful experiments are added into the culture's standard of living. Thus, for example, compact discs are a successful experiment while 8-track tapes are not. These experiments presumably started at the dawn of history as brave (and/or foolish) individuals experimented with different types of food, shelter, and tools.

The rate of change in standards of living depends on whether a society places an "irrational" premium on custom or on novelty; the amount of interaction with other societies; the presence or absence of a "scientific spirit"; the degree to which an economic system grants "formal freedom" to the consumer; the amount of economic surplus with which experiments can be performed; and the relative absence of rigid social classes, since social fluidity gives more impetus to experimentation.

The direction of change is more indeterminate. It requires some knowledge of one's self. However, education is probably necessary to find one's "consumption calling," and education is a scarce good. Figuring out new patterns of consumption also requires time, which may be one of the scarcest goods. Because of these limitations on true innovation, one may find the following reactions to an increase in income. First, a rising income could be used to acquire more of the same goods that already form part of the standard of living, or higher quality versions of goods already existent could appear. Second, individuals with a lower standard of living might simply emulate the standards of living enjoyed by those in a higher class. Third, for individuals in the highest class, there might simply be no way to spend all the income. Kyrk uses this point to elaborate on the underconsumption possibilities discussed by Hobson.

Kyrk's final chapter moves into the issue of what constitutes a high standard of living. Such a determination may be as vague as saying that a high standard is one that allows a person the means to carry out whatever activities are important for well-being. Economists may be more inclined to designate standards of living as high when they consume a lot of resources. Such "high" standards can have the effect of preventing population problems and giving extra bargaining power to labor. Additionally, a high standard of living can serve as an impetus to get people to work hard. Kyrk clearly prefers the first, vague description of what a "high" standard of living is. But this need not leave us with nothing to say:

> Consumption will cease to be a backward art and will begin to show improvement as these conditions are appreciated and policy shaped

> in accordance with them. The first prerequisite for progress in standards of consumption is, it is believed, a critical analysis of existing standards. A necessary preliminary to the raising of our standards is a survey, as objective as we can make it, of existing concepts of what is desirable and essential, of how our present standards came to be and what values constitute a part of them. This is the business of human intelligence—to criticize and to remake human valuations. Our valuations come to us in large part ready-made; our attitudes and reactions follow established behavior patterns. But life upon the level of intelligence means that we examine and if necessary, remake our valuations. This is the scientific spirit applied to life; this is scientific knowledge and human experience applied directly to the problems of living. There is no doubt that many values now well entrenched in our standards would disappear in the course of this critical analysis. They have so little rational basis and they are fundamentally so "wasteful" that they cannot stand the light of impartial inquiry into their source. They shrivel up and die as soon as the dissecting scalpel touches them. A decided step toward economy and elimination of waste will, then, be taken when we are ready to scrutinize our standards and see whence they have come and of what they are made. . . . The second step toward greater wisdom in consumption and toward the establishment of a high standard . . . is the formulation with some degree of precision of the ends which are sought and the scheme of life to be carried into effect. It is in this connection that recourse must be had to the best advice we can get upon the whole art of living from sages of the past and present. What interests and activities are worth while? It is in making this decision that the consumer as such has always been weak. He has scarcely attacked this his most difficult problem, the setting up of definite ends to be pursued. (287–88)

In short, we will never be able to definitively determine what constitutes a high standard of living, but surely a systematic discussion on the subject would have to lead to a general improvement in standards of living.

Kyrk's Methodological Stance toward Her Subject

If one reads Kyrk from the control stance, parts of her argument will be familiar. She offers what sounds like concrete policy recommendations. In order to achieve a high standard of living (Kyrk's policy goal), Kyrk recommends a system that retains consumer sovereignty due to the importance of freedom of choice.[22] She believes that economic growth is useful insofar as it gives consumers greater scope for exploring their true interests in life, although she does not say whether the government has any particular role to play in this regard.

The rest of her "recommendations" are incoherent if one reads them from the control stance. She continues her discussion of what would be necessary to achieve a high standard of living. Consumers would spend more time thinking about the ultimate purposes they have in life. They would utilize information generated by economists about standards of living to sort out what elements of their standard of living are truly useful. And there would be greater awareness of the "business of consumption": the importance of budgeting and being a "good" shopper (being well-informed about goods and so on). Insofar as she has already ruled out government policy as a means for implementing these kinds of proscriptions, one has to ask what she does intend.

Kyrk's position is much more coherent if one looks at it from the conversational stance. In the conversational stance, the main purpose of the economist is to provide information to individuals in the economy rather than to some "policy maker" outside the system. The research agenda outlined in the preceding lengthy quote, is the type of information Kyrk would like to be able to provide. The recommendations she makes about wise decision making and so on are the ones suggested by her theory. If individuals think her theory makes sense, they might choose to adopt her recommendations. Essentially, Kyrk is trying to initiate a serious public discussion about the purposes of consumption and the ways we form our preferences. That discussion (and any research associated with it) is not likely to lead to any particular set of government policies. But it has the potential of helping people "set better policies" (if you will) for their own lives.

As already noted, Kyrk does discuss policy issues. One could simply argue that in those sections of her book she is writing from the control stance. However, I would argue that even when she is writing on policy issues, the conversational stance informs her discussion. Rather than making recommendations to a policy maker, Kyrk raises various issues that "we" might consider as "we" try to reach social decisions. In other words, this information is again intended for individuals within

22. She is not an absolutist on this point, but her inclinations are toward laissez-faire.

the economy. This time, however, it is for use in their public rather than their private lives. The ultimate policy decisions will be the result of the bargaining and compromise that is inherent in the democratic process—these decisions will not be the result of a decision by an omniscient policy maker. Note that Kyrk does not formulate the definitive policy recommendations that are characteristic of the control stance.

I have related Kyrk's ability to outline a full research program concerning consumer behavior to her adoption of the conversational stance. Such a research program appears much more useful when one considers it as a source of information to be used directly by consumers (if they choose). In the control stance, the information from such a research program might eventually be useful, but only if the severe analytical difficulties of determining a standard of consumer welfare and a method for measuring it can be overcome. In this vein, it is interesting to note that at least one other economist who succeeded in a lengthy exploration of consumer behavior also adopted at least elements of the conversational stance.

In *The Joyless Economy* (1976), Tibor Scitovsky also produces a theory of economic behavior that draws heavily on the work of psychologists. Like Kyrk, Scitovsky writes from the conversational stance, addressing individuals within the economy: "But is there not another reason for our increasing frustration with our freely chosen lives? Could it not be that we seek our satisfaction in the wrong things, or in the wrong way, and are then dissatisfied with the outcome?" (4). Toward the end of the book, he writes: "How well do we Americans use our resources to achieve satisfaction? And where does this book leave the reader, who, aided or unaided, must face the economic problems around him?" (282). The similarity of tone between Scitovsky and Kyrk is striking. Unlike Kyrk, Scitovsky comes close to explicitly recognizing his use of the conversational stance. Early in the book he points out that economists have been willing to see themselves as advisors to business and he then wonders whether a new role for economists as advisors to consumers might not also be possible (6–7).

4. Conclusion

Methodology affects the problems we choose to study. The methodological stance adopted by mainstream economics has tended to foreclose the possibility of really exploring consumer behavior. One need not connect the idea of the control stance versus the conversational stance with feminist theory. However, it is worth noting that, while the control stance embodies the masculine values of detachment and control, the conversational stance embodies the feminine values of connection and conversational egalitarianism. Feminist economic theory does not argue that all women would adopt the conversational stance and all men would adopt the control stance. Rather, it argues that economists as a group value masculine qualities more highly than feminine qualities and that this valuation contributes to the choice of methodologies that reflect masculine values. This article is an example of the types of changes in methodology (and hence in the types of questions studied) that we might expect to see as we all become more willing to value feminine qualities in our work as highly as we already value masculine qualities.

References

Belenky, Mary Field, Blythe McVicker Clinchy, Nancy Rule Goldberger, and Jill Mattuck Tarule. 1986. *Women's Ways of Knowing: The Development of Self, Voice, and Mind.* New York: Basic.

Bordo, Susan. 1987. *The Flight to Objectivity: Essays on Cartesianism and Culture.* Albany: State University of New York Press.

Chodorow, Nancy. 1978. *The Reproduction of Mothering: Psychoanalysis and the Sociology of Gender.* Berkeley: University of California Press.

Cowen, Tyler. 1993. The Scope and Limits of Preference Sovereignty. *Economics and Philosophy* 9:253–69.

Dinnerstein, Dorothy. 1976. *The Mermaid and the Minotaur: Sexual Arrangements and Human Malaise.* New York: HarperPerennial.

Easlea, Brian. 1980. *Witch Hunting, Magic and the New Philosophy: An Introduction to Debates of the Scientific Revolution.* Atlantic Highlands, N.J.: Humanities.

Fox Keller, Evelyn. 1983. *A Feeling for the Organism: The Life and Work of Barbara McClintock.* New York: Freeman.

———. 1985. *Reflections on Gender and Science.* New Haven, Conn.: Yale University Press.

———. 1995. *Refiguring Life.* New York: Columbia University Press.

Friedman, Milton. 1953. *Essays in Positive Economics.* Chicago: University of Chicago Press.

Gruchy, Allan. 1947. *Modern Economic Thought: The American Contribution.* New York: Prentice Hall.

Hahnel, Robin, and Michael Albert. 1990. *Quiet Revolution in Welfare Economics.* Princeton, N.J.: Princeton University Press.

Harding, Sandra. 1995. Can Feminist Thought Make Economics More Objective? *Feminist Economics* 1:7–32.

Hausman, Daniel. 1984. Introduction to *The Philosophy of Economics: An Anthology*, edited by Daniel Hausman. Cambridge: Cambridge University Press.

Hirschfeld, Mary L. 1994. The Old Home Economics: Hazel Kyrk's Institutionalist Theory of Consumption. Paper presented at the History of Economics Society conference at Babson College, Massachusetts.

Hutt, William H. 1936. *Economists and the Public: A Study of Competition and Opinion*. London: Jonathan Cape.

Kauffman, Stuart. 1995. *At Home in the Universe: The Search for Laws of Self-Organization and Complexity*. Oxford: Oxford University Press.

Kyrk, Hazel. 1923. *A Theory of Consumption*. Boston: Houghton Mifflin.

———. 1950. The Income Distribution as a Measure of Economic Welfare. *American Economic Review* 40 (Part 1): 342–55.

Lane, Robert. 1991. *The Market Experience*. Cambridge: Cambridge University Press.

Magrabi, Frances M., Young Sook Chung, Sanghee Sohn Cha, and Se-Jeong Yang. 1991. *The Economics of Household Consumption*. New York: Praeger.

McCloskey, Donald N. 1985. *The Rhetoric of Economics*. Madison: University of Wisconsin Press.

———. 1993. Some Consequences of a Conjective Economics. In *Beyond Economic Man: Feminist Theory and Economics*, edited by Julie Nelson and Marianne Ferber. Chicago: University of Chicago Press.

Merchant, Carolyn. 1980. *The Death of Nature: Women, Ecology and the Scientific Revolution*. San Francisco: Harper and Row.

Mitchell, Wesley C. 1937. *The Backward Art of Spending Money and Other Essays*. New York: Augustus M. Kelley.

Nelson, Julie A. 1996. *Feminism, Objectivity and Economics*. London: Routledge.

Nelson, Julie A., and Marianne A. Ferber, eds. 1993. *Beyond Economic Man*. Chicago: University of Chicago Press.

Penz, G. Peter. 1986. *Consumer Sovereignty and Human Interests*. Cambridge: Cambridge University Press.

Pickering, Andrew. 1995. *The Mangle of Practice*. Chicago: University of Chicago Press.

Pujol, Michele. 1992. *Feminism and Anti-Feminism in Early Economic Thought*. Aldershot: Edward Elgar.

Rothenberg, Jerome. 1968. Consumer Sovereignty. In vol. 3 of *International Encyclopedia of the Social Sciences*, edited by D. L. Sills. New York: Macmillan.

———. 1991. G. Peter Penz's *Consumer Sovereignty and Human Interests. Economics and Philosophy* 7.2:322–29.

Samuels, Warren. 1988. An Essay on the Nature and Significance of the Normative Nature of Economics. *Journal of Post-Keynesian Economics* 10:347–54.

Scitovsky, Tibor. 1976. *The Joyless Economy: An Inquiry into Human Satisfaction and Consumer Dissatisfaction*. Oxford: Oxford University Press.

Seiz, Janet. 1993. Feminism and the History of Economic Thought. *HOPE* 25.1:185–201.

Stanfield, J. Ron. 1983. Institutional Analysis: Toward Progress in Economic Science. In *Why Economics Is Not Yet a Science*, edited by Alfred Eichner. Armonk, N.Y.: M. E. Sharpe.

Veblen, Thorstein. 1899. *The Theory of the Leisure Class*. New York: Mentor.

Persuading by the Numbers: The Balance Sheet in Late-Victorian Financial Journalism

Timothy L. Alborn

Since at least the time of W. S. Jevons and Alfred Marshall, economists have recurrently found themselves caught between the conflicting virtues of empirical fit and formal rigor. When the goal to describe accurately how people make "real-world" economic decisions meets the goal to achieve logical consistency at all costs, the result is often methodological confusion, if not worse. Such confusion has appeared as both a subject and an obstacle for historians of economics, who have often noticed the tensions that beset orthodox economists without always fully escaping those same tensions themselves. Important problems within the intellectual project of late-nineteenth-century economics are revealed, for instance, by Bruna Ingrao and Giorgio Israel's pursuit of the "dialectic between the descriptive and the normative approaches" of such theorists as León Walras and Vilfredo Pareto (Ingrao and Israel 1990, 52), and by Philip Mirowski's discussion of metaphorical misfittings between the economics of Jevons and Marshall and the "energetics" program of turn-of-the-century physics (Mirowski 1989). But while each of these approaches has produced incisive critical readings of economic thought over an impressive range of periods and research schools, they both have also left the underlying tension between empiricism and formalism naggingly unresolved. Ingrao and Israel conclude their book with a methodological flourish that promises much but offers few concrete strategies for challenging the orthodox formal theory of general equilibrium, the analytical strengths of which the authors themselves admit to be great. Mirowski has followed his original foray into the inappropriate use of metaphors in economics with a series of further efforts to replace the economists' old borrowings with new, better-fitting models from the natural sciences. If not energetics, perhaps chaos theory or evolutionary biology, seems to be the suggestive but still exploratory constructive complement to the more purely critical approach in *More Heat than Light* (see, e.g., Mirowski 1990, 1994).

One reason for the relative lack of resolution that has followed the appearance of these promising studies five years ago is that neither of them, nor much kindred work, has moved very far beyond a strictly internal critique of orthodox economic thought and methodology. Appearances to the contrary, formalism remains a dominant value for the new historians of economics, who have been much more willing to absorb the findings of *other* types of intellectual history (history of science, anthropology) than to notice what social and cultural history has had to say about the social world occupied by the economists who populate their books.[1] What recent work in social and cultural history has to offer the history of economics is the technique of reading back from "classic" disciplinary texts (in the social sciences, for instance) to the more obviously problematic texts and practices that preceded them. This strategy means more than searching the past for precursors to "modern" thought, and it means more than repeating the efforts of standard histories to celebrate the coherence of present-day disciplinary thinking by contrasting it with the muddle of preprofessional "real-world" discourse. Rather, by focusing on the subjective tensions that emerge clearly in predisciplinary practices, the point is to hold up these tensions as a mirror to reflect latent contradictions in modern social science that have hitherto been successfully obscured by the process of professionalization (see, e.g., Alborn 1995; Robbins 1990).

Perhaps the most methodologically explicit of these works has been Christopher Herbert's *Culture and Anomie*, which evaluates nineteenth-century ethnographic writings in order to challenge the hegemony of the

1. In a less historical vein, the same can be said regarding the importance for more connections to be drawn between economic thought and methodology, on the one hand, and such works in the ethnology and sociology of the economics profession that exist, on the other (e.g., Klamer and Colander 1990). An important exception in the history of economics to my comments in this paragraph is Maloney 1985.

idea of "culture" in present-day anthropology and related disciplines. The point of his project, he argues, is "to make visible certain aspects of our own exploitation of the culture idea which usually go unrecognized, for reasons both of rhetorical expediency and of historical amnesia." By tracing "culture" back to such sources as missionary writings, Henry Mayhew's London enthnographies, and Anthony Trollope's novels, he concludes that the concept's "explanatory power (to the extent that this is genuine to begin with) may turn out to have affinities with other modes of power which we would prefer to disavow" (Herbert 1991, 1). Diverting the gaze of anthropologists, critical or otherwise, from the language structures they have created and imposed on other societies, Herbert argues, can at the very least serve "to highlight the often-dissimulated rhetorical urgency of such writing, and to locate its origin in the problematics of the theory of the complex whole" (6–7).

An example of how this method works in practice is Herbert's chapter on Methodist missionaries in Fiji, which he uses to undermine the "ethnographic creed" of modern anthropology. He first cites Malinowski's declaration in *Argonauts of the Western Pacific* (1932) that Victorian ethnographers were "full of the biassed and pre-judged opinions inevitable in the average practical man, whether administrator, missionary, or trader; yet so strongly repulsive to a mind striving after the objective, scientific view of things" (cited in Herbert 1991, 152). He then turns this critique of moralism against itself, identifying "this not-disinterested mythic narrative as *a moral liberation* as well as a perfecting of scientific technique" (152), and drives the point home by contrasting Malinowski's "objective" public face with the copious references to "niggers" and "savages" in his private ethnographic diaries (154). More is going on here than a simple accusation of hypocrisy, as becomes evident when Herbert turns to the missionaries who earned Malinowski's scorn. Where most commentators have only seen cultural imperialism in the missionaries' practices and writings, Herbert reveals something far more problematic: the missionaries' discovery that native souls could not be saved without jeopardizing the souls of the savers. To comprehend Polynesians well enough to convert them, missionaries obsessively catalogued their language and culture. And the more they catalogued, the more their objects of study came to serve as a "projection of the original, innate depravity in themselves which their religion teaches them to ponder incessantly, to regard with horror and to repress with utmost vigilance" (169). By exposing the wretched travails of missionaries who were forever tempted to "go native," Herbert suggests that the only crucial difference between ethnography then and now is that modern anthropologists are not nearly as bothered by contradictions between their private feelings and their public scientific claims.

In *Visions of the People* (1991) and later work, Patrick Joyce has employed a similar method to challenge historians who have borrowed heavily from social scientists' static conceptions of class. Instead of opposing standard appeals to class by importing an alternative construct from social science, Joyce examines the historical emergence of class against the backdrop of a wide array of alternative popular forms of discourse. This strategy leads him to discuss at length the nineteenth-century development of dialect almanacs (inexpensive, widely read annuals written in local slang), broadside ballads, and music hall performances. From there he traces the complicated process of translation that accompanied such documents as they made their way from "the people" into more refined climes of scholarly debate (e.g., folklore studies) or toned-down "middle-class" renditions. Joyce's survey of the interplay among different types of "working class" discourse and their problematic cooptation by "middle-class" publishers and academics leads him not only to criticize standard applications of "class" to social history but also to question efforts by such historians as Gareth Stedman Jones to impute a single "language of class" to whole sectors of the population. "Even when looking at so decidedly a proletarian group as textile workers, and at the dialect literature that expressed so many of their concerns," he concludes,

> we find that what seems at first glance to be the possession of a particular group could be pressed into service not only by many sorts of workers, but also by many who were not manual workers. . . . The discourse of "the people" did not express some higher "class" identity or unity. It mattered in its own right. Language mattered in its own right. The notion of "languages of class" carries great dangers. (Joyce 1991, 333)

Here we find the same warning against reification that we find in Herbert, with "class" filling in for "culture" as the dangerous category that conceals as much as it describes.

What is the relevance of these warnings for the history of economics? One obvious lesson concerns the keen interest displayed by many recent historians of thought with the themes of language, metaphors, and the like. Needless to say, references to anthropologists like Mary Douglas and literary critics like Northrop Frye mark a significant and positive departure from where history of economics was even ten years ago. But they also beg certain questions that the more historicist approaches of Herbert and Joyce seek to reopen. In particular, economists who focus so much on the internal structure of economic language (e.g., McCloskey) or on the trade in metaphors between different forms of scientific discourse risk falling into the same sin of "rhetorical urgency" that orthodox economists commit in their pursuit of formal models—or, for that matter, which similarly saddles anthropologists and literary critics. In the rest of this article, and in necessarily schematic fashion, I want to suggest some strategies for building on the relatively restricted hermeneutics of existing histories of economic thought. I start with a set of tensions within early neoclassical economics that Mirowski reveals in *More Heat than Light* and move from there to a parallel set of tensions that are more obviously on display in the pages of the *Economist* under the editorship of Walter Bagehot. Specifically, I look at the rhetorical services performed by the published balance sheets in that newspaper, which offered businessmen and economists alike a crucial source of the economic information that they used to come to terms with their social surroundings.

Reading back from Jevons and Marshall

A strong case can be made that the early British neoclassical economists took the same ambivalent interest in financiers and financial journalism that second-generation anthropologists took in missionaries' ethnographies, or that folklorists took in working-class ballads and almanacs. One of the best-known neoclassicals (and among the more sympathetic toward financial journalism) was W. S. Jevons, who appealed directly to the realm of economic practice to justify his claim in *The Theory of Political Economy* that the "numerical data" available for mathematical economics "are more abundant and precise than those possessed by any other science, but that we have not yet known how to employ them" (1871, 13). He required a long list just to categorize the various sources in which this abundant but "perplexing" data lay hidden:

> The private account books, the great ledgers of merchants and bankers and public offices, the share lists, price lists, bank returns, monetary intelligence, Custom-house and other Government returns, are full of the kind of numerical data required to render Political Economy an

exact mathematical science. Thousands of folio volumes of statistical, parliamentary, or other publications await the labour of the investigator. (13)

It is possible to read into this comment an implicit criticism of the people who used such data in their daily life without sufficiently appreciating its rich potential as an aid to theory. It was, after all, "chiefly a want of method and completeness in this vast mass of information," wrote Jevons, "which prevents our readily employing it in the investigation of the natural laws of Political Economy" (13). Alongside his real frustration at the seeming impenetrability of financial numbers in the mid-Victorian period, however, was a sense of optimism regarding the ability of economic theorists to work with financial journalists, whom Jevons saw as occupying an important middle ground between the unrefined mass of information and his own formal mathematical models. Jevons was a regular contributor to newspapers like the *Economist* and forums like the London and Manchester Statistical Societies where bankers, merchants, and journalists did their best to make sense of the incoming stream of data. He also personally intervened in the careers of several such men, including bankers R. H. Inglis Palgrave and John Lubbock and statistician William Newmarch, to reinforce their efforts with public acclaim (Alborn 1991, 297–303; *Economist* 25 (1867): 161).

Later economists were more careful to protect their own claims to expertise from the possibility that these "practical" economists would take too much credit for converting numbers into a usable form. In public, and especially in his early career in Bristol, Marshall was quick to praise the constructive role to be played in economic thought by those with personal contact with the business world. As a lecturer in Bristol in the late 1870s, he hoped to provide businessmen with the "true literary education" that would allow them "to play an important part in making this age a great intellectual age" (cited in Whitaker 1972, 23), and he contributed a preface to the student's edition of Bagehot's *Postulates of English Political Economy* in 1885, proclaiming that the author "was excellently qualified" owing to his possession of "a well-trained scientific mind, and a large experience of City life" (Bagehot 1968–86, 11:196).[2] Behind the scenes, however, Marshall was less warmly disposed to the abilities and presumptions of businessmen. He confessed to a friend that his preface to *Postulates* was more a favor to Bagehot's widow than a sincere re-

2. On Marshall in Bristol, see also Groenewegen 1995, 288–92.

flection of his views (Whitaker 1975, 1:31), and when Palgrave asked him to write entries for his *Dictionary of Political Economy*, he declared himself "a neutral . . . who is so engaged on Domestic politics (his own books) that he can't go in for an active policy in foreign affairs" (quoted in Alborn 1991, 297).[3] More generally, Marshall condescendingly referred in private to the "historical men" (a group that included Bagehot and many other journalists and statisticians) as "intelligent, more or less earnest, but not very profound"; they were "Kittle-Kattle," he wrote to J. N. Keynes, "and yet important" (quoted in Maloney 1985, 43).

Such anxiety had both intellectual and political sources. Intellectually, the infuriating prospect of "practical" men mishandling data threatened to derail the economists' epistemological fantasy of determining in precise detail the unfolding of economic laws. Mirowski has referred to this utopia as the Laplacian Dream, which he describes as "a thoroughgoing determinism that would allow the mapping of future evolution of the economy on paper" (1989, 275). The chief source of this dream, he concludes, was a similar, but fast-disappearing, urge among physicists to master the laws of motion. As the latter dream faded under pressure of further observation and calculation, so, too, was the economists' determinism destined to wane: "The elaboration of the Laplacian Dream led inexorably to its dissolution" (275). To a large degree, though, both the dream of a complete map of the economy and the threat of its destructive elaboration also had much to do with the expanse of data that was filling up so many blue books and newspaper columns by the end of the nineteenth century. Just as the economists did their best to ignore changes in physics that challenged their goals, so did they valiantly turn a blind eye to any possible long-term tensions between marginalist theory and commercial practice. As John Maloney has observed, Marshall postponed the conflicting values of "universality and accuracy" into a vaguely reconciliatory future and thereby managed to "forget the need to choose between economics the pure science and economics the profession with humanity as its client" (Maloney 1985, 55).

Politically, economists faced a similar problem of increasingly elaborate data leading to a dissolution of the ideal economic world described in their theories. Here the problem was that the best numbers were private, and hence immune to perfect comprehension, while both the normative

3. Such views of Bagehot have survived into the present day: see the comment by Mark Blaug that Bagehot "fails to maintain any abstract argument for more that [*sic*] a few sentences at a time" (1988, 5).

and intellectual dictates of neoclassical economics forbade the institutional revolution that would make all such data public (or even accessible to a restricted class of experts). Topping Jevons's list of useful numbers were "private account books" and "the great ledgers of merchants and bankers and public offices," none of which were available for thorough scientific scrutiny; Marshall was similarly wistful about the "unpublished history of business" that was in the possession of the "troublesome" class of nonacademic economists (quoted in Maloney 1985, 41). On reflection, though, the trouble stemmed less from the businessmen themselves than from the information network that was a necessary part of an ideally "free" market. Neoclassical economics was grounded on the assumption that optimal markets required freely competing independent agents, who would be at a competitive disadvantage if they were to expose their balance sheets to public scrutiny. If the economists' intellectual utopia required an all-seeing expert capable of perfectly digesting all the available information, its institutional corollary was a Benthamite panopticon capable of requiring every subject to submit complete and honest financial returns. That such a panopticon did not come close to existing in late-nineteenth-century England is clear from the economists' frequent complaints about the imperfect nature of what government data did exist; that economists would not have approved of such a panopticon is clear from their frequent praise of the light administrative burden performed by the British government, in contrast to its European and American counterparts.

Making the Balance Sheet Public

The conflict between the ideals of completely public economic information and completely atomistic economic relations only rarely came to the surface in neoclassical economic thought. If recent trends in the history of economics has taught us anything, it is that economists have always been good at concealing methodological and political tensions by framing their theories in the seemingly more pristine language of the physical sciences. Such techniques of concealment were not as readily available to the financial journals, whose job it was to publish as comprehensively as possible the information upon which financiers and merchants relied to make economic calculations, while at the same time opposing too much government interference in the daily lives of its intended audience. Far from endlessly putting off the problem of inaccessible data into an indefinite future, journalists like Bagehot at the *Economist* held up the businessman's private store of facts as a moral measuring rod, a tacit standard by which to judge both the organization and the accuracy of all published facts and figures.

It was in this sense that the numbers published in journals like the *Economist* and the *Statist* embodied a sort of "dialect literature" that was self-consciously intended to be valued in a special way by a limited category of readers. If only certain regions or trades were expected to make sense of almanacs filled with Yorkshire typography, as Joyce compellingly argues, the same sort of claim can be made for the financial journals. The sense of requisite initiation into the world of "dry" financial statistics was evoked in an 1863 column by *Banker's Magazine* editor David Morier Evans, who summoned the childhood image of "the strange feeling of dread inspired by my father, who was a fundholder, emphatically desiring me, as fathers can do, to look under the head of the money market, and read to him the two or three first paragraphs respecting the state of the stocks" (1864, 84). Evans next remarked that "to wade, as I then thought, through a dreary column devoted to facts and prices, was an ordeal second only to that of returning to school after the customary month's vacation." He then took the reader through his step-by-step illumination, initiated by his mother's patient explanation as to the "interest-bearing capacity of the funds" and culminated by a tour of the City with his father—whereupon "much of the hazy film, which had previously covered my young and inexperienced eyes, was suddenly removed" (84–86).

Such splitting off between initiates and outsiders, whether in Evans's metaphorical style or more straightforwardly, was especially prominent in what Wayne Parsons has referred to as the "first generation" of financial journals, the main object of which was to win political campaigns like the repeal of protectionism (1989, 28–44). In these situations it made political sense to encourage solidarity by emphasizing shared skills and experiences, among which facility at manipulating financial figures ranked high. This strategy was evident in an *Economist* piece from 1860 entitled "Statistical Mares' Nests," which started as an attack on Tory historian Archibald Alison's butchery of trade statistics in a recent protectionist diatribe, but concluded by extending equal condemnation to a critique of Alison by a journalist in the Whig *Edinburgh Review*, who was not "quite familiar with the practice of handling official tables" and consequently "falls into a confusion himself." Neither historian nor reviewer, owing to their lack of practical experience, possessed the "care, special training, and . . . exceptional degree of conscientiousness" that was needed to manipulate statistics honestly and productively (*Economist* 18(1860): 532). This sense of "us against them" in the financial journals faded as the nineteenth century progressed, as both their function and audience shifted. As Parsons has argued, the purpose of the financial press in both England and America changed by the turn of the century from being mainly propagandistic to being putatively neutral providers of information—in particular, financial "tips" for investors in public companies. I will return at the end of this article to discuss some more general implications of this shift; for the moment, it is enough to observe its impact on the assumption of tacit knowledge among the *Economist*'s readership that is apparent through its first two decades.

Having suggested some of the social functions performed by numbers in Victorian financial journals, what of the numbers themselves? Although most of the rest of this article focuses on balance sheets, it is important to mention in passing a different sort of quantitative information that vied for position in the pages of the *Economist* and kindred publications: chronological comparisons of prices or trade returns (i.e., time series). This category has been the subject of recent work by Judy Klein (forthcoming), who has shown how the intellectual problems introduced by these early time series persisted in the econometric work of people like Irving Fisher. In the issues of the *Economist* I examined, weekly chronological comparisons encompassed the volume of cash transactions at the London Bankers' Clearing House; the number of Londoners on indoor and outdoor poor relief; the going interest rate on mercantile paper, bank deposits, and foreign securities; import and export totals for numerous varieties of grain, cotton, sugar, livestock, and coal at a variety of British ports; and prices of all those commodities, as well as share prices and dividends for railways, mines, banks, and colonial loans. Most of these tables included a column that compared the previous week's price or volume with that from the same week as reported a year earlier. Also, starting in 1863 the *Economist* commissioned statistician William Newmarch to compile its weekly series into an annual tabular "commercial history." These numbers certainly had their moral and political component, since they were frequently called into play as a means of celebrating Britain's dominant commercial status—or, after 1880, as a means of taking sides in the debate over whether other countries were catching up to Britain at a faster or slower rate (see Friedberg 1988, 38–45).

With the exception of these uses, though, the numbers in such tables most often "spoke for themselves," to borrow from the parlance of the time; they appeared in the back of each issue without any commentary. By the time they had reached this state, such trade and share statistics were more successful than balance sheets at concealing the tension between public display of knowledge and the demands of privacy imposed by a free-market system. That is not to say, however, that such tensions were nonexistent in their case, only that they had been negotiated at a point prior to publication. In the case of Bankers' Clearing House statistics, for instance, it was not until 1867 that Sir John Lubbock, upon taking over as that body's secretary, convinced his fellow members to consent to weekly publication of aggregate data. More generally, each listing in the weekly trade returns represented the culmination of negotiations, either among a self-governing body of private traders (such as the Bankers' Clearing House or the various local trade associations and chambers of commerce) or between traders and a public intermediary like the Board of Trade. When such negotiations led to the appearance of new statistics in the *Economist*, or led to a change in their format, the paper departed from its usual straightforward equation of the numbers with either progress or decline to mention the social processes that went into their compilation. A move toward more intelligible accounts received the paper's (not unmixed) blessing, for instance, when the Board of Trade revised its export tables in 1871. While lamenting that the change forced people "to compare two things not precisely identical" and hence required "considerable explanation," the editorial conceded that the reduced expense and improved clarity of the new tables would be worth some short-term confusion. Significantly, the requisite explanation in this case involved assuring the reading public that exports had not in fact fallen as dramatically since the previous year as the returns suggested (*Economist* 29 (1871): 161).

In contrast to aggregate trade statistics, balance sheets appeared in the *Economist* less frequently but drew attention to themselves much more often. This was due both to the type of institutions that presented the numbers and to the location and form in which balance sheets appeared in the paper. Unlike trade statistics, which nearly always referred to private traders in the aggregate, published balance sheets were by definition limited to specific cases. These cases, furthermore, were by convention only public bodies (municipal corporations or national and foreign budgets) or quasi-public firms (banks or railways). Although it would not have been impossible for a private firm to allow its balance sheet to be published, it would have been (and today still would be) considered commercial suicide for a firm to reveal more information about itself than was offered by its competitors. Consequently, the only time the rule against publishing a private firm's balance sheet was broken was in the fatally exceptional case of bankruptcy, when its failure to compete brought on the ultimate ignominy of forced exposure by the bankruptcy judge (see, e.g., *Economist* 18 (1860): 161).

Those balance sheets that did appear in print showed up in one of three different locations in the *Economist*: in the editorial leaders, usually in reference to national or local government accounts; in special weekly departments devoted to the national budget and the Bank of England; and in paid advertisements for banks and other companies on the last two or three pages of the paper. The fact that printed balance sheets in the *Economist* were the exclusive preserve of public or quasi-public bodies, while an obvious point, is also crucial for comprehending the moral economy of publishing quantitative information. The reason for this is clear once it is recalled that balance sheets that appeared in the *Economist* did not come close to exhausting the total number of balance sheets (unpublished as well as published) that existed in the presumed experience of the paper's primary readership. Even more important, the *Economist* took it for granted that the documents that did appear in their pages, especially the ones on which they saw fit to comment, were in varying degrees inferior to the private balance sheets that never circulated beyond the hands of any given set of partners. The *Economist*, in other words, constantly and openly presented those balance sheets which it published as falling well short of an ideal type, concrete examples of which were assumed to be readily but not *publicly* available to its readers. This ideal represented a vanishing point toward which the *published* balance sheets tended, upward from government documents through public companies to (by the end of the nineteenth century) a handful of private banks that published their accounts.[4]

If private accounts stood invisibly atop the heap of published balance sheets in the financial journals, the accounts that were available for all to see were organized beneath them in an informal moral hierarchy. Emerg-

4. On the latter case, see "Balance-Sheets Published by Private Banks," *Banker's Magazine* 52 (1891): 817–25.

ing victorious in this struggle for relative supremacy in organization and accuracy of accounts were the public companies who paid for space at the back of the *Economist*'s pages. The distinctive (if obvious) feature of advertised balance sheets was that they lacked any of the negative commentary that accompanied most other published balance sheets in the financial press. By accepting their advertising money, the paper was tacitly endorsing the accuracy of their financial statements. There was, of course, a strictly commercial reason for doing this since the proceeds from such large advertisements added up much more quickly than two-inch ads for books or patent medicine; for journals with lesser reputations than the *Economist* or the *Times*, this lucrative motive for "puffing" any company that was willing to pay dominated all others (see Nevett 1986). In journals like the *Economist*, however, which had a sufficient circulation to be more selective about the ads it ran and which had a decades'-old reputation to uphold, the strictly commercial motive for standing by the accuracy of advertised accounts was less important than the moral function served by their prominence in its columns.

What this moral function was can be more precisely described by analyzing two paid advertisements from 1871: a full-page National Provincial Bank advertisement, which the company purchased for £15, and the annual report of the Standard Life Assurance Company, which spilled over into one and a third pages and cost just over £20.[5] Aside from the opportunity these advertisements allowed for the chairman (or manager, in the latter case) to comment favorably on the year's finances, the revenue account and balance sheet—of which the chair's comments were both an exegesis and a buildup—stood as a tribute to the orderly architecture of Britain's financial sector. The revenue account ("prepared," as the National Provincial announced, "in the usual form") took the reader through the doggedly repetitive process of bringing forward profits, allowing for expenses, dividends, bonuses, and (in the bank's case) "doubtful debts." The National Provincial's account culminated with the comforting phrase "leaving reserve invested in Government securities" followed by the healthy and precise-sounding sum of £388,015, 8s/6d, while the Standard's ended with an announcement of the "amount of funds at the end of the year, as per second schedule"—which exceeded the amount at the beginning of the year, and top of the account, by over

5. *Economist* 29 (1871): 592, 526–27. Prices are calculated from the paper's published weekly rate chart.

£70,000. From the revenue account, both reports proceeded to the balance sheet proper, which paired off assets against liabilities, again down to the last penny. It was at this point that the appearance of order most often fell short of an orderly investment portfolio, since much could be concealed by phrases like "bills discounted, loans, &c." or "landed estate and fee-duties." But while the *Economist* occasionally used editorial space to criticize what was left unsaid in such reports, such comments were relatively rare in an era when company reports of any kind were completely voluntary. For business leaders, certainly, but also for creators of financial opinion like the *Economist*, the alternative of carefully defined government standards for company reporting was a fate worse than the occasional omission. Also, from the mid 1860s on, the paper ran special supplements in which all available company reports ran side by side and could at least be judged according to thoroughness relative to one another.

By the time readers reached the paid-for balance sheets at the back of each issue of the *Economist*, they might have already seen what was, in the editor's view, a poor replica of such numbers in a leader devoted to government spending. Balance sheets composed by English government officials fell short of the higher standard of public companies (and still more, the even higher tacit standard of private firms' books) on several fronts. One of their leading faults, ironically, was that the ministers or magistrates who put them together were required by statute to be more specific about their component assets and liabilities. Especially in 1860, before Gladstone had ironed all the bugs out of the pre-1846 tariff codes, he had to put up with exposures of budget items that, in the *Economist*'s words, showed "how absurdly insignificant the gain to the revenue of many of the articles now subject to duty in fact is" (*Economist* 18 (1960): 165). Such articles included, on one occasion,

	£	s	d
Hats or bonnets of straw, yielding	882	11	10
Opera glasses, and all marine and race glasses, not being telescopes	2609	6	6
Toys	4158	15	11

A more straightforward shortcoming of government accounts when measured against their private-sector counterparts related to their relative lack of order. This was a special concern of the *Economist* in the 1870s, when the beginning of what would become a steep rise in municipal spending foregrounded the haphazard nature of local record keeping. As Bagehot observed in 1871 in a piece on "Local Burdens," "the number of spending bodies in the country is immense; they make up their accounts under different heads, on discordant principles, and very often not for the same period" (*Economist* 29 (1871): 405).

Like the problem of inconclusive company reports, though, Bagehot tended to accept haphazard government accounts as a fact of life in a laissez-faire economy, and very much worth whatever annoyance they might cause. The only alternative to such accounts, after all, "would be to abolish Local Government, and to make some kind of despotic *prefet* determine in each district what should be done, and what should be spent" (*Economist* 29 (1871): 406, 566). Secure in his assumption of a common readership, Bagehot could confidently declare that "no evil would be so great in Englishmen's eyes as this. . . . They would submit to anything rather than have county and parish business settled by a 'Jack in office' from London, to whom it would be constantly necessary to bow and cringe"[6] (406).

If Bagehot was so ready to concede that inefficient accounting was a necessary price to pay to stave off administrative despotism, in part this was due to the elevated status this problem conferred on the profession of financial journalism. A fully equipped central accounting office, after all, would have rendered irrelevant much of the work of elucidation that went into the *Economist*'s frequent discussions of local and national government balance sheets. And the paper was quick to draw attention to exactly how much work such summaries required, and what a great public service it was performing in exerting the requisite labor. When the Corporation of London published its finances for the first time in 1870, the *Economist* praised the development but added that "the accounts are . . . not adapted to show the broad result which would be of so much interest." The "abstract which we publish," on the other hand, would not only be of interest to its readers but "may perhaps be useful to members of the Common Council themselves, who often complain of the difficulty of understanding the accounts" (*Economist* 29 (1871): 3). As long as such comments were limited to national or local government accounts,

6. This attitude toward "non-English" centralized accounting was also apparent in the *Economist*'s reporting on foreign balance sheets—for example, the accounts of the French government during the Franco-Prussian War, those of the Paris Commune ("one of the most singular documents in a singular period of French history") and those of colonies and Latin American republics (*Economist* 29 (1871): 406, 566).

the paper was safe in continuing to assume that its readers shared a common access to and understanding of private balance sheets. The "dialect literature" of the balance sheet was not endangered by explications of government finances, since few readers would have had reason to feel that their own diligence and ability to read accounts was being impugned by a suggestion that London magistrates might gain from summaries of municipal expenses. This was especially the case because businessmen were not expected to have much time left over from their private affairs to spend on poring over government accounts.

It was hence possible for financial journals to reconcile their elucidation of "inferior" government balance sheets with their carefully constructed moral hierarchy of financial figures; it was more difficult for them to combine, at a more general level, such claims of public expertise with their utopia of atomistic entrepreneurs whose expertise sat squarely in the realm of tacit knowledge. And as the *Economist* and kindred journals moved, after the 1870s, toward increasing the breadth of its editorial elucidation, this more general tension grew in prominence. As the readership and institutional context of the financial press changed by the end of the nineteenth century, out-of-the-way government statistics gave way to company accounts as the chief source of balance sheets on display for commentary. This was part of the move toward "tipsterism," which, Parsons has observed, took place not only in the *Economist* but also in newer journals like the *Statist* and the *Financial Times*. The institutional corollary to tipsterism was a transition (more gradual in England than in America) from private family firms toward public companies, and a consequent rise in the blind investor who lacked personal knowledge either in specific firms or general principles of bookkeeping. As early as 1866–67 Bagehot included in the *Economist* a series entitled "What to Buy," in which he claimed that "nobody ought to put their money where they do not understand" and promised to substitute "homely illustrations" for "columns of figures which frighten many" (Bagehot 1968–86, 10:484). This was a far cry from the paper's usual tactic of letting firms' "columns of figures" speak for themselves at the back of each issue, and it was a harbinger of the paper's editorial function in the last third of the century. The columns of figures did not disappear from the paper (and still have not), but they now vied with increasingly sophisticated analyses of stock options and economic indicators. Ultimately, and for all practical purposes, the result was a partial inversion of the old moral hierarchy, whereby the figures produced by public companies (and conforming increasingly closely to government standards) counted for more than the unpublished private balance sheet (see Bryer 1993). This was so simply because the public figures generated by institutions would, taken en masse, become more important to that part of the economy catered to by the financial press.

As Parsons observed, the move toward "tipsterism" in the British financial press coincided with the rise of neoclassical economics, and he explains the coincidence in terms of the depoliticization of both forms of discourse. What I have tried to show here is that these two changes were also related at a deeper level, involving the meanings and the moral significance of the numbers that appeared in their pages. While I have only traced this shift in meaning in any detail for the financial press, a similar and in many ways even more dramatic shift was also taking place for the economists who followed Jevons. As marginalism and its accompanying mathematical program edged out "literary" economics, the participating economists self-consciously rejected the assumption that they shared a common language with the capitalists whose agency continued to impel the system they described.[7] Their importation of metaphors from physical science, with its even narrower currency, only reinforced this more general strategy. If this shift was more dramatic (and ultimately more problematic) than the parallel shift in the financial press, it was because the numbers they imagined to belong in their mathematical formulae continued to harken back to the older atomistic moral hierarchy dominated by relatively inaccessible private balance sheets. The financial press, meanwhile, was churning out numbers faster than ever, but these numbers inverted the older moral hierarchy which framed the formulas bred by the marginalist revolution. It should not be surprising, then, that economists like Jevons and Marshall expressed frustration at the numbers and the men who produced them, since the promise of empirical completeness that lay hidden within their pages could not overcome the divergence in meaning that came to separate the financial press from the economics profession.

References

Alborn, Timothy L. 1991. The Other Economists: Science and Commercial Culture in Victorian England. Ph.D. diss., Harvard University.

———. 1995. The Moral of the Failed Bank: Professional Plots in the Victorian

7. On this point, see also Tribe 1991 and contributions to Kadish and Tribe 1991.

Money Market. *Victorian Studies* 38:199–225.
Bagehot Walter. 1968–1986. *The Collected Works of Walter Bagehot*. 15 vols. Edited by Norman St. John-Stevas. Cambridge: Harvard University Press.
Blaug, Mark. 1988. *Great Economists before Keynes: An Introduction to the Lives and Works of One Hundred Great Economists of the Past*. Cambridge: Cambridge University Press.
Bryer, R. A. 1993. The Late Nineteenth-Century Revolution in Financial Reporting: Accounting for the Rise of Investor or Managerial Capitalism? *Accounting, Organizations and Society* 18:649–90.
Evans, David Morier. 1864. *Speculative Notes and Notes on Speculation, Ideal and Real*. London: Groombridge.
Friedberg, Aaron L. 1988. *The Weary Titan: Britain and the Experience of Relative Decline, 1895–1905*. Princeton, N.J.: Princeton University Press.
Groenewegen, Peter. 1995. *A Soaring Eagle: Alfred Marshall 1842–1924*. Aldershot: Edward Elgar.
Herbert, Christopher. 1991. *Culture and Anomie: Ethnographic Imagination in the Nineteenth Century*. Chicago: University of Chicago Press.
Ingrao, Bruna, and Giorgio Israel. 1990. *The Invisible Hand: Economic Equilibrium in the History of Science*. Cambridge: MIT Press.
Jevons, W. S. 1871. *The Theory of Political Economy*. London: Macmillan.
Joyce, Patrick. 1991. *Visions of the People: Industrial England and the Question of Class, 1848–1914*. Cambridge: Cambridge University Press.
Kadish, Alon, and Keith Tribe, eds. 1993. *The Markets for Political Economy: The Advent of Economics in British University Culture, 1850–1905*. London: Routledge.
Klamer, Arjo, and David Colander. 1990. *The Making of an Economist*. Boulder, Colo.: Westview.
Klein, Judy. Forthcoming. *Time and the Science of Means: The Statistical Analysis of Changing Phenomena 1830–1940*. Cambridge: Cambridge University Press.
Maloney, John. 1985. *Marshall, Orthodoxy and the Professionalisation of Economics*. Cambridge: Cambridge University Press.
Mirowski, Philip. 1989. *More Heat than Light: Economics as Social Physics; Physics as Nature's Economics*. Cambridge: Cambridge University Press.
———. 1990. From Mandelbrot to Chaos in Economic Theory. *Southern Economic Journal* 57:289–308.
———, ed. 1994. *Natural Images in Economics: Market Read in Tooth and Claw*. Cambridge: Cambridge University Press.
Nevett, Terry. 1986. Advertising and Editorial Integrity in the Nineteenth Century. In *The Press in English Society from the Seventeenth to the Nineteenth Centuries*, edited by M. Harris and A. Lee. London: Fairleigh Dickinson University Press.
Parsons, Wayne. 1989. *The Power of the Financial Press*. Aldershot: Edward Elgar.
Robbins, Bruce. 1990. Telescopic Philanthropy: Professionalism and Responsibility in *Bleak House*. In *Nation and Narration*, edited by H. K. Bhabha. London: Routledge.
Tribe, Keith. 1991. Political Economy to Economics via Commerce: The Evolution of

British Academic Economics 1860–1920. In *Discourses on Society: The Shaping of the Social Science Disciplines*, edited by P. Wagner, B. Wittrock, and R. Whitley. Dordrecht: Kluwer.
Whitaker, J. K. 1972. Alfred Marshall: The Years of 1877 to 1885. *HOPE* 4:1–61.
———, ed. *The Early Economic Writings of Alfred Marshall, 1867–1890*, 2 vols. London: Macmillan.

"What Is Truth" in Capital Theory? Five Stories Relevant to the Evaluation of Frank H. Knight's Contributions to the Capital Controversy

Ross B. Emmett

> I am absolutely convinced that such theories are completely wrong, but—what is truth!—Frank H. Knight to Erwin Graue (speaking of Austrian capital theory), 5 October 1933 (FHK box 59, folder 26)

At the conclusion of "Economic Theory and Nationalism," Frank H. Knight called for the scientific community of economists to eschew self-promotion and institutional allegiances, avoid public displays of dissension among themselves, and devote themselves exclusively to the self-sacrificial vocation of truth seeking. Only a unified search for better economic knowledge, guided by the criteria of the scientific method

An expanded version of this article was presented at the Kress Seminar in the History of Economic Thought and the History of Economics Society annual meeting in Vancouver. The expanded version has been constructed as an experimental web page: the URL is http://www.augustana.ab.ca/~emmer/Capital/. A previous version was presented at the York University History of Economic Thought Seminar, the University of Manitoba economics department seminar, and the European Conference on the History of Economics in Rotterdam. I wish to thank Avi Cohen and Jack Birner for their discussion of the earlier version's argument, Greg Ransom for his help in interpreting Hayek, and Robert Leonard and Phil Mirowski for their remarks on the expanded version. The Harvard University Archives, the special collections department of the University of Chicago, and the Christian Theological Seminary Library extended permission to cite from unpublished sources. I also gratefully acknowledge the support of the Humanities and Social Sciences Research Council of Canada in funding the research for this article.

operating in a context in which other interests such as public esteem and power were held apart, offered hope for liberal society in a beleaguered world (Knight 1935a).

Standard histories of the interwar years of "high theory," written in the "absolutist" tradition of historiography in economics, sometimes imply that economists actually heeded Knight's call: the development of economic theory is told as a progressive process, efficiently guided (with only a few unfortunate disruptions) by the criteria of scientific truth seeking. However, despite the texts we use in classes, many historians of economics today recognize that a multiplicity of stories about "progress" can be told about the interwar period. The unity and progress of economic science is also being questioned on other grounds. For one thing, the recent challenge to "Methodology" (the identification of a unified set of scientific criteria for truth seeking) has undermined the possibility of defining "progress" in any meaningful way, and suggests that historians need to look closely at the particular criteria operating in specific situations, whether or not these criteria correspond to current notions of "proper" scientific method. For another, recognition of the role of institutional allegiances, personal biographies, public debate, cultural "mindsets," and the like in scientific communities suggests that interests other than truth seeking are not held apart. Scientific practice, like all human activity, is a tissue of paradox in which interests conflict and competing criteria of evaluation are employed. We do not live "by truth alone," and our historical accounts of scientific communities cannot artificially assume that we do.

In what follows, some of these recent insights are reflected back on the study of Knight's work during the 1930s—the decade of Knight's controversy with the Austrians over the theory of capital. At the center of the study are five interrelated stories about the themes that occupied Knight's attention during the 1930s. In the interplay among these five stories, we will see several things: that theoretical debate can reflect differences in scientific criteria; that the justification of theoretical arguments is informed by a variety of concerns; and that the line between personal biography and scientific pursuit becomes blurred. Taken together, the close intertwining of the five stories of Knight's work makes it impossible to separate scientific activity from other activities: At what point is Knight qua economist separable from Knight qua social philosopher or Knight qua educator or even Knight qua spouse/ex-spouse and father?

Theme 1: Personal Crisis

Knight's appointment to the University of Chicago in 1927 was accompanied by his divorce and deteriorating health. Most of the story of the family separation remains hidden in family letters, but the *Daily Iowan* reported that Knight wanted "congenial and more intellectual companionship" and freedom from family responsibilities. In a subsequent letter to his mentor Frederick Kershner, Knight said: "I may say that there was no violent or acute special occasion for the step. . . . Whatever 'fault' there was was on my side, [but] it is not clear to me how far one is to blame for being what one is" (F. H. Knight to F. D. Kershner, 30 March 1929, FDK). Minerva Knight and their four children stayed in Iowa City, where she continued to work and study at the University of Iowa. Frank Knight provided financial assistance to the household throughout the 1930s (apparently more than the courts of the time would have required), until the children went on to their university studies.

The related details of Knight's relationship with Ethel Verry, whom he married in 1929, are better known. A student in one of Knight's first classes upon his return to Chicago, she was for years the director of the Chicago Child Care Society. They were married in September 1929 and spent six months during 1930 in Europe on a Guggenheim Foundation fellowship (Knight visited Vienna during this trip).

Shortly after moving to Chicago in 1928, Knight began to experience serious health problems. Health complaints are common in his letters to both family and friends during the late 1920s and early 1930s, and he apparently considered taking disability leave from the University in 1928. While the intensity of the pains he experienced eventually diminished, he never fully recovered his health; in letters to friends throughout the rest of his life he complained of tiredness and either being overworked or not being able to work for health reasons.

Behind this sketchy story lies an emotional and financial crisis that we know little about. While the increase in real income Knight experienced over the decade of the 1930s (because of President Robert Hutchins's promise of stable faculty salaries) ensured that he could continue to support two households, providing support to Minerva Knight's household undoubtedly constrained his ability to support his own new, and growing, family (Frank and Ethel had two children, born in 1933 and 1936). In what ways did his abandonment of his family parallel his abandonment of liberalism? Was his decision the search for better conversation, an exercise of free choice in personal relations, or an act of force and coercion—the epitome of what he believed the demise of liberalism had brought us to? To what extent were Knight's health problems the result of, or an addition to, the chaos of his personal life? And are we to "discount" Knight's aggressive response to the Austrians and nihilistic comments about the state of economics and liberal democracy as the remarks of an emotionally, financially, and physically stricken man?

Theme 2: Historical and Institutional Economics

> You may or may not have heard echoes of the fact that I have become more or less involved in controversy in economic theory, the theory of capital and interest in particular. I came to Chicago expecting . . . "institutionalism" to be my main field of work. But Viner went to Geneva two different years, leaving me the main course in theory. . . . The controversy referred to grew especially out of my growing realization that the treatment of capital and productive factors generally in this material and in all my previous teaching is simply "wrong." A year ago I started in seriously to re-work this material, but found myself wrestling with unsolved problems over virtually the whole field of traditional theory. Really, I haven't made very much headway with the whole project, except for getting some of my ideas more or less straightened out, but chiefly finding out how muddled they (and those of the élite in the field generally) really are.—Frank H. Knight to Talcott Parsons, 1 May 1936 (TalP HUG(FP) 42.8.2, box 2)

When Frank Knight returned to the University of Chicago in 1927, he did not intend to assume the mantle of theorist. Indeed, he had no need to—Chicago was already blessed with one of the best theorists of Knight's generation, Jacob Viner. Knight's role was to complement Viner's instruction in theory with courses in the history of economic thought, economics and social policy, and historical or institutional economics. The latter, in particular, was an emerging area of interest for Knight, and one toward which he intended to direct the majority of his attention.

"But Viner went to Geneva," and once Knight began a reevaluation of modern economics, he found it difficult to stop. Furthermore, in the course of teaching the history of economic thought, he realized that many of the difficulties he saw in contemporary economics were related to "errors" inherited from classical economics. Chief among these were the ongoing adherence to utilitarianism, which led marginalism to focus on "subjective" utility evaluations rather than "objective" alternative cost evaluations (Knight [1935] 1951), and the vestiges of the classical notion that production was the creation of commodities rather than a stream of services (see Knight [1935] 1956).

Knight's reevaluation of value and distribution theory also led him to revisit his treatment of the nature and limitations of equilibrium price analysis. In his earlier writings on economic method (especially Knight 1921 and [1924] 1935), he had identified economic theory as an exercise of abstraction and analysis: abstraction in the sense that economics studied a constructed realm which bore little resemblance to the real world, but which, if the process of abstraction was successful, isolated the underlying, unchanging forms of reality; and analysis in the sense that, once isolated, the underlying forms could be examined within the context of the constructed realm in terms of both their individual impact and their interaction. The central purpose of the scientific discipline of abstraction and analysis was the pursuit of truth—understood in "definitional" rather than "empirical" terms. "Good" theories were like "good" definitions; if the elements that polluted analysis were successfully stripped away, then the theory was true—it correctly captured the meaning of the particular aspect of human experience under consideration. Economics was "scientific," therefore, because it followed the discipline of abstraction and analysis, not because of its "empirical" content. Whether the truths of economic theory were applicable to the particularities of the "real" world was not ultimately the concern of the economist qua theoretical scientist. The art of application (judging how the truths of economics and other social sciences were relevant to an immediate situation) was the task of economic policy makers and, more important, of every citizen.

Knight's notion of economic theory as a process of abstraction and analysis was associated with his early advocacy of the method of successive approximations. However, in his reworking of equilibrium theory during the early 1930s, Knight weakened the relationship between abstraction and approximation. Despite occasional references to the usefulness of the approach (for example, Knight 1944, 28), in practice Knight abandoned the method in favor of a clear dichotomy between the abstractions of economic theory and the study of the changing institutional structure of capitalist society. No process of successive approximation would enable us to move from the abstract realm characterized by the absence of uncertainty to the conditions of real life in which change brought uncertainty; instead, the two realms required different types of investigation.

The transition from the method of successive approximation to the clear division between different realms is found in Knight's attempts to articulate the difference between the "static" analysis of equilibrium price theory and the need for a new "dynamic" analysis. Knight argued that any changes in the conditions of the economy that displayed an underlying stability fit within traditional "static" analysis, but that most changes did not display such stability because they were the result of free choices made by human beings. The nonmechanistic nature of those changes would frustrate any attempt at a "dynamic" science—abstraction and analysis did not work in the realm of change. Because theorizing was the process of abstraction and analysis, "static" equilibrium price analysis, therefore, was all that economic science could offer. Unfortunately, the reality of change and the uncertainty it created meant that the time horizon for the predictions of any static analysis was extremely short. The study of the economy in a changing world required supplementing theory with an examination of the evolution of the economy's underlying conditions—changes in its wants, resources, and technology; the distribution of resource ownership and monetary conditions; and the political, legal, and moral system (Knight [1930] 1935, 172–74). Central to that examination would be a historical study of the institutional structures by which the underlying economic conditions were created and continually reshaped. For that historical examination, equilibrium analysis was practically irrelevant.

> Our general conclusion must be that in the field of economic progress the notion of tendency toward equilibrium is definitely inapplicable to particular elements of growth and, with reference to progress as a unitary process or system of interconnected changes, is of such limited and partial application as to be misleading rather than useful. This view is emphasized by reference to the phenomena covered by the loose term "institution." All speculative glimpses at trends in connection with price theory relate to a "competitive" or "capitalistic" economic system. But all the human interests and traits involved in this type of economic life are subject to historical change. Moreover, no society is or could be entirely and purely competitive. The roles of the state,

> of law, and of moral constraint are always important and that of other forms of organization such as voluntary co-operation may be so. Business life in the strictest sense never conforms closely to the theoretical behavior of an economic man. Always history is being made; opinions, attitudes, and institutions change, and there is evolution in the nature of capitalism. In fact evolution toward other organization forms as the dominant type begins before capitalism reaches its apogee. Such social evolution is rather beyond the province of the economic theorist, but it is pertinent to call attention to the utter inapplicability to such changes, i.e., to history in the large, of the notion of tendency toward a price equilibrium. (Knight [1930] 1935, 184)

However, three things mitigated against Knight's efforts to develop an alternative institutionalism. The first was his own fault: he usually spent so much time preparing the ground for his examination of the evolution of the institutions of modern society that he seldom ended up with much time or word-space to examine their evolution. Hence, despite the fact that he was the translator for the first of Max Weber's works to appear in English (Weber 1927), that he reviewed numerous books by historicists and institutionalists, and that he developed a course on institutionalism (Economics 305: Economics from an Institutional Standpoint—first taught in the summer quarter of 1932), his institutionalist work appears preliminary.

The second and third mitigating factors relate to the changing context of American social science during the 1930s and early 1940s. On the one hand, the emergence of national socialism and communism in Europe in the midst of capitalism's worst depression cast a long shadow over any discussion of the evolution of the market. Some of Knight's best institutional analysis, therefore, took place in the context of a comparative study of the institutional structures of capitalism and socialism (for example, in Knight [1940] 1947 and [1939] 1947). On the other hand, the type of economic study Knight envisioned became increasingly rare among economists as the discipline became more formal and mathematical in its orientation (his institutionalist work was labeled "social philosophy", obviously outside the realm of economics). Ironically, Knight's radical separation of economic theory from any form of historical analysis, and his focus on theory in both his economic and historical work, helped to contribute to the discipline's emerging ahistorical orientation (Ross 1991, 427)—a result he personally was unhappy with.

Theme 3: Capital, Time, and the Interest Rate

> In the large, I think I understand what the drift of [your response] is, and it serves to emphasize the fundamental problem in my mind these days, which is the question whether there is any profit in the discussion of fundamental issues in economics. . . . In this connection, I recall the observation in your letter, that systematic exposition rather than the meeting of specific questions is the way to "advance knowledge." I am strongly convinced of the opposite.—F. H. Knight to F. A. von Hayek [December] 1934 (FHK box 60, folder 10)

Knight's capital theory contributions consist of a string of conversations with other theorists in which his own reworking of the relevance of equilibrium price analysis to the problem of capital is intertwined with his questions for other approaches to the same issues. This combination has caused some problems for commentators because it does not fit the "standard" model of scientific argumentation, which calls for theorists to set out their own approach in comprehensive and systematic fashion. Fritz Machlup, for instance, indirectly called on Knight to stop asking questions and systematically set out his own theoretical position for comparison and criticism in his rejoinder to Knight (Machlup 1935b). Nicholas Kaldor was less gracious when he described Knight's persistent questioning of the Austrian position as akin to the launching of a military offensive and remarked that Knight's arguments were "frequently clothed in paradoxical sentences which are intended to challenge the mind but without a sufficient indication of where to turn in order to uncover those mental processes which must have led up to them" (Kaldor 1937, 201, 202–3).

For Knight, however, conversations and questions were an integral part of his own theoretical work, which was an ongoing process with an incomplete product. If theorizing is like the creation of a good definition, then asking questions of other treatments of the topics which point toward polluted elements in their analysis—rather than the systematic modeling—was essential to the scientific task. Of course, there was a need to pause occasionally and assess what the definition/theory now looked like. But in Knight's case, the guiding principle in that assessment was not "Which theory best corresponds to empirical reality?", but "Have we correctly defined what marginal theory has to tell us, and are we aware of the limitations that the process of abstraction and analysis place upon us?" The result has been that those searching for a new theoretical position in Knight's capital theory articles have found his approach "very difficult to understand and, also, either apparently or really, contradictory" (Lutz 1967, 104).

A case in point is Knight's conversation about capital with the Austrians. Knight took the opportunity provided by the call for a contribution to the *festschrift* for Gustav Cassel to examine the "Jevons-Böhm-Bawerk-Wicksell" capital theory in light of his reformulated opposition to the "classical" theory of production. His contribution (Knight 1933) was constructed around the definition of terms such as production, wealth, income, value, and capital. For each of these terms, Knight's goal was to strip away extraneous meanings that prevented economic theorists from correctly characterizing these notions. In the process, however, Knight also sought to reveal the limitations of equilibrium theory by identifying the difference between their meaning in a stationary economy and their meaning in a dynamic economy. Capital proved to be the central term in relation to the time dimension of a dynamic economy, and its proper definition both falsified the Böhm-Bawerk theory and identified the need for an alternative (but yet here unspecified) method for examining capitalistic production.

In the two initial articles aimed at identifying the extraneous elements that polluted the Austrian theory of capital, Knight (1933, 1934a) focused his attention on two questions: What is meant by the period of production? Why must one relate the quantity of capital to a period of production, however defined? Knight believed that a properly defined theory of interest removed the need for the concept of a period of production by basing the interest rate on the relation between the marginal productivity of capital and the momentary supply of capital (moving beyond the moment would, as indicated already, require a historical, rather than an equilibrium, analysis). Böhm-Bawerk's theory, on the other hand, required the notion of a period of production because it related the interest rate to one's willingness to abstain from using a specific quantity of potential capital for consumption purposes: one would want to know minimally the average length of time one's funds might be tied up. But, Knight argued, the definition of a period of production provided in Austrian theory depended on elements of classical economics that conflicted with the basic facts of economic production recognized by modern economic theory. In order to convince Knight, therefore, the Austrians would have to redefine the period of production in a manner consistent with a marginalist capital theory freed from these classical errors.

Knight's attack on the foundations of the Austrian theory of capital required a response, and both Machlup (1935a, 1935b) and Friedrich von Hayek (1936) took up the task. However, while Machlup sought to defend Austrian theory against Knight's attack, Hayek's engagement with Knight formed a part of Hayek's own reformulation of capital theory. In the Knight-Hayek debate, then, we will see two theorists reworking their understanding of equilibrium theorizing and arriving at different points. Are they simply talking past each other, or are their different formulations the result of the application of different criteria of evaluation?

The Knight-Hayek debate is particulary interesting because of the correspondence that exists between the two men during this time (FHK box 60, folders 10–11), the similarity in their concerns as theorists, our knowledge of the fundamental shift in Hayek's own thinking that occurred during the 1930s, and the relation of Hayek's theoretical innovations to the postwar emergence of a dominant neo-Walrasian mode of theorizing. Like Knight, Hayek in the mid 1930s sought to make sense of the relevance of equilibrium theorizing for a world characterized by change and the presence of collectivist institutional structures. Part of Hayek's response assigned a role to knowledge in relation to individual choice reminiscent of Knight's (1921) treatment of imperfect knowledge and entrepreneurial choices—in the real world, human action is contingent on our expectations of others' actions; hence, uncertainty is systemic and creates the potential for systematic misinterpretation of market signals. The systematic misunderstandings of price signals imply that equilibrium will not be achieved; nevertheless, because entrepreneurs are free to respond quickly, the market process naturally has a tendency toward equilibrium. In contrast, the slowness of bureaucratic response in a centrally planned economy would create economic havoc from even the smallest errors (Hayek 1937).

To show why equilibrium would not be achieved in the contingent world, the nature of the errors that could be made and their consequences, and why the differences between entrepreneurial and bureaucratic responses were important, Hayek (like Knight) adopted a notion of theorizing that departed from the common method of successive approximation. Furthermore, Hayek successfully redefined capital theory in terms which did not depend on the classical tripartite division of the factors of production—one of Knight's main requirements. Nevertheless, Hayek's development of a pure logic of intertemporal equilibrium (Hayek 1936, 1941) was still unacceptable to Knight, although it is difficult to provide a clear and consistent account of the reasons for their disagreement. One is left with the unsettling impression that while they are obviously talking past each other at one level, the issues that continue to divide them are real but entangled in a multitude of other concerns, especially their respective evaluations of the prospects for liberal society.

The debate began with Hayek's first attempt to restate Austrian capital theory in a form that would not be susceptible to the type of criticism Knight raised (Hayek 1934). Knight apparently initiated discussion of their differences in correspondence shortly after that article, but he became increasingly disillusioned about the chances for agreement over the course of their correspondence. Eventually Knight published his criticism of Hayek, reiterating the questions he had asked Machlup, the necessity of defining capital as a perpetual fund, and his frustration with the Austrian's unwillingness (as he saw it) to provide a satisfactory answer to his argument about the symmetrical relation among the factors of production (Knight 1935b). The correspondence continued until shortly after Hayek's response, in which he clearly breaks with the Böhm-Bawerk theoretical framework. Knight's final letters indicate that, although he recognized Hayek's new direction, there were still significant outstanding issues at stake between them; issues which, for Knight, emerged from Hayek's refusal to accept the notion of a perpetual fund of capital. Resorting back to publication, Knight concludes his side of the debate with another reassessment of capital theory, once again emphasizing the importance of the perpetual fund (Knight 1936).

Because the notion of a perpetual fund of capital appears as the key theoretical point of contention between Hayek and Knight, we can use their disagreement on this notion to explicate their different understandings of equilibrium theorizing. In his response to Knight's critique, Hayek agreed with Knight that the Jevons-Böhm-Bawerk theory was "responsible for much of the confusion which exists on the subject" (Hayek 1936, 200), but he went on to say:

> But Professor Knight, instead of directing his attack against what is undoubtedly wrong or misleading in the traditional statement of this theory, and trying to put a more appropriate treatment of the time element in its place, seems to me to fall back on the much more serious and dangerous error of its opponents of forty years ago. In the place

> of at least an attempt of analysis of the real phenomena, he evades the problems by the introduction of a pseudo-concept, devoid of content and meaning, which threatens to shroud the whole problem in a mist of words. . . .
>
> This basic mistake—if the substitution of a meaningless statement for the solution of a problem can be called a mistake—is the idea of capital as a fund which maintains itself automatically, and that, in consequence, once an amount of capital has been brought into existence the necessity of reproducing it presents no economic problem. According to Professor Knight "all capital is normally conceptually, perpetual," "its replacement has to be taken for granted as a technological detail," and in consequence "there is no production process of determinate length, other than zero or "all history," but "in the only sense of timing in terms of which economic analysis is possible, *production and consumption are simultaneous*." . . .
>
> Against this I do indeed hold that . . . all the problems which are commonly discussed under the general heading of "capital" do arise out of the fact that part of the productive equipment is non-permanent and has to be deliberately replaced on economic grounds, and that there is no meaning in speaking of capital as something permanent which exists apart from the essentially impermanent capital goods of which it consists. (Hayek 1936, 200–4; emphasis in original)

Hayek's own response to the nonpermanence of capital goods was the construction of an intertemporal equilibrium theory in which individual capital goods were assigned different prices at different times and places. The problem of valuation was resolved in Hayek's model by the logical relations among the intertemporal own rates of return of current nonpermanent production goods (each good's own rate of return being a relation between time preference and productivity and therefore unrelated to past events). According to Hayek, the trade-offs among time-discounts, the duration of individual capital goods, and their productivity help us understand the nature of exchange over time when the existing capital goods need to be maintained or replaced and new capital goods created. If the trade-offs are known, then a dictator with control over all resources could construct a perfect intertemporal plan of action—Hayek's intertemporal equilibrium is a purely logical construct. However, the imperfections and contingencies of entrepreneurial plans in the real world cause the actual course of a market economy to depart from the flawless coordination of the perfectly planned economy.

In contrast, Knight's approach asks us to consider the output of the economy to be like a choral music production (Knight 1934a). The choir's act of producing the music we enjoy is simultaneous with our act of consumption. Production is the creation of a stream of enjoyable services; consumption is the enjoyment of the stream of services—although we often distinguish between them, the two processes occur at the same moment. In fact, the value of the services is entirely determined at the moment of production/consumption: there is no value produced or consumed prior to, or after, the choir's performance. Of course, economic activity is a continuous process of production/consumption without interruption—a never-ending song. Investment is the diversion of a portion of the endless stream of consumption services into increasing our capacity to produce more services. Under the normal assumptions of perfect competition, once capital has been added to the economy, nothing can destroy it except the discontinuation of the stream of production/consumption. Because modern society has accumulated over its history an enormous set of productive capacities, the addition or loss of a small amount of capital will not effect the overall flow of consumption services. Only a major dissolution of the institutions that sustain the stream of capitalistic production/consumption could interrupt or end its flow; an event that lies outside of economics because economic theory takes the institutional structure of society as given. Thus, capital is perpetual, although its value (the interest rate) is always determined at the moment of production/consumption.

Despite the obvious differences in their theoretical frameworks, Hayek and Knight share several key things. First, they both abandon the method of successive approximation in favor of a sharp division between the constructed realm of theory and the contingent world of lived experience. For Hayek, the theoretical realm is completely separate from reality, yet modeled as a process of dated goods existing through time. For Knight, theory captures one element of our lived experience at the moment and has no relevance beyond the allocative aspect of that moment. Second, for both authors, the difference between the realm of theory and the realm of lived experience is primarily based on the presence of uncertainty in the real world. Third, both men share a rejection of the Böhm-Bawerk theory of capital. Hayek moves to an intertemporal microeconomic theory, while

Knight continues to treat society's output in the aggregate, although it would be better to say that he treats society's output as a nondivisible whole. Yet, neither Knight nor Hayek is willing to accept the other's reformulation of capital theory. Knight thinks Hayek is perpetuating the classical error of treating output as definable commodities rather than a stream of services, and Hayek labels Knight's perpetual fund a "mythology."

Fourth, behind both men's reconstructions of capital theory lie their concerns for the state of liberal society. Hayek's intertemporal equilibrium construct allows him to identify the key ingredient to understanding the difference between capitalism and socialism as the contingent nature of individual decisions about nonpermanent capital goods. Knight's emphasis on the relevance of equilibrium theorizing for the moment only allows him to focus attention on the historical evolution of capitalist and socialist institutions and their comparative impact on society's wants, resources, and technologies. If there is a significant difference in their social outlook, it is that Hayek believes market processes tend toward equilibrium, while Knight cannot hold out that promise. Hayek's intertemporal equilibrium theory shows what equilibrium over time would look like if achievable; Knight increasingly refuses to model equilibrium over time because change in the presence of uncertainty would not only create a moving equilibrium, but would alter the institutional structure which equilibrium theorizing takes as given.

These themes in Knight's theoretical framework provide the backdrop for his reassessment of capital theory in a two-part article at the end of the Austrian controversy (Knight 1936). Similar in nature to the two articles that preceded his debate with the Austrians, the follow-up article reiterates Knight's central issue—the limits of equilibrium theorizing in relation to economic life (612). Continuing to insist that static equilibrium models could capture the maximization problem, but increasingly reluctant to draw implications of equilibrium analysis apart from the immediate moment of exchange, Knight included a diagrammatic presentation of the supply and demand for capital, but claims that there was "no grounds for drawing a supply curve for capital" (463), effectively reducing the supply curve to a point (628) and vitiating any attempt to apply equilibrium price theory to the determination of capital and the interest rate over time. "There is absolutely no presumption," he concluded, "that actual changes in historic time will tend to establish equilibrium" (463). Finally, in his insistence that economic theory does not need to treat the possibility of a "decadent" society in which significant disinvestment occurs, he identified the relationship between his understanding of equilibrium theorizing and the massive realignment of the institutional structure of society that would occur in a "decadent" society—nothing less than the creation of humans who no longer have an interest in getting ahead (457–58).

Theme 4: Modern Education

Knight's tenure as professor of economics at the University of Chicago (fall 1927 to spring 1951) overlapped almost exactly with the tenure of one of the university's most famous and controversial presidents, Robert M. Hutchins (1929 to December 1950). During the years of Hutchins's presidency, the University stood at the forefront of educational reform in the United States. In the graduate faculties around which the University was built, these years saw increased specialization and academization accompanied by interdisciplinary dialogue and initiatives (such as the creation of the Committee on Social Thought, of which Knight and Hutchins were founding members). Whatever the successes of earlier years (and they were many), these were the years that enshrined the University as one of the premier research universities in the world in the social and natural sciences. At the undergraduate level, the creation in 1930 of Hutchins's New College Program, initially as a two-year program of general education intended to be followed by specialized study in a discipline and then (in 1942) as a four-year general education degree program, provided a paradigm of undergraduate education that is still a model for colleges and universities across North America (McNeill 1991, 41–71; Dzuback 1991, 109–228).

The successes were enmeshed in controversy, however. The controversy took several forms, but at its core lay the following question: Does American society need its higher educational system shaped by the modern methods and knowledge of the sciences (both natural and social) or by the classical methods and knowledge of the liberal arts, especially philosophy? The dispute took on new intensity as the depression deepened, the threat of war emerged in Europe, and the Chicago university community realized that America's economic, social, and political structures were in crisis. The future of the American dream, and therefore all of Western civilization, was at stake, and it was just as important for the "battle" to be won on the educational front as in Europe and Asia.

The chief proponents of the classical liberal arts were Hutchins and Mortimer Adler, who Hutchins brought with him from Yale Law School. While Hutchins worked to create a general education program which gave its place of prominence to the Western tradition of philosophical thought rooted in the "great books," Adler provoked Chicago's scientists in both public and private debate with his doubts about the truth claims of science. Adler's provocations reached a peak in the 1933–34 academic year when he debated physiologist Anton Carlson before an overflow crowd in Mandel Hall (McNeill 1991, 58–59). During the same year, he held a year-long seminar in the division of social sciences in which he castigated the division's members for their failure to understand and accept the Aristotelian underpinnings of a proper, unified social theory. Later, on the eve of America's entrance into the war, Adler declared in a public lecture at a conference in New York that America's greatest danger lay not in the external threat of Nazism in Hitler's Germany, but in the internal threat posed by its atheist professors (Adler 1940).

Knight was a key opponent of the Hutchins-Adler educational program. His friend and colleague Harry Gideonese was appointed to the College in 1931 to participate in designing and teaching the new year-long Introductory General Course in the Study of Contemporary Society. In consultation with Knight and other members of the division of social sciences (the graduate faculty), Gideonese and his College colleagues created a course that had as its operating principle not the elucidation of timeless truth available in the "great books" but "the notion that human beings had accumulated amazing knowledge and skill across the centuries by using the power of reason to overcome irrational impulses and institutional stupidity" (McNeill 1991, 55)—including those of traditions such as Judeo-Christianity and Aristotelianism. The section of the course that introduced the students to economics was anchored by a set of introductory economics material that Knight had first developed in 1924–25 while still at the University of Iowa (eventually published as Knight 1951).

Knight was also the author of an influential defense of modern thought against the charge of "anti-intellectualism." The article was rejected by the pro-Adler campus newspaper the *Daily Maroon*, but was eventually published in the university's alumni magazine (Knight 1934b). More important, it was given a place of prominence in the reading packet for Gideonese's general social sciences course throughout the 1930s.

Yet Knight's defense of modern thought was not necessarily a defense of his scientific colleagues. For years he had been resisting the objectivist or naturalistic tendencies of American social scientists, and although he joined them now in opposing a greater threat—the moralistic approach to social problems which characterized the new medievalism of Hutchins and Alder—he retained his skepticism about their project of recreating American liberalism under the authority of science (see Knight 1932). Indeed, while he was responding to Adler's attack on the professors, he also launched a scathing attack on T. W. Hutchison's introduction of logical positivism into economics (Knight [1940] 1956). Thus, we have the anomaly of Knight siding with the positivists and pragmatists in defense of educational reforms which bring the insights of modern natural and social scientific knowledge to bear on the problems of society but, at the same time, decrying the impact of that knowledge on society. Unfortunately, in an era when positivism offered the certainty of science in place of the rejected authorities of religion and the classical liberal arts, and pragmatism was the chief intellectual option for Americans struggling to live with uncertainty, Knight's unwillingness to seek common ground with either party marginalized him even from those who might have become his allies.

Theme 5: The Dilemmas of Liberalism

Knight's faith in liberalism was fundamentally shaken by his disputes with other economists and social scientists, the beginning of the depression, his interchanges with those he described as "new medievalists" and "positivists," and the political changes of the early 1930s in the United States and other industrial countries. Six days before the 1932 election in the United States, Knight gave a talk for a group of students on the University of Chicago campus entitled "The Case for Communism: From the Standpoint of an Ex-liberal" (Knight [1933] 1991).

While the title of the talk may have been a joke, its central theme—the self-contradictory nature of liberalism—showed up in several other essays and lectures. One of the ways Knight found to express this theme emerged from his concern for the relation between theorizing and truth seeking. As a liberal committed to the right of individuals to seek knowledge independently of the constraints of any tradition (religious or otherwise), Knight valued both the pursuit of truth and the right of individuals to hold different views. Unfortunately (from Knight's perspective), the fact that truth is only one among many values in the liberal framework forces those pursuing truth to compete for resources with those pursuing other values, and eventually even to compete with each other. This competition interferes with the pursuit of truth because it turns the free discussion which marks the joint production of truth into a debate in which the participants seek to assert the primacy of their own positions at the expense of others. The self-contradictory nature of liberalism is exposed, Knight argued, when its greatest achievement—the freeing of truth seeking from the shackles of tradition—is reduced to the search for applause or the quest after control of the coercive power of the state. Because ultimately the quest for power and applause cannot be reconciled with the quest for truth, liberal society will eventually have to either give up democracy or replace the quest for truth with the manipulation of public opinion (see "Capital as Roundaboutness," FHK box 1, folder 23). In the 1930s, Knight believed that society was in the process of doing both of these things simultaneously, and hence that liberalism was in its death throes.

Conclusion

The introduction to this article closed with a question: At what point is Knight qua economist separable from any other aspect of Knight's life? Fives stories have been told here to suggest that no separation exists, and that an account of his scientific practices will need to examine the interplay between his work as a theoretical economist, his social philosophy, his interest in modern education, and his personal life in order to be complete. Despite his quasi-religious call to the intellectual "priesthood," Frank Knight did not live "by truth alone."

I wish to push the issue somewhat further, however. If human activity is a tissue of paradox, ought we to expect that the interplay of these themes in Knight's activities flow seamlessly together? Most of the stories ended with a puzzle: How can Knight claim to be interested in a historical study of economics when his theoretical work occupies so much of his attention? Why was he not able to articulate a theory of capital that was at least consistent? What are we to make of the way he marginalized himself among social scientists and social philosophers with regard to modern educational reform and the prospects for liberal democracy? Can we form a consistent whole if we put the themes together? If not, will gathering more stories of Knight's life during the 1930s "solve" the puzzles and provide a unified story? Or is the story of each theme a mirror of the fragmentation of the others—each raising more questions than it solves?

More important, should we expect order and unity in the stories? The requirements of academic publication necessitate the construction of a linear account which puts each element in its place, but is that not just the "tyranny of science" all over again? Perhaps the conjunction of seemingly disparate elements can reveal the truth. But, then, what is truth?

References

Private Manuscript Collections Cited

FDK The Frederick D. Kershner Papers at the Christian Theological Seminary, Christian Theological Seminary Library, Indianapolis

FHK The Frank H. Knight Papers at the University of Chicago, Special Collections, University of Chicago Library

TalP The Talcott Parsons Papers at Harvard University, Harvard University Archives

Published Material Cited

Adler, Mortimer. 1940. God and the Professors. *Daily Maroon* (University of Chicago), 14 November (Supplement): 1–2.

Dzuback, Mary Ann. 1991. *Robert M. Hutchins: Portrait of an Educator*. Chicago: University of Chicago Press.

Hayek, Friedrich von. 1934. On the Relationship between Investment and Output. *Economic Journal* 44 (June): 207–31.

———. 1936. The Mythology of Capital. *Quarterly Journal of Economics* 50 (February): 199–228.

———. 1937. Economics and Knowledge. *Economica* (n.s.) 4 (February): 33–54.

———. 1941. *The Pure Theory of Capital*. London: Macmillan.

Kaldor, Nicholas. 1937. Annual Survey of Economic Theory: The Recent Controversy on the Theory of Capital. *Econometrica* 5 (July): 201–33.

Knight, Frank H. 1921. *Risk, Uncertainty, and Profit*. Boston: Houghton Mifflin.

———. [1924] 1935. The Limitations of Scientific Method in Economics. In *The Ethics of Competition*. New York: Harper and Bros.

———. [1930] 1935. Statics and Dynamics: Some Queries Regarding the Mechanical Analogy in Economics. In *The Ethics of Competition*. New York: Harper and Bros.

———. 1932. The New Economics and the Control of Economic Activity (review article on *Modern Economic Society*, by Sumner H. Slichter). *Journal of Political*

Economy 40 (August): 433–76.
———. 1933. Capitalistic Production, Time and the Rate of Return. In *Economic Essays in Honour of Gustav Cassel*. London: George Allen and Unwin.
———. [1933] 1991. The Case for Communism: From the Standpoint of an Ex-liberal. In *Research in the History of Economic Thought and Methodology*, edited by Warren J. Samuels. Greenwich, Conn.: JAI Press.
———. 1934a. Capital, Time, and the Interest Rate. *Economica* (n.s.) 1 (August): 257–86.
———. 1934b. Modern Thought: Is It Anti-intellectual? *University of Chicago Magazine* 27 (November): 20–21, 23.
———. 1935a. Economic Theory and Nationalism. In *The Ethics of Competition*. New York: Harper and Bros.
———. 1935b. Professor Hayek and the Theory of Investment. *Economic Journal* 45 (March): 77–94.
———. [1935] 1951. Notes on Utility and Cost. In *The Economic Organization*. New York: Augustus M. Kelley.
———. [1935] 1956. The Ricardian Theory of Production and Distribution. In *On the History and Method of Economics*. Chicago: University of Chicago Press.
———. 1936. The Quantity of Capital and the Rate of Interest, I–II. *Journal of Political Economy* 44 (August, October): 433–63, 612–42.
———. [1939] 1947. Ethics and Economic Reform. In *Freedom and Reform*. New York: Harper and Bros.
———. 1940. God and Professor Adler and Logic. *Daily Maroon* (University of Chicago), 14 November (supplement): 5.
———. [1940] 1947. Socialism: The Nature of the Problem. In *Freedom and Reform*. New York: Harper and Bros.
———. [1940] 1956. "What Is Truth" in Economics? (review article on *The Significance and Basic Postulates of Economic Theory*, by T. W. Hutchison). In *On the History and Method of Economics*. Chicago: University of Chicago Press.
———. 1944. Diminishing Returns from Investment. *Journal of Political Economy* 52 (March): 26–47.
———. 1951. *The Economic Organization*. New York: Augustus M. Kelley.
Lutz, F. A. 1967. *The Theory of Interest*. Chicago: Aldine.
Machlup, Fritz. 1935a. Professor Knight and the "Period of Production." *Journal of Political Economy* 43 (October): 577–624.
———. 1935b. The "Period of Production": A Further Word (reply to comment by F. H. Knight). *Journal of Political Economy* 43 (October): 808.
McNeill, William H. 1991. *Hutchins' University: A Memoir of the University of Chicago, 1929–1950*. Chicago: University of Chicago Press.
Ross, Dorothy. 1991. *The Origins of American Social Science*. Cambridge: Cambridge University Press.
Weber, Max. 1927. *General Economic History*. Translated by Frank H. Knight. Adelphi Economic Series. London: George Allen and Unwin; New York: Greenberg.

Part 4

Dynamics of the Development of Ideas

Economists' Responses to Anomalies: Full-Cost Pricing versus Preference Reversals

Daniel M. Hausman and Philippe Mongin

One feature of scientific disciplines historians and philosophers of science have often studied is how members respond to apparent disconfirmations. This feature has attracted so much attention because philosophers of science hold that a discipline cannot be a respectable empirical science unless it is appropriately sensitive to disconfirming evidence. If a discipline is so constituted that empirical difficulties with its theories are always ignored, then the discipline cannot justifiably claim to be a science, and it cannot justifiably claim that its theories are well-supported.

Philosophers are still arguing about what sort of sensitivity to disconfirming evidence is "appropriate" and what sort is not, and a further reason for studying how apparently empirical disciplines have responded to disconfirming evidence is that the historical record may guide one in formulating reasonable normative criteria. A variety of criteria are to be found in the philosophical literature. On a naive construal of Karl Popper's falsificationism, the only acceptable response to disconfirming evidence is to abandon the theory or to modify it in a content-increasing way. Presumably this need not be done overnight, and if a theory is doing some important job, scientists may legitimately continue to make use of it even after they have recognized that it is unsatisfactory and needs to be

The authors are grateful to Roger Backhouse, John Davis, Uskali Mäki, and Max Steuer for useful comments.

replaced. Historians have had any easy time establishing that scientists do not behave this way. Any sophisticated version of Popper's falsificationism will distinguish between prima facie disconfirming evidence—anomalies—and actually disconfirming evidence—refutations. For Imre Lakatos, the difference between the two depends on whether there exists a content-increasing alternative to the given theory. The notion of refutation in effect coincides with that of a methodologically justified rejection. On this construal, the maxim that refuted theories should be abandoned is unproblematic, since a theory is not refuted until it is abandoned. The issue then shifts to how to define content-increasing changes.

Although Thomas Kuhn writes history of science rather than prescriptive philosophy of science, he clearly believes that scientists have done their jobs in more or less the right way and that one thus can draw normative conclusions from the historical record. He finds that theories always confront apparently disconfirming data and that scientists are largely undisturbed by such empirical problems. They recognize that it is difficult to bridge the gap between theory and data and that it may take a long time to figure out how to apply their "paradigmatic" theory in a way that will eliminate the conflict with the data. But scientists are not always unperturbed about apparent disconfirmations. Given their commitments to certain theories, apparatus, mathematical techniques, and so forth, some empirical problems will be deeply disturbing. With respect to *these* phenomena, the theory ought to give the right answers. More and more work will (and should) go into studying such anomalies, and this work leads unwittingly to scientific revolutions.

Although Lakatos's work is usually regarded as more normatively demanding than Kuhn's, he may actually demand *less* of scientists in response to apparent disconfirmations than does Kuhn. If one adopts a stringent notion of increasing content, like one suggested by Lakatos himself, then few anomalies will become refutations, and sophisticated falsificationism might in practice underwrite scientific conservatism. This paradoxical consequence might also result from a weakness in Lakatos's characterization of "theoretical progress." On one plausible interpretation, Lakatos demands only that scientists modify their theories in a content-increasing way so as to cope with some disconfirmation or other. Thus, a "scientific research program" can arguably make splendid progress, even though its practitioners completely ignore almost all anomalies. The problem here is that his methodology leaves us with little guidance concerning how to appraise how "central" or "important" a given anomaly may be.

This essay is concerned with how economists respond to anomalies. As the above thumbnail survey makes clear, we cannot borrow from the philosophical literature a well-established rule stating how economists ought to respond to empirical problems. Lacking clear-cut normative guidance, we shall "look and see" how economists have in fact responded to anomalies, and shall leave our appraisal until the end of the paper. It seems obvious that economists do not completely dismiss all disconfirming data and that data conflicting with detailed models are sometimes taken to require serious modification in those models. Beyond that, to diagnose how sensitive economists are to evidence that apparently disconfirms fundamental theories, we will make use of two detailed case studies, the first by Philippe Mongin (1992) on the "full-cost" controversy and the marginalist controversies of the 1940s and 1950s, and the second by Daniel Hausman (1992) on economists' reactions to the discovery in the 1970s of the "preference reversal" phenomenon. These two case studies suggest relevant conclusions about the evolution of economic methodology.

1. The Full-Cost Pricing Controversy

In 1939 the Oxford economists R. L. Hall and C. J. Hitch published an essay arguing on the basis of questionnaire data that firms set prices by marking up average costs (at some reference level of output) by some fixed percentage. In the wake of this essay, other economists, mostly in Britain and America, found evidence of this "full-cost" policy, particularly in oligopolistic markets. Although Hall and Hitch were ambivalent about whether such pricing behavior could be incorporated into profit-maximizing models of the firm, full-cost pricing came to be seen as a radical challenge to orthodox models of the firm, and for roughly a decade and a half a lively controversy raged. The controversy was resolved in the early to mid 1950s with the vast majority of economists convinced that the essentials of firms' pricing policies were compatible with the standard profit-maximizing theory. Some disagreement remained concerning exactly to what extent companies employ full-cost pricing policies, but this disagreement was of little importance, since there was a consensus that the answer did not bear on the adequacy of the standard theory.

From a normative perspective, this controversy leaves a great deal to be desired. The contending positions were never clearly defined, and those committed to the standard theory often defended its assumptions about the motivation of the firm by confusing them with much weaker and less controversial assumptions, such as that the firm *takes into account* the advantages and disadvantages of particular decisions. This conflation of the optimizing models of the then-prevailing theories of imperfect competition with a watered-down and commonsensical view of business decisions has been dubbed "benign marginalism" by Mongin (1990–91, 1992); it is perhaps the single most important phenomenon of the controversy. For example, in responding to a passage in which another heterodox economist from the Oxford group, P. W. S. Andrews, had described entreprencurs as rationally deciding not to undersell their competitors, Austin Robinson concluded: "I find it hard to distinguish this balancing of the advantages and disadvantages of price cutting . . . from the balancing process which the theories of imperfect competition have assumed" (1950, 778). In fact, Andrews had in mind a rational but completely unspecific method of reaching decisions.

Not only was there this confusion, but also there was little serious use of evidence. Data on costs and demand were scanty, and statistical methods were then underdeveloped, but the hypothesis that theories of imperfect competition could encompass full-cost pricing could have been tested. All parties claimed the empirical evidence for themselves, but nobody thought to carry out any serious tests. Urgent empirical questions suggested by the questionnaire data (concerning, for example, the role of demand and the determination of output) were never followed up by either side. And when the controversy died out, the initial theory remained with remarkably little conceptual or empirical progress having been made.

As the full-cost debate was taking shape, a related controversy took place in the *American Economic Review* of 1946–1948. It started with two strongly antagonistic essays by R. A. Lester and F. Machlup, and evolved into a lively and fairly inconclusive discussion of the strengths and weaknesses of the prevailing theory of the firm. This "marginalist controversy" included an assessment of full-cost pricing by Machlup but also touched on related issues, such as the shape of cost curves, the prevalence of oligopolistic behavior, and the role of quantity and price adjustments versus other adjustments to exogeneous changes.

One important consequence of the full-cost and marginalist controversies was that economists grew more conscious of the gulf between the terms in their theories—profits, prices, marginal costs, and so forth—and the prices, profits, and costs that make up the reality of business life.[1] Related to this realization was a lasting (and controversial) methodological contribution. Economists increasingly came to hold that their theories were to be judged exclusively by their predictions concerning prices and quantities. This view has a twofold implication. First, economists should not be concerned with the way in which business decisions are made; only the final results of the agents' deliberations matter, not the procedures. Second, not all of the results matter either; only price and quantity changes really count. Adjustments to changes in cost and demand such as selling efforts, increased efficiency, or bargaining with the working force and competitors, should be seen as negligible or as mediated by quantity and price adjustments. This restrictive doctrine became influential toward the end of the controversies, and it made economists receptive to the related methodological views defended by Milton Friedman (1953) and Machlup (1955) (on this connection see Mongin 1986, 1992).

Though there is much to criticize, at least there was a controversy. Economists discovered an anomaly, and the profession was galvanized to discuss it. The anomaly was certainly not ignored. On the contrary, it attracted attention from leading theorists in leading journals and at important conferences, and the confidence of the profession in some of the central theories of economics was seriously, if temporarily, shaken. Economists clumsily attempted to make sense of the anomalous data, while grappling with the problem of how to operationalize claims about marginal revenue or marginal cost curves or about the differences between competitive, monopolistic, and oligopolistic markets.

2. Preference Reversals

The second reaction to unfavorable evidence with which we are concerned belongs to an altogether different context. In a 1968 study of how individuals evaluate gambles, psychologists Paul Slovic and Sarah

1. It is instructive to compare Joan Robinson's (1933) discussion of the basic concepts of the theory of the firm with Machlup's (1967) late exposition of the same topic. Robinson was aware of the semantic gap between the technical notions of a commodity and of an industry and their counterparts in ordinary language, but she could write rather boldly that "a firm is a concern very similar to the firms of the real world" (1933, 17). By contrast, Machlup insisted that the economic theorist's firm is primarily a "theoretical construct." In the intervening time the controversies had exercised their disenchanting influence.

Lichtenstein were led to claim that it should be possible to find pairs of gambles with the following counterintuitive property: agents who claim to prefer one will be willing to pay *more* for the other. Consider, for example, a gamble that pays off $4 with probability 35/36 and requires one to pay $1 with probability 1/36. The expected monetary value is $3.86. A second gamble pays off $16 with probability 11/36 and with probability 25/36 requires one to pay $1.50. Its expected value is almost the same—$3.85. Slovic and Lichtenstein predicted that among those people who claim to prefer the gamble with the $4 payoff, many will offer to pay more for the other gamble! They also claimed that one would not find such "preference reversals" in the other direction—that is, that one would not find people who say they prefer the gamble with the $16 prizc and who are willing to pay more for the gamble with the $4 prize.

These claims were predictions of novel facts, and they were confirmed by experiments reported in a 1971 article. The results were strikingly replicated in an experiment in which the gambles were actually played on the balcony of the Four Queen's Casino in Las Vegas. More than two-thirds of individuals who prefer gambles with low prizes and low risk (such as the gamble that pays off $4) assign a higher price to gambles such as the one that pays off $16. Although these results were discovered by psychologists, their relevance to economics is evident. If people's preferences between two gambles depend on the mode of elicitation, then the axioms of ordinal utility theory are pointless or refuted. Economists noticed Slovic and Lichtenstein's findings, and in a 1979 article in the *American Economic Review*, David Grether and Charles Plott set out to show that these results would not hold in experiments that more accurately reflected the environment in which economic choices are made. Instead, they wound up replicating Lichtenstein's and Slovic's results. Grether and Plott recognized that these findings constitute a striking disconfirmation of the theoretical core of orthodox economics, but since there is no alternative with the same extremely wide scope, they did not recommend abandoning or modifying the theory, or even diminishing one's reliance on it.

After Grether and Plott's report, the preference reversal phenomenon attracted a good deal of attention, and the *American Economic Review* published a number of articles devoted to it. Very few of these essays took seriously the psychological theorizing that had motivated Slovic and Lichtenstein's prediction: subjects would, Slovic and Lichtenstein maintained, focus much more on the size of the prizes in pricing gambles than in choosing among them, hence the discrepancy. Different practical tasks evoke different forms of cognitive processing. Nor were economists impressed by the fact that the psychologists had predicted the phenomenon before it was observed. Indeed, some of these essays showed only a faint grasp of what the phenomenon is (Cox and Epstein 1989). The bulk of the work was devoted to efforts (which were sometimes extremely ad hoc) to make the phenomenon go away or to show that it did not, after all, refute ordinal utility theory. Given that the choices involve gambles, it is not altogether surprising that economists, such as E. Karni and Z. Safra (1987), tried to interpret the preference reversal phenomenon as another failure of the empirically weak link in expected utility theory: the von Neumann–Morgenstern independence axiom. Others put the blame on the "reduction of compound lotteries" axiom (Segal 1988). There have also been suggestions that preference reversals could be accommodated by versions of utility theory that permit intransitivities (e.g., Loomes, Starmer, and Sugden 1989).

Another intellectual factor had a more important role in dulling the impact of preference reversals: economists who studied this anomaly internalized an implicit constraint on the *scope* of acceptable economic explanations. The reason Grether and Plott were not more deeply disturbed at having replicated the findings of reversals is that they take it for granted that a competitor to orthodox theory must, like orthodox theory itself, have an extremely wide scope: "The fact that preference theory and related theories of optimization are subject to exception does not mean that they should be discarded. No alternative theory currently available appears to be capable of covering the same extremely broad range of phenomena" (1979, 634). For this reason, Grether and Plott could not be impressed by Slovic and Lichtenstein's explanatory hypothesis: a theory which applies only to pricing gambles is simply not a competitor.

3. Some Similarities in the Reactions to Anomalies

In the case of preference reversals, unlike the case of full-cost pricing, there has been no active controversy. Yet, unlike the consensus view of full-cost pricing, preference reversals appear to pose a serious empirical problem for the fundamental theory.

Before addressing this puzzle, we will point out the many important similarities in the reactions of economists to both problems. First, in neither case was the evidence seriously denied. Admittedly, Machlup in

1946 cast doubts on the data collected by the antimarginalists, particularly on the grounds that they were unrepresentative and biased by the questionnaire technique. But this strategy of denying the evidence was not consistently pursued, even by Machlup in his 1946 article. R. F. Heflebower's 1953 report, which brought the American part of the controversy to an end, contains a careful summary of all existing evidence on full-cost pricing (see Heflebower 1955). He concluded that the existence of this pricing method was well-established on certain types of oligopolistic markets, but only on those; it was widespread but not as universal as the Oxford economists had claimed. Similarly, if Grether and Plott's initial reaction was to suspect that Slovic and Lichtenstein's data were spurious, they changed their mind after replicating the data. Later experimental work by economists on preference reversal led them to qualify claims about the frequencies of reversals (Reilly 1982), but never to deny that reversals of the kind predicted occur on a significant scale. Even if economists are by and large more interested in theorizing than in searching for new data, they do not disregard evidence.

Second, in each case there were attempts to reconcile the evidence with existing theory. These attempts had similar weaknesses: only part of the evidence was taken into account, the attempted reconciliations depended on unsupported auxiliary hypotheses, and models were juxtaposed in an unsystematic way. Different defenders of orthodoxy maintained that different constructions in Joan Robinson's "box of tools"—such as the standard monopoly, long-term competition, and various oligopolistic construals—were relevant to full-cost pricing, but nobody showed that full-cost pricing could formally be derived from standard theory with the help of any of these. In addition, the required auxiliary assumptions were not subjected to independent tests; most of the time they *could not be tested* because they had not even been clearly stated in the reconciliating "model." There were fewer but much more precisely articulated reconciliating attempts in the preference reversal case. The most typical one was the already-mentioned strategy of reducing the reversals to another case of expected utility violation. Auxiliary hypotheses were clearly stated, but they remained unsupported and apparently ad hoc. Part of the evidence was left out, notably the crucial fact that "unpredicted" reversals (preferring the high-prize gamble but pricing the other higher) rarely occur.

Third, in both cases defenders of accepted theory attempted to blunt the criticisms by denying that any alternative theory accounted for the anomalies. Hall and Hitch's survey was taken by many, especially in England, as suggesting a new industrial doctrine: hence, the curious expression, full-cost *principle*. This portentous reconstruction of the Oxford economists' work partly reflected their own meaning. For instance, in Andrew's *Manufacturing Business* (1949), full-cost pricing was elevated to the level of a behavioral postulate competing with "marginal revenue equals marginal cost." This theoretical twist of the controversy in England facilitated its resolution there: one reason full-cost pricing was declared to be an unimpressive anomaly was that the theoretical alternative to which it apparently led—to take full-cost pricing as the fundamental decision-theoretic assumption of the theory of the firm—was grossly unsatisfactory. The conflation of the full-cost *anomaly* with the expression of a new *doctrine* that marred the British debate also shows itself in the American debate, even though the latter was more thorough and brought out a few novel facts in the course of the discussion. In the case of preference reversals, many economists have remained complacent on the grounds that no alternative—or at least none that economists are willing to entertain—accounts for the phenomenon either. In the 1980s, this methodological argument was sufficiently well-known to be made briefly and crushingly. The defense of orthodox theorizing on the grounds that no "satisfactory" alternative exists is regarded by many economists as one of the indisputable contributions in Friedman's (1953) controversial essay. There were numerous occurrences of this strategy from the late 1950s onward (e.g., Koopmans 1957).

4. Explaining the Dissimilarities

The common features of the economists' reactions to the two anomalies are perhaps not so striking as the dissimilarities. One would have thought that the preference reversal phenomenon ought to have mattered to economists more than full-cost pricing. The theory it casts in doubt is more central. The phenomenon itself is better established, and its bearing on theory is less ambiguous. Yet preference reversals have been of interest to relatively few economists, while work on full-cost pricing gave rise to a major debate. If the full-cost pricing and marginalist controversies show the profession awkwardly coming to terms with an ill-defined phenomenon of dubious relevance, the discussion of preference reversals finds the profession reluctantly establishing that a certain phenomenon does indeed disconfirm the central theory of contemporary economics, and then treating this conclusion as of no great importance.

What explains this apparently striking difference? The first thing to emphasize is that the work on full-cost pricing was done by economists and concerned behavior that was believed to be clearly within the purview of economics. The work on preference reversals, in contrast, was initially done by psychologists, and the importance of preference reversals in market contexts is questionable. One reason why there was a controversy over full-cost pricing (but not over preference reversals) is that full-cost pricing seemed to challenge conclusions traditionally regarded as *economic*, while preference reversals did not. Indeed, Grether and Plott's starting point was the conviction that preference reversals were artifacts of psychologists' experiments and that they would not occur in a context where actual buying and selling took place. Since Grether and Plott's replication of the preference reversal phenomenon conflicts with this conjecture, it would seem that we have not yet clarified the difference in reactions to anomalies from one controversy to the other.

Here is perhaps a better formulation: in the face of suitable replications, economists might concede that preference reversal could be seen as a phenomenon that actually occurs in economic contexts; but at the same time, they might deny that such problems should shake their confidence in standard theorizing. They might say, "Obviously the fundamental principles of economics are a great oversimplification. If one takes them literally, they're false. The serious question is whether they do their job of explaining and predicting market phenomena well." By contrast, the full-cost pricing data *directly* bore on those market-related predictions which economists have always regarded as central. By claiming that full-cost pricing policies are really explained by the fact that "producers cannot know their demand or marginal revenue curve," Hall and Hitch had suggested that pricing is insensitive to changes in demand. This was a direct challenge to the optimizing model set up by Joan Robinson: that marginal revenue equals marginal cost.

We have no doubt that this difference in the "bearing" of full-cost pricing and of preference reversals goes a long way toward explaining why preference reversals have been of so little concern. But this explanation is shallow as long as it is not put in historical perspective. What is within the purview of economic theory is not simply given. It depends on methodological decisions. This explanation presupposes that economists are only concerned about implications concerning changes in prices and quantities. When mentioning this doctrine in section 1, we made the point that its canonical formulation, in particular in Machlup (1955), was not independent of the full-cost pricing and marginalist controversies. It did not preexist the initial reactions to Hall and Hitch's or Lester's findings, and it was very much influenced by the way the discussion evolved. On the other hand, this doctrine—that only the predictions of theories concerning (changes in) prices and quantities matter—could be taken for granted a generation later when preference reversals came to be discussed.

A second and related explanation for the differences in the economists' reactions is that full-cost pricing appeared to be of immediate relevance to economic *policy*, while the relevance of preference reversals is dubious. We think that there is something to this explanation, but that it also is superficial. Like many empirical studies of pricing pursued in the 1930s, Hall and Hitch's inquiry was motivated by the main economic riddle of the time: Why had industrial prices remained sticky after the Great Crash, leaving output and employment to adjust to the new conditions? The Oxford group was unavoidably concerned with possible remedies to price stickiness, typically in terms of regulating competition on oligopolistic markets. It is thus readily understandable why full-cost pricing attracted so much attention.

But does the preference reversal phenomenon have no policy implications? The dependence of preference on mode of elicitation could matter to the firms' advertising policy and even to the way in which they determine the quality of products. This might have consequences on regulation of competition and consumer protection. By and large, the greater and more systematic the defects in individual decision making, the more tenuous the case for laissez-faire. At a more theoretical level, much of welfare economics is based on a "willingness-to-pay" measure of individual advantages and disadvantages, and would simply crumble if that measure were not also indicative of a preference ranking. One wonders what would be left of the notion of a Pareto-improving transfer if more than one preference concept were required. Even if, unlike full-cost pricing, preference reversals do not bear immediately on contemporary policy discussions, it would be surprising if economists could not look beyond the moment's debate and see the policy relevance of a major challenge to their fundamental theory. A passage in Grether and Plott's article (1979, 624) shows that at least some of them did. Even more than the first, the second explanation raises more questions than it answers.

A third—and, in our view, more important—explanation is that there have been significant methodological changes within the economics profession. First, the profession has become more sensitive to the need for testing and to the requisites of good tests. Although there have been some episodes since the full-cost pricing controversy in which concerns about testing have played a surprisingly small part—witness the so-called Cambridge controversy (Hausman 1981)—one would expect contemporary economists to discuss full-cost pricing evidence more carefully than did their predecessors. Second, the profession is on average more hostile to survey data than it was fifty years ago. A study such as Hall and Hitch's would have a hard time getting a hearing today, even if it relied on a larger sample and a more sophisticated design. The hostility has tapered off over the last decade, but it seems fair to say that thc average economist is still deeply suspicious of surveys.[2] These two methodological changes help explain why a major debate concerning full-cost pricing might not take place nowadays, but they obviously do not explain why the preference reversal phenomenon has been largely ignored.

The methodological change we would like to emphasize connects with the following finding: the exact interpretation of fundamental theory was not yet settled during the period of the full-cost pricing controversy. As explained, even major theorists such as Austin Robinson and Ronald Coase did not clearly distinguish between profit maximizing and "rationality" in some less clearly delineated sense. At a rather late stage of the discussion, E. H. Chamberlin could write approvingly of the full-cost "principle" on the grounds that it showed the profit-maximization assumption to be dispensable in the analysis of industrial competition. Chamberlin's statement makes it clear in retrospect that there had been a gulf yawning between his own *Theory of Monopolistic Competition* (1933) and Joan Robinson's *Economics of Imperfect Competition* (1933). Still, the two approaches were often conflated in the 1940s under the label "theories of imperfect competition."

At the same time as the content of economic theory has been made definite, the work of neoclassical economists has become more tightly constrained by theory and less eclectic. In the late 1930s many economists were more open-minded. For example, the extent to which they regarded the shape of average cost curves as an empirical matter is evidence that

2. At least when economists do the surveys. As Robert Goldfarb has pointed out, economists have few qualms about employing government statistics, which are often the results of surveys.

they were prepared to give up part of the traditional framework. A leading economist such as Stigler could accept the full-costers' conclusion that (contrary to the Robinsonian picture) the average cost curve is flat on the relevant operating interval. Some major economists—Roy Harrod (1952) is one striking example—were even prepared to consider the possibility that the standard theory of the firm might be badly mistaken. In the 1980s, in contrast, economists were much more firmly convinced that their theory, though not necessarily fully correct, was nevertheless the best possible first approximation.

5. Some Philosophical Conjectures

The discussion above highlights the differences between the two episodes, but at the same time it points to subtle similarities in the way economists respond to anomalies. We would like now to elaborate on this dialectical point. The reader will have noticed that in their responses to the two anomalies economists made some of the same arguments, even if the novelty, degree of explicitness, and relative weight of these arguments varied from one case to the other. Analyzing these common arguments, we are led to highlight the following two features, which are already invoked by Hausman (1992) as part of his general assessment of economic theory.

First, economists often defend their particular *theories* by arguing that their *discipline* is separate from other modes of social inquiry. Most of the economists' research on the preference reversal phenomenon was driven by the question, Is it possible that the psychologists' findings survive in *an economic setting*? More discretely, but already there, this commitment to a separation of economics underlies the controversies over the firm. Witness the following pronouncement by Joan Robinson at the outset of her treatise:

> The single assumption which it is necessary to make . . . is that the individual firm will always arrange its affairs in such a way as to make the largest profits that can be made. . . . It is this assumption that makes the analysis of value possible. If individuals act in an erratic way, only statistical methods will serve to discover the laws of economics, and if individuals act in a predictable way, but from a large number of complicated motives, the economist must resign his task to the psychologist. (1933, 6)

It might be asked, would it be such a disaster if economists resigned their investigation of motives to statisticians and psychologists? Robinson's paradigmatic answer is that in no circumstances should economists resign because if they did, economics would not exist as a distinct science.

The controversies suggest that separation can be seen in two ways: either as a primarily methodological concept, related to the "formal" definition of economics by Robbins and others, or as a substantial constraint on what causal factors one attends to, in a way consistent with John Stuart Mill's philosophy of the social sciences. Hausman's (1992) account emphasizes the latter view. Either way, separation provides a key to the puzzling question of how economists can live with anomalous phenomena within the usual territory of economics (in "situations where economic theory is generally applied" to use Grether and Plott's words).

Second, potential economic theories face a maximal scope constraint, which also helps keep economics separate from other fields of inquiry. Remember the way Grether and Plott discredited the psychologists' accounts of preference reversals. A similar scope requirement is implicit in Joan Robinson's consideration of a "single" fundamental assumption throughout her theory. Machlup's final word against Lester is that "The 'mental ruts' of the marginalists are equipped to take care of all the economic considerations which Professor Lester has mentioned as factors in business decisions. This makes marginal analysis less simple but more revealing than a theory which tries to explain the volume of employment in the firm solely with reference to its sales possibilities" (1947, 154). Lester's unconventional hypothesis (that employment is determined by sales prospects) is disqualified on the grounds that it does not apply to the same broad range of situations as profit maximization. The Robinsons rejected Harrod's and Andrews's suggestions that full-cost pricing be taken as a primitive assumption for a similar reason: it would cover only a limited range of industrial situations. They added the related but distinct point that even in its range, the full-cost "principle" would not explain everything. This last distinction helps clarify the scope requirement as follows: not only should the alternative hypothesis apply to at least as many phenomena as does the existing theory but it should also explain them with at least the same precision. Notice the analogy between the full-cost "principle" and Slovic and Lichtenstein's behavioral hypothesis: the latter lacks not only a broad scope but also precision. For example, it does not say how a "preference reverser" would compose a portfolio of $-bets and P-bets if he or she were given the choice.

The separation and the maximal scope arguments play an overt role in the preference reversals case. This study shows that they were *also* present in the earlier controversies. Having identified these common factors, we would like to offer a speculative answer to our major puzzle: Why were economists so much more dogmatic in one case than the other? In the preference reversal case, the two methodological points just identified are mutually supporting: psychological explanations happen to be partial in the sense excluded by the scope constraint, so that this requirement strengthens the effect of the disciplinary or causal separation strategy. By contrast, in the full-cost pricing case, only the maximal scope requirement is fully binding. The other argument, that economics should be separate, is effective, but not to the same degree; in effect, it served only to exclude the more procedural interpretations of profit maximization without going to the heart of the full-cost debate. The major problem in the full-cost and related cases was not the fact that firms did not make calculations in the way marginalism had suggested, but the apparently anomalous reactions of firms to changes in economic conditions. Hence, the need for a reinterpretation of at least *some* of the negative evidence. In sum, economists were consistent with their long-term commitments by being completely unwilling to consider the alternative theory in one instance, and merely reluctant to do so in the other.

In comparing reactions to the two anomalies, we have tried to be primarily descriptive. But such self-constraint has its limits, and we would like to close with some comments on whether we think economists' reactions have been justified. In our view, though economists cannot take much pride in either episode, those who want to dismiss economics as ideological pseudo-science should be taken aback. In particular, the view that economists pay no attention to evidence is refuted by our narrative. Moreover, we can see some limited form of progress—particularly in the appreciation of what counts as a model and what counts as a test—as well as in the appreciation of the need for testing. The comparison between the two episodes is, however, for the most part disquieting, if only because it confirms the pervasive role of the separation and scope constraints in stopping controversies before they really take off.

As noted in the introduction, contemporary philosophy of science provides no precise guidelines concerning how scientists should respond to anomalies. So one cannot draw on any established philosophical rules to say whether economists have responded as they should have. But useful hints may be drawn from the works of Popper, Lakatos, and Kuhn. For instance, we noted Kuhn's point that anomalies influence the articulation of a paradigm, even if for a long time they coexist with unchanged formulations of accepted laws and facts. One finds little such influence of full-cost pricing or preference reversals. There are few echoes of either in textbooks or treatises in industrial economics or choice theory. The fact that conventional economics tends to ignore past anomalies points, we think, to a failure of economics as a science rather than a failure of philosophy of science to advise economists.[3]

In this context we can do little more than to *assert* these normative judgments. We must also hasten to add that very recently one finds some conflicting trends in the methodological development of economics. The hostility toward questionnaires is perhaps fading, as survey results are once again appearing in major journals. At the same time that economists are, on the whole, more focused on implications concerning price and quantity data than they were in the 1930s, there is also a great deal more experimenting and theorizing that is specifically concerned with the fine grain of decision making, and sometimes even with the *procedural* side of decisions.[4] The growing importance of this body of work should redirect attention toward other things than market prices and quantities.

References

Andrews, P. W. S. 1949. *Manufacturing Business*. London: Macmillan.

Chamberlin, E. H. 1933. *The Theory of Monopolistic Competition*. Cambridge: Harvard University Press.

Cox, J., and S. Epstein. 1989. Preference Reversals without the Independence Axiom.

3. Full-cost pricing is still discussed, and sometimes even actively, outside conventional, "neoclassical" economics. Managerial economics is one example. "Post-Keynesian" economics is another; on this particular connection, see F. S. Lee 1984, and the winter 1990–91 issue of the *Journal of Post-Keynesian Economics*. Post-Keynesians have followed Andrews in basing an alternative doctrine of price decisions on full-cost pricing. However, it could be argued that Post-Keynesians do not study the anomalies faced by the full-cost doctrine any more than orthodox economists do the anomalies faced by the standard theory of the firm! To make this criticism in any detail would have distracted us from our main point. But we would like to suggest that there is a sense in which economics at large, not only conventional economics, ignores the past anomalies.

4. On the experimental side, see in particular the collection recently edited by J. K. Kagel and A. E. Roth (1995). Among many other things, this volume contains a thorough discussion of evidence relative to the preference reversal phenomenon.

American Economic Review 79:408–26.
Friedman, M. 1953. The Methodology of Positive Economics. In *Essays in Positive Economics*. Chicago: University of Chicago Press.
Grether, D., and C. Plott. 1979. Economic Theory of Choice and the Preference Reversal Phenomenon. *American Economic Review* 69:623–38.
Hall R. L., and C. J. Hitch. 1939. Price Theory and Business Behavior. *Oxford Economic Papers* 2:12–45.
Harrod, R. 1952. *Economic Essays*. London: Macmillan.
Hausman, D. 1981. *Capital, Profits and Prices: An Essay in the Philosophy of Economics*. New York: Columbia University Press.
———. 1992. *The Inexact and Separate Science of Economics*. Cambridge: Cambridge University Press.
Heflebower, R. F. 1955. Full Costs, Cost Changes, and Prices. In *Business Concentration and Price Policy*. Princeton, N.J.: Princeton University Press.
Kagel, J. K., and A. E. Roth. 1995. *Handbook of Experimental Economics*. Princeton, N.J.: Princeton University Press.
Karni, E., and Z. Safra. 1987. "Preference Reversal" and the Observability of Preferences by Experimental Methods. *Econometrica* 55:675–85.
Koopmans, T. 1957. *Three Essays on the State of Economic Science*. New York: McGraw-Hill.
Lee, F. S. 1984. The Marginalist Controversy and the Demise of Full-Cost Pricing. *Journal of Economic Issues* 18:1107–32.
Lester, R. A. 1946. Shortcomings of Marginal Analysis for Wage-Employment Problems. *American Economic Review* 36:62–82.
Lichtenstein, S., and P. Slovic. 1971. Reversals of Preference between Bids and Choices in Gambling Decisions. *Journal of Experimental Psychology* 89:46–55.
———. 1973. Response-Induced Reversals of Preference in Gambling: An Extended Replication in Las Vegas. *Journal of Experimental Psychology* 101:16–20.
Loomes, G., C. Starmer, and R. Sugden. 1989. Preference Reversal: Information-Processing Effect or Rational Nontransitive Choice. *Economic Journal* (conference supplement) 99:140–51.
Machlup, F. 1946. Marginal Analysis and Empirical Research. *American Economic Review* 36:519–54.
———. 1947. Rejoinder to an Antimarginalist. *American Economic Review* 37:148–54.
———. 1955. The Problem of Verification in Economics. *Southern Economic Journal* 22:1–21.
———. 1967. Theories of the Firm: Marginalist, Behavioral, Managerial. *American Economic Review* 57:1–33.
Mongin, Philippe. 1986. La Controverse sur l'enterprise (1940–1950) et la formation de l'irréalisme méthodologique. *Economie et Sociétés* 5:91–151.
———. (1990–91). The Early Full-Cost Debate and the Problem of Empirically Testing Profit Maximization. *Journal of Post-Keynesian Economics* 13 (winter): 236–81.

———. 1992. The Full-Cost Controversy of the 1940s and 1950s: A Methodological Assessment. *HOPE* 24:311–56.

Reilly, R. 1982. Preference Reversal: Further Evidence and Some Suggested Modifications in Experimental Design. *American Economic Review* 72:576–84.

Robinson, A. 1950. The Pricing of Manufacturing Products. *Economic Journal* 60:771–80.

Robinson, J. 1933. *The Economics of Imperfect Competition*. London: Macmillan.

Segal, U. 1988. Does the Preference Reversal Phenomenon Necessarily Contradict the Independence Axiom? *American Economic Review* 78:233–36.

Slovic, P., and S. Lichtenstein. 1968. Relative Importance of Probabilities and Payoffs in Risk Taking. *Journal of Experimental Psychology Monograph* 78, part 2: 1–18.

Responses to Arbitrariness in Contemporary Economics

S. Abu Turab Rizvi

> The near emptiness of general equilibrium theory is a theorem of the theory.—Christopher Bliss, "Oil Trade and General Equilibrium"

In the 1970s, Hugo Sonnenschein, Rolf Mantel, and Gerard Debreu established a series of results regarding the properties of aggregate excess demands arising in Walrasian general equilibrium models of the Arrow-Debreu-McKenzie type. They showed that, despite the usual assumptions made on preferences, endowments, and technology, the aggregate excess demands were arbitrary, save that they satisfied Walras's Law and continuity (Sonnenschein 1972, 1973a, 1973b; Mantel 1974, 1976, 1977; Debreu 1974). Although some other authors made striking additions to this characterization (especially Alan Kirman and Andreu Mas-Colell and their collaborators—Kirman and Koch 1986; Mas-Colell 1977; McFadden, Mas-Colell, Mantel, and Richter 1974), we can call this body of work SMD theory after the initials of the three originators.

I am grateful to Roy Weintraub, Nancy Wulwick, Marcel Boumans, and Jim Hartley for their reflections on earlier versions of this essay. The article also benefited from comments by Phil Mirowski, Roger Backhouse, and Philippe Mongin, as well as other participants of the Annual *HOPE* Conference, "New Economics and Its Writing," at Duke University, March 31, 1996. Elise Josserand provided superb research assistance.

SMD theory has important implications. It shows that good behavior at the microeconomic level is consistent with arbitrary behavior at the macroeconomic level. Therefore, the many economists who looked for microfoundations of systematic aggregate phenomena could not find them in these general equilibrium models. SMD theory also means that general results on, for example, uniqueness (Mas-Colell 1977; Ingrao and Israel 1990, ch. 11), stability (Sonnenschein 1973a; Ingrao and Israel 1990, ch. 12), comparative statics (Kehoe 1985), econometric identification (Diewert 1977; Stoker 1984a, 1984b), imperfectly competitive general equilibrium (Roberts and Sonnenschein 1977), and microfoundations of macroeconomics (Rizvi 1994b), are unobtainable on the basis of the commonly accepted Walrasian microfoundations. The general equilibrium research program, which has been running since the 1950s on the fumes of a huge variety of existence theorems for its general results and on particular case after particular case in other areas, has finally run out of gas.

The growing realization that this is the case has led to a variety of responses in recent economic writing. This article explores one of these—the distinctive contributions of the European economists, Werner Hildenbrand, Jean-Michel Grandmont, and their collaborators. In doing this, I want to more generally describe a change in attitude among economists. This shift is not uniform, certainly, but it is occurring among a significant number of practitioners and will have to be dealt with by their detractors. The new attitude is characterized by an empirical turn, a modesty concerning goals, an openness toward using a variety of methods and data, and—above all—an abandonment of strict microfoundations (which were based as much as is possible on individualistic assumptions). My argument is that these changes have been precipitated by a clearer understanding of the importance of SMD theory.

Section 1 sketches the history of attitudes toward SMD theory and to microfoundations, and demonstrates that initial skepticism regarding SMD theory has turned into a growing if grudging acceptance. This acceptance is inversely related to adherence to strict microfoundations. Section 2 looks at Hildenbrand's and Grandmont's work on market demand. This work signifies a very large change in what is the appropriate method for dealing with aggregate economic phenomena. The implications of this change are discussed in section 3, after which I conclude the paper.

1. Attitudes toward SMD Theory and Microfoundations

During the 1970s and into the first half of the 1980s, the acceptance of the importance of the SMD results remained weak to skeptical (Rizvi 1994b, 361), outside of a small group of general equilibrium theorists such as Herbert Scarf (1973) and Egbert Dierker (1974). The belief in microfoundations—that all statements about the macroeconomy should be derived from microeconomic data considered individually—remained correspondingly strong in this period. E. Roy Weintraub, in his book on microfoundations, could accurately state that "even those few economists who argue that current microeconomics *does not generate* macroeconomics have been extremely shy in their attempts to convince their colleagues of the seriousness of their concerns" (1979, 5). There seemed to be consensus around Allan Drazen's view that "explanations of macroeconomic phenomena will be complete only when such explanations are consistent with microeconomic choice theoretic behavior and can be phrased in the language of general equilibrium theory" (1980, 293). These views were so common that by 1986 James Tobin lamented their ubiquity and their exclusive use in publication, peer review, and hiring (350).

Matters started to change slowly in favor of SMD theory's acceptance in 1982. In that year, Wayne Shafer and Hugo Sonnenschein codified the arbitrariness results in a chapter of the *Handbook of Mathematical Economics*, and the SMD results and their robustness should have been apparent to a wide audience of economists. SMD theory began to be mentioned in macroeconomic contexts following this publication (Rizvi 1994b, 361, n. 2). Things came to a head at the end of the 1980s with the publication of Alan Kirman's 1989 article on the "intrinsic limits" of general equilibrium theory, and the process of dealing with the SMD results continues to this day. By now, however, even such erstwhile stalwarts of general equilibrium theory as Christopher Bliss compare that theory to theology (1993, 227).

Moreover, it can be argued that a great deal of the methodological pluralism in microeconomics since the mid 1980s has resulted from the theoretical dead end made obvious by the SMD results. For example, there is evidence that the turn to game theory around 1985 was directly influenced by the realization that SMD theory blocked progress in the general equilibrium mode (Rizvi 1994a, 2–6). Some authors, such as Donald Saari (1991) and adherents of the Santa Fe School, have embraced the complexity that SMD theory derives, and they have not sought regularities at the aggregate level (Rizvi 1994b, 370–73). The European work on the "law of demand" as well is directly inspired by the SMD results, and it is to this work that we now turn.

2. Market Demand from Distributional Restrictions

Werner Hildenbrand and Jean-Michel Grandmont have been interested in demonstrating conditions under which the "law of demand"—the inverse monotonic relation between price and quantity demanded at the aggregate level (or more precisely, that the changes of price and of quality demanded point in opposite directions)—holds true. In his Alfred Marshall lecture called "Facts and Ideas in Microeconomic Theory," Hildenbrand considers the law of demand to be "fundamental and indispensable," since it is needed to do comparative statics, "which is the ordinary job of the economist" (1989, 252). However, both authors understand that SMD theory demonstrates that this cannot result from general equilibrium theory as ordinarily construed (Hildenbrand 1989, 252; 1994, preface; Grandmont 1992, 2). Thus, for both economists, a substantial change in approach is required to proceed.

Their approach contrasts with the standard approach in getting definite results at the aggregate level. The usual approach was to consider individual data and to place more and more restrictions on them—for example, the assumption of homotheticity in the area of preferences—until regularity resulted at the aggregate level. Grandmont describes this as putting "constraints on the range of the agents' allowable characteristics" and rejects its use as being too restrictive (1992, 3). Hildenbrand also rejects the usual approach, in quite forceful terms, on epistemological grounds. For him, assumptions such as homotheticity at the individual level cannot serve as a basis for monotone market demand since "individual preference relations are not observable and we have no criterion to judge assumptions on preferences as 'reasonable' "; he asks, rhetorically, "Do good looking indifference curves describe typical behavior?" (257). He continues, "For this reason, the axiomatic individualistic approach—which consists in making ad hoc assumptions on *individual* preferences or demand functions in order to derive properties of the market demand function—cannot, in my opinion, lead to a satisfactory foundation of the Law of Demand. An economic foundation of the Law must, as much as possible, be based on observable entities" (257).

Grandmont also considers that an empirical basis for market demand is preferable. Moreover, it is possible since the approach of wanting to "impose qualitative and quantitative restrictions on the shape of their distribution" can in principle be verified (1992, 3). Before turning to the empirical results that Hildenbrand discusses, let us consider the sort of restrictions Grandmont and Hildenbrand have in mind. There have been two main approaches (Grandmont 1992, 6). One is to assume some minimal sort of rationality at the individual level, and then combine this with observable distributional restrictions at the macro level. The other is to assume no rationality at all, only satisfaction of budget constraints, but this approach has fewer testable implications.

Hildenbrand takes the first approach (1983, 1989, 1994). The minimal rationality corresponds to his "ideas," the distributional restrictions to "facts." Although Hildenbrand is quite skeptical of untestable rationality assumptions, he assumes that individual demands derive from preference maximization or satisfy Weak Axiom of Revealed Preference only for "lack of a better alternative." In any case, Hildenbrand's approach is empirically based only to some extent, although he is very clear about this "limitation." Yet given the Weak Axiom, the individual Slutsky-substitution matrices are each negative semidefinite. The mean of these individual substitution-effect matrices, which refers to the aggregate level, is then also negative semidefinite (Hildenbrand 1989, 252). There is thus no impediment to downsloping aggregate demand here for substitution-effect reasons. The problem arises with the matrix of the means of the individual Slutsky income-effect matrices, which cannot be assumed in general to be positive semidefinite. At this point, Hildenbrand relies on an argument from John Hicks's *Revision of Demand Theory*, which claims that the heterogeneity of consumer characteristics implies that individual income effects will balance one another at the aggregate level, leaving the well-behaved substitution-effect to predominate (Hicks 1956, 144; Hildenbrand 1989, 258–59). Thus regularity might be expected to occur at the macro level, *because of aggregation*, and which could not be expected at the individual level.

Hildenbrand investigates this idea formally and empirically. For instance, he demonstrates that the mean demand of a continuum of consumers will be downsloping in prices if the distribution of incomes is independent of prices (this is a strong assumption, of course, but Hildenbrand has used it consistently) and if the density of the income distribution is downsloping—that is, wealthier consumers are fewer than poorer consumers (Hildenbrand 1983). Empirically, these hypotheses could be violated without violating the result, since the aggregate income-effect matrix or related matrices can be estimated directly (Hildenbrand 1989, 266). Using the United Kingdom's Family Expenditure Survey for 1969–83, Hildenbrand shows the matrix to be positive semidefinite for all years for expenditures (not quantities) of nine commodity groups such as housing, food, clothing, and footwear. In Hildenbrand (1994), he reports similar results for French consumption.

Thus, for Hildenbrand, the Law of Demand is a hybrid of theory and facts. On the one hand, "it rests on standard theoretical, yet more or less ad hoc and untested, hypotheses on individual behavior" and, "on the other hand, it rests on observable regularities of consumption patterns of large populations" (1989, 275).

Grandmont's (1987, 1992, 1993) approach is less amenable to empirical testing, but it is a more radical departure from standard theory in that it forsakes individual rationality altogether. Grandmont is inspired by Hildenbrand's theoretical demonstrations of downsloping aggregate demand, calling Hildenbrand (1983) an "outstanding methodological achievement in that it shows by way of example the applicability of the distributional viewpoint to demand analysis" (1992, 3). In regard to rationality, Grandmont recalls Gary Becker's (1962) demonstration that if choices are uniformly distributed on the budget plane (!), then demand is downsloping, equally distributed among commodities, and of the Cobb-Douglas type. This is clearly too special, but Grandmont preserves Becker's idea that consumers' choices simply respect their budget constraints and need not be derived from constrained maximization. Grandmont then describes a metric on the space of consumers' characteristics, and using it, he can say what it means for those characteristics to become more dispersed. Grandmont's results are that increasing dispersion among consumers results in downsloping aggregate demand, and also yields other desirable aggregate properties. These properties are all the result of aggregation itself, based on a particular distribution of characteristics among individuals in society. Nothing so well-behaved is going on at the micro level.

3. Implications of the New Approach

An important feature of these approaches is that they are no longer based on strict microfoundations. *Societal* characteristics are used to underpin the analysis of other macroeconomic regularities (Kirman 1989, 138). Very little attention is paid to restricting the nature of individual characteristics—quite a lot to their distribution in the population. Without realizing it, perhaps, these authors have rediscovered the probabilistic approach that was popular in other social sciences many decades ago. In general, Hildenbrand and Grandmont pay little attention to the antecedents of their approach. However, both Hildenbrand and Grandmont refer to Becker (1962). Recently, Hildenbrand (1995, 329), in a reply to critical review by Hendrik Houthakker of *Market Demand*, pointed out that Houthakker himself (in Houthakker 1955) used the distributional approach in an analysis of the production function (to demonstrate that it would be Cobb-Douglas if the distribution of firms had a particular shape) and that this was crucial in influencing his own work. Edmond Malinvaud (1993) also refers to Houthakker 1955 as "one of the first applications of the [distributional] approach" (125) and mentions Pareto's law of income distribution and Schumpeter's admiration for it (129–30). A more inclusive list of antecedents in the economics of the post–World War II period would need to include Karl Borch (1953) and Benoit Mandelbrot's (1961) work on the Pareto distribution (Rizvi 1994, 371–72). It seems that the distributional approach enjoyed a brief resurgence among European expatriate economists in the United States in the early post–World War II period. Nancy Wulwick (personal communication) has also brought to my attention work by Basmann, Battalio, and Kagel (1976)—published in Europe and largely overlooked—which is very much concerned with a distributional approach to macro level regularities. Indeed, such an approach was indicated by Rutledge Vining over fifty years ago:

> Distributions of economic variates in as large groups as can be obtained should be studied and analyzed. . . . That is to say, statistical economics is too narrow in scope if it includes just the estimation of postulated relations. Probability theory is fundamental as a guide to an understanding of the nature of the phenomena to be studied and not merely as a basis for a theory of the sampling behavior of estimates of population parameters, the characteristics of which have been postulated. In seeking for interesting hypotheses for our quantitative studies we might want to wander beyond the classic Walrasian fields and poke around the equally classic fields once cultivated by . . . Lexis, Bortkiewicz, Markov, and Kapteyn. (Vining 1949, 85)

Claude Ménard (1987) has investigated why the classic probabilistic approach did not become popular in economics, and its revival also needs to be explained. At all events, it is clear that the taboo against using preexisting societal regularities in the investigation of other social phenomena is being lifted in economics. In addition, the use of a continuum of agents to justify the price-taking assumption in general equilibrium theory—a large concern of Hildenbrand's in the 1970s—may have made working with distributions in the present context easier for a number of economists brought up on general equilibrium theory.

The distributional restrictions can be investigated both empirically, as Hildenbrand has done, and theoretically. Both Kirman (1989) and Grandmont (1992) have called for the study of elements of social cohesion that are not based in market interactions, but which can give rise to the distributional restrictions envisaged in market-demand theory. This call is again quite a change as it puts nonmarket interactions among agents at the forefront, instead of as exceptions to the analysis. Kirman and his coworkers have pursued this approach, building on H. Föllmer (1974). In addition, S. Abu Turab Rizvi and Rajiv Sethi (forthcoming) show how the complicated interaction of imitation, habit formation, and the pursuit of novelty in consumption might lead to relatively simple limiting behavior of consumption in the aggregate.

The writings on market demand also signal a shift in economists' attitudes toward rationality. Essentially, rational behavior is employed only grudgingly—as by Hildenbrand (1994, 10–14)—if at all. It is considered either unscientific or irrelevant to the goal of establishing aggregate regularities. In Grandmont's models, rational behavior is not postulated at all. This, of course, creates some "embarrassment of riches" for him, as it suggests that individual "rationality" may not be as necessary as some economists would like to believe to the construction of a "sound macroeconomic theory" (1992, 6–7). Grandmont expands on this idea in a passage that shows how big the change wrought by SMD theory really is:

> The present analysis raises again some (old) questions about the actual status of the postulates of *individual* "rationality" in the Walrasian paradigm. It suggests in particular that such postulates might not be as necessary as some would like to believe to the construction of a sound quantitative macroeconomics. An alternative research strategy would be indeed to actually *reverse* the traditional Neoclassical research pro-

> gramme, and to try to obtain some form of *aggregate rationality* as in the present paper (but surely *not* the existence of a "representative" consumer!) by relying more on particular features of the distribution of behavioral characteristics among the members of the system under consideration. (Grandmont 1992, 33)

The literature on the criticism of methodological individualism and rational behavior is, of course, quite immense; and even general equilibrium theorists have been contributing to the criticism of this "touchstone of accepted economics" (Arrow 1994, 1, in his Ely Lecture). But it is striking that the main thrust in Hildenbrand's and Grandmont's rejection of the use of individual rationality is that it is neither necessary nor sufficient to aggregate economics: not sufficient, because of the SMD results, not necessary because of distribution-based approach. Their change seems much less due to criticisms and doubts about the rationality approach at a methodological or philosophical level than it does to its lack of fruitfulness.

It is hard to overemphasize the nature of the change to theory made by an abandonment of rationality assumptions. In particular, one point has not been sufficiently emphasized, although it has been alluded to (Hildenbrand 1989, 251): the utility basis for economics traditionally serves two purposes: it motivates choice behavior *and* it provides an indicator of welfare. When Hildenbrand, Grandmont, and others abandon rationality assumptions, they also lose the welfare or normative basis of neoclassical economics. This is why Gustav Cassel's approach of beginning with individual demand functions as being elementary (to which Hildenbrand 1994 returns) was not popular. None of the "invisible hand" results—the two welfare theorems—can be demonstrated in a nonoptimizing framework. Thus the distribution-based approach is more subversive than it at first might seem. This observation also indicates why the distribution-based approach has not met with universal acclaim.

Specifically, a divide seems to be forming between those American economists who understand SMD theory but have not committed to a systematic approach to aggregate economics in response to it, and the European economists who are willing to jettison large chunks of received theory. Some Americans seem quite reluctant to give up this theory. Arthur Lewbel (1994b), in an illuminating exposition and critique of Hildenbrand's *Market Demand*, begins with a long list of authors on demand theory to which Hildenbrand does *not* refer, emphasizing the renegade aspects of the book. He also repeatedly points out Hildenbrand's reluctance to use behavioral (rationality) assumptions. Lewbel's attitude carries over from his earlier description of Hildenbrand's work as making insufficient reference to traditional aggregation theory. Specifically, Lewbel charges that Grodal and Hildenbrand (1991) "fail to acknowledge how much their work borrows from the exact aggregation literature" (Lewbel 1994a, 129). Here, Lewbel specifically mentions his own work (Lewbel 1991) as being not adequately cited. Similar tensions surface in a review by Houthakker (1995) of Hildenbrand's book. The review is quite revealing since it is followed by a reply by Hildenbrand (1995) and a rejoinder to that by Houthakker. Houthakker chides Hildenbrand for "some sweeping assertions concerning past research that need examination" (327) and also for rejecting the usual methodology of economics, which he asserts is up to the task posed by demand analysis (327–28). Hildenbrand's response makes it clear that he is undeterred by these criticisms and, what is more, that he is currently working on developing his work into a "dynamic theory of market," which explicitly takes the time-dependence of demand into account.

The new approaches discussed in this article are indeed a far cry from the choice-theoretic, general equilibrium approach of fifteen years ago. Not surprisingly, the attitude toward macroeconomics has also changed in the European economics milieu. Evidence for this can be seen in Malinvaud's 1989 presidential address to the European Economic Association, "Observation in Macroeconomic Theory Building." This address shares the characteristics of the recent views of Grandmont and Hildenbrand: an empirical turn to economic writing (Malinvaud 1989, 218), a yearning to be practical and relevant (205), a broadening toward what might be an acceptable observation base for economics (216–18; this includes panels of national data, expectations surveys, evidence of disequilibrium, historical approaches, experimental data, and socioeconomic structures), all combined with an avowed sense of the modesty of the whole exercise.

Malinvaud begins with an acknowledgment that "it was repeatedly found with uneasiness that the properties derived from pure theory are too inconclusive" and describes the twin crises caused for macroeconomics by the disputes over the role of rationality in model building and the challenges made against the probability approach of its allied econometrics (1989, 207, 206–13). He wants to avoid a macroeconomics that has "become a detached intellectual play" (205) and feels that the methodological strictures of strict microfoundations—that one should recognize "only constraints, behaviour and equilibrium conditions" (207)—went too far: "Clearly, such a stand is too dogmatic, even if it is induced by the normal teaching of microeconomic theory. . . . If we can correctly identify elementary behaviour, this is perfect; but when we cannot, we have to stick to observing results of a more complex sort, and we should not impose on the data an unfounded preconception" (207). He now favors eclecticism over rigor: "But the notions of proper concepts, true models and true facts cannot and should not be interpreted strictly; somewhat tentative notions or constructs are not ruled out. This open-mindedness and eclecticism is again consistent with the view that one tries to benefit, as much as is possible, from present knowledge, even from that part which is not hard and fast" (209). Malinvaud's assessment of the strict microfoundations impulse is quite harsh:

> The same general idea of a discipline that theoreticians ought to impose on lousy macroeconomics often occurs in less extreme form. In particular it was often stated that disequilibrium models were not admissible as long as the rationale for sticky prices had not been elucidated, or as long as the price and wage dynamics had not been derived from the study of elementary behaviour behind it. The indisputable impact that such claims had in the profession reveals a kind of methodological perversity about which one ought to reflect. (212)

In an essay on the macroeconomic implications of microeconomic theories, Malinvaud (1992) again considers this issue. He argues that the differences in perspective between microeconomics and macroeconomics invalidate any easy transposition from the micro to the macro level. For microeconomic "speculations" to be fruitful, they must be formulated in a macroeconomic framework and tested and validated against the data (12–13). He takes comfort in the fact that "As W. Hildenbrand's (1989) research seems to show, aggregated relations could well appear commonly less complex than what certain segments of mathematical economics suggests" (18; trans. Elise Josserand) while at the same time, he suggests that such an approach ought to take production factors more closely into account (20–21; Malinvaud 1993). In a recent article on rationality, Malinvaud (1995) dismisses the easy fiction of a representative agent. He considers Grandmont's (1992) work to be "special but revealing" in its approach to aggregation, where "the emphasis must shift" to "bear in mind the observed properties of statistical distributions of the individual characteristics of agents and of their behaviors. Werner Hildenbrand's recent book (1994) perfectly shows the efficacy of this method" (535; trans. Elise Josserand). In these ways Malinvaud's writings show a distancing from the exclusive focus on microeconomics of the past, a concern with empirical validity as opposed to deductive speculation, and a cautious but respectful attitude toward the work of Grandmont and Hildenbrand.

The relative autonomy of recent European writing on aggregate economics can be seen in a number of other ways as well. Several issues of *Ricerche Economiche* in 1993 are devoted to the new approaches to aggregation I have been discussing. This includes Malinvaud's (1993) essay on aggregation, in which he highlights the distributional approach (calling it the statistical approach) and gives it equal footing to other, more traditional approaches to aggregation. He indicates that contributions in this vein "are not only interesting in themselves, but also show the way for a very promising trend" (125). Roger Backhouse (1995) has argued along different lines for the distinctiveness of European macroeconomics. He also points out to me (personal communication) that European economists are becoming more self-aware of their distinctiveness, as is indicated for example by the special issue of *Kyklos* (1995, 48.2) devoted to European economics. While there certainly are American responses to SMD theory (such as, it can be argued, complexity approaches, experimental economics, and game theory), so far they do not concern reformulating macroeconomics. For example, as Jim Hartley has observed (personal communication), even when Joseph Stiglitz (1992) mentions SMD theory, he does so only in passing. The recent work by Dhananjay Gode and Shyam Sunder (1993), building on Becker (1962), seems also to be motivated by concerns other than macroeconomics. There is, however, an interesting exception to the rule of Europeans pursuing statistical approaches to market phenomena. I refer to Duncan Foley's (1994, 1996) work on statistical equilibria. He, however, *derives* statistical regularities from certain assumptions instead of imposing them as distributional restrictions. For instance, he supposes that there are many agents with each offer set, and that each action within an offer set is equally likely. This setup permits Foley to characterize equilibria statistically, as the outcome most likely to be realized. It is clear, therefore, that the center of gravity of the distributional approach to aggregate phenomena lies in Europe.

4. Conclusion

The thesis of this article, that it is much easier to understand contemporary work in economics by looking at the impact of SMD theory, can be encapsulated by contrasting Drazen's comments in 1980 and Malinvaud's in 1989, both quoted earlier here. Whereas Drazen felt that "explanations of macroeconomic phenomena will be complete only when such explanations are consistent with microeconomic choice theoretic behavior and can be phrased in the language of general equilibrium theory," Malinvaud characterizes such a view as methodologically perverse. It is a significant comment on what causes change in modern economics that the economists mentioned here, who are now led to hold such "revisionist" sentiments about microfoundations, have probably long had doubts about the foundational problems with their earlier approach. Moreover, the very path they now take had been pointed out a number of times before, as instanced by Vining's comments quoted above. Yet it seems clear that the factor that directly motivates the shift to the new work is that the attempt to uphold the earlier methodological strictures failed, and it was found that progress along those lines was not possible. The theoretical vacuum created by the SMD results then elicited the distinctive European approach to the relation between micro variables and macroeconomic regularities.

References

Arrow, Kenneth J. 1994. Methodological Individualism and Social Knowledge. *American Economic Review* 84:1–9.

Backhouse, Roger E. 1995. *Interpreting Macroeconomics: Explorations in the History of Macroeconomic Thought.* London: Routledge.

Basmann, R. L., R. C. Battalio, and J. H. Kagel. 1976. An Experimental Test of a Simple Theory of Aggregate Per-capita Demand Functions. *Schweizerische Zeitschrift für Volkswirtschaft und Statistik* 112:153–73.

Becker, Gary S. 1962. Irrational Behavior and Economic Theory. *Journal of Political Economy* 70:1–13.

Bliss, Christopher. 1993. Oil Trade and General Equilibrium: A Review Article. *Journal of International and Comparative Economics* 2:227–42.

Borch, K. 1953. Effects on Demand of Changes in the Distribution of Income. *Econometrica* 21:325–41.

Cassel, Gustav. 1932. *The Theory of Social Economy.* New York: Harcourt Brace.

Debreu, Gerard. 1974. Excess Demand Functions. *Journal of Mathematical Economics* 11:15–23.

Dierker, Egbert. 1974. *Topological Methods in Walrasian Economics.* Berlin: Springer-Verlag.

Diewert, W. E. 1977. Generalized Slutsky Conditions for Aggregate Consumer Demand Functions. *Journal of Economic Theory* 15:353–62.

Drazen, Allan. 1980. Recent Developments in Macroeconomic Disequilibrium Theory. *Econometrica* 48:283–306.

Foley, Duncan K. 1994. A Statistical Equilibrium Theory of Markets. *Journal of Economic Theory* 62:321–45.

———. 1996. Statistical Equilibrium in a Simple Labor Market. *Metroeconomica* 47:125–47.

Föllmer, Hans. 1974. Random Economies with Many Interacting Agents. *Journal of Mathematical Economics* 1:51–62.

Gode, Dhananjay K., and Shyam Sunder. 1993. Allocative Efficiency of Markets with Zero-Intelligence Traders: Markets as a Partial Substitute for Individual Rationality. *Journal of Political Economy* 101:119–37.

Grandmont, Jean-Michel. 1987. Distributions of Preferences and the "Law of Demand." *Econometrica* 55:155–62.

———. 1992. Transformations of the Commodity Space, Behavioral Heterogeneity, and the Aggregation Problem. *Journal of Economic Theory* 57:1–35.

———. 1993. Behavioural Heterogeneity and Cournot Oligopoly Equilibrium. *Ricerche Economiche* 47:167–87.

Grodal, Birgit, and Werner Hildenbrand. 1991. Cross-section Engel Curves, Expenditure Distributions, and the "Law of Demand." In *Aggregation, Consumption, and Trade: Essays in Honor of H. S. Houthakker*, edited by Louis Phlips and Lester D. Taylor. Dordrecht: Klüwer Academic.

Hicks, John R. 1956. *A Revision of Demand Theory.* Oxford: Clarendon.

Hildenbrand, Werner. 1983. On the "Law of Demand." *Econometrica* 51:997–1020.

———. 1989. Facts and Ideas in Microeconomic Theory. *European Economic Review* 33:251–76.

———. 1994. *Market Demand.* Princeton, N.J.: Princeton University Press.

———. 1995. Reply to Professor Houthakker's Review. *Journal of Economics/Zeitschrift für Nationalökonomie* 62:329–32.

Houthakker, Hendrik S. 1955. The Pareto Distribution and the Cobb-Douglas Production Function in Activity Analysis. *Review of Economic Studies* 23:27–31.

———. 1995. Review of Hildenbrand, W.: *Market Demand* and Rejoinder to Professor Hildenbrand's Reply. *Journal of Economics/Zeitschrift für Nationalökonomie* 62:324–29, 332.

Ingrao, Bruna, and Giorgio Israel. 1990. *The Invisible Hand: Economic Equilibrium in the History of Science.* Cambridge: MIT Press.

Kehoe, Timothy J. 1985. Multiplicity of Equilibria and Comparative Statics. *Quarterly Journal of Economics* 100:119–48.

Kirman, Alan P. 1989. The Intrinsic Limits of Modern Economic Theory: The Emperor Has No Clothes. *Economic Journal* (supplement) 99:126–39.

Kirman, Alan P., and K. J. Koch. 1986. Market Excess Demand in Exchange

Economies with Identical Preferences and Collinear Endowments. *Review of Economic Studies* 53:457–63.

Lewbel, Arthur. 1994a. Book review of *Aggregation, Consumption, and Trade: Essays in Honor of H. S. Houthakker*, edited by Louis Phlips and Lester D. Taylor. *Journal of Economic Literature* 32:128–30.

———. 1994b. An Examination of Werner Hildenbrand's "*Market Demand*." *Journal of Economic Literature* 32: 1832-41.

Malinvaud, Edmond. 1989. Observation in Macroeconomic Theory Building. *European Economic Review* 33:205–23.

———. 1992. Implications macroéconomiques des théories microéconomiques modernes. *L'Actualite Économique* 68:11–22.

———. 1993. A Framework for Aggregation Theories. *Ricerche Economiche* 47:107–35.

———. 1995. Sur l'hypothèse de rationalité en théorie macro-économique. *Revue Économique* 46:523–36.

Mandelbrot, B. 1961. Stable Paretian Random Fluctuations and the Multiplicative Variation of Income. *Econometrica* 29:517–43.

Mantel, Rolf. 1974. On the Characterization of Aggregate Excess Demand. *Journal of Economic Theory* 7:348–53.

———. 1976. Homothetic Preferences and Community Excess Demand Functions. *Journal of Economic Theory* 12:197–201.

———. 1977. Implications of Microeconomic Theory for Community Excess Demand Functions. In *Frontiers of Quantitative Economics*, edited by Michael D. Intriligator. Amsterdam: North-Holland.

Mas-Colell, Andreu. 1977. On the Equilibrium Price Set of an Exchange Economy. *Journal of Mathematical Economics* 4:117–26.

McFadden, Daniel, Andreu Mas-Colell, Rolf Mantel, and Marcel K. Richter. 1974. A Characterization of Community Excess Demand Functions. *Journal of Economic Theory* 9:361–74.

Ménard, Claude. 1987. Why Was There No Probabilistic Revolution in Economic Thought? In *The Probabilistic Revolution.* Vol. 2: *Ideas in the Sciences*, edited by Lorenz Krüger, Gerd Gigerenzer, and Mary S. Morgan. Cambridge: MIT Press.

Rizvi, S. Abu Turab. 1994a. Game Theory to the Rescue? *Contributions to Political Economy* 13:1–28.

———. 1994b. The Microfoundations Project in General Equilibrium Theory. *Cambridge Journal of Economics* 18:357–77.

Rizvi, S. Abu Turab, and Rajiv Sethi. Forthcoming. Novelty, Habits and Imitation in a Scitovskian Model of Consumption. In *The Active Consumer*, edited by Marina Bianchi. New York: Routledge.

Roberts, John, and Hugo Sonnenschein. 1977. On the Foundations of the Theory of Monopolistic Competition. *Econometrica* 45:101–13.

Saari, Donald G. 1991. Erratic Behavior in Economic Models. *Journal of Economic Behavior and Organization* 16:3–35.

Scarf, Herbert. 1973. *The Computation of Economic Equilibria*. New Haven, Conn.: Yale University Press.

Shafer, Wayne, and Hugo Sonnenschein. 1982. Market Demand and Excess Demand Functions. In *Handbook of Mathematical Economics*. Vol. 2, edited by Kenneth J. Arrow and Michael D. Intriligator. Amsterdam: North-Holland.

Sonnenschein, Hugo. 1972. Market Excess Demand Functions. *Econometrica* 40:549–63.

———. 1973a. Do Walras' Identity and Continuity Characterize the Class of Community Excess Demand Functions? *Journal of Economic Theory* 6:345–54.

———. 1973b. The Utility Hypothesis and Market Demand Theory. *Western Economic Journal* 11:404–10.

Stiglitz, Joseph. 1992. Methodological Issues and the New Keynesian Economics. In *Macroeconomics: A Survey of Research Strategies*, edited by Alessandro Vercelli and Nicoli Dmitri. Oxford: Oxford University Press.

Stoker, Thomas M. 1984a. Completeness, Distribution Restrictions and the Form of Aggregate Functions. *Econometrica* 52:887–907.

———. 1984b. Exact Aggregation and Generalized Slutsky Conditions. *Journal of Economic Theory* 33:368–77.

Tobin, James. 1986. The Future of Keynesian Economics. *Eastern Economic Journal* 13:347–56.

Vining, Rutledge. 1949. Methodological Issues in Quantitative Economics. *Review of Economics and Statistics* 31:77–94.

Weintraub, E. Roy. 1979. *Microfoundations: The Compatibility of Microeconomics and Macroeconomics*. Cambridge: Cambridge University Press.

New Economics and Its History: A Pickeringian View

John B. Davis

Until fairly recently, the history of economic thought as generally taught and researched tended to end around 1940, more than a half century ago. Some textbooks, of course, went further with a few chapters on "recent developments," but more often than not, I suspect these latter chapters were rarely taught or were compressed into one or two, hurried, end-of-the-term lectures. At the same time, until a few years ago contributions to journals and conference programs on the history of economic thought almost never left the terrain of past thought. Indeed, since the *History of Political Economy* appeared nearly three decades ago, it seems as if most historians of economic thought have concluded that they no longer speak to other economists, and might accordingly focus entirely on thought that is no longer actively pursued by contemporary economists and on which history has closed the door. Certainly, for a time, historians tried to keep feet in both domains, arguing to their colleagues that new ideas often recapitulated old ones and that a study of past thought improved current theorizing. I doubt, however, that many people today find this theme of eternal recurrence still persuasive. Our colleagues in graduate programs don't seem to have given it so much as even a passing thought, as they have systematically eliminated the history of economic thought from the

Thanks to Roger Backhouse, Zohreh Emami, Wade Hands, and Philip Mirowski for helpful comments on earlier versions of this article.

Ph.D. curriculum in economics. Indeed, were undergraduate education in many colleges and universities not tied to some vision of the liberal arts, the history of economic thought might cease to be taught altogether in most places.

In the last several years, a small minority of historians have begun to make recent, ongoing economics a primary subject of research. Roy Weintraub's *Stabilizing Dynamics* (1991) brought his story of general equilibrium theory right up to the temporal backdoor of current economics. Philip Mirowski's recent work, for example, on scientific constants and the Santa Fe Institute (1995, 1996), even anticipates the direction of ongoing research. At the same time, however, nonhistorians have not hesitated to chart recent Whig history in survey article after survey article across a variety of generalist journals. Indeed, the American Economic Association's *Journal of Economic Perspectives* might well be seen as a history of recent economic thought journal. Most articles describe the recent development of economic ideas, the task at which historians generally excel. Yet historians, who are capable of bringing deeper insights to such surveys, rarely even appear in the journal, and when they do it is usually in the "Features" section. How is it, then, that historians have come to focus almost exclusively on past thought and do not expect and are not expected to contribute the history of current economics?

Clearly, one reason historians of thought focus on past thought is that they have seen their charge as explicating the texts of the "greats"—Smith, Ricardo, Marx, Keynes, and the others. This view of the history of ideas is surprisingly resilient in light of literally centuries of critical thinking about the complexity of the historical process, and it may be that attachment to the view on the part of so many historians of economic thought is a function of something more contemporary—namely, their isolation in the economics profession. The rise of formalism in economics in the last half century (predicated on disdain for the concrete, the qualitative, the normative, and history) no doubt reinforces the notion that great texts are the historians' exclusive domain. Thus, on the one hand, in response to the lack of engagement with historical thought on the part of other economists, historians may sniff defensively that there are no "greats" in recent thought and that they keep better company with their nonliving colleagues. On the other hand, caught up themselves in the profession's modernist obsession with the demonstrable and certain, historians may find it most acceptable to turn to their own, private well-sealed realm—namely, a handful of texts that possess a logic to be investigated apart from attention to the complicated histories of their producers and their times. Yet an attachment to the "greats" and their texts, while it may have temporary defensive advantages in an increasingly narrow and hostile profession, is no excuse for poor historiography. Historians of economic thought, as argued by Margaret Schabas (1992), simply ought to be better historians.

The matter might be put this way: How are historians of economics to avoid becoming keepers of an increasingly dusty museum of economic thought rarely visited except by undergraduates? Giving credit where credit is due, we might start by noting that the spirit behind the myth of eternal recurrence, if not the myth itself, seems deserving of rehabilitation. That is, if historians focus on what's living in past economic thought, why not also explain what's living in current economics and attempt to understand the present from a historical perspective? Presumably, some will allow this might be a good tactic in a battle with colleagues for resources and respect, but they will still deny it is good strategy. Strategy implicates deeper goals, and the seeming absence of "greats" on the contemporary scene will make the recommendation intellectually suspect and opportunistic to some. Such a reply, it seems fair to say, presupposes an artificial conception of the historical process and the contributions individuals make to the history of ideas. But perhaps the most effective way of making this obvious to doubters is for historians of thought to produce histories of current, ongoing economics in which it cannot be ignored that economists and their texts (or their models) are embedded in concrete historical circumstances. This is not to say that historians should give up work on Smith, Ricardo, and the others. Rather, their work on those individuals and their times should proceed with the same attention to historical context that we would more naturally (I believe) adopt toward our own time. In short, I recommend a more contextually informed history of economic thought that pursues the past and the present on essentially the same historiographic basis, where the goals are, first, to expand the space in which historians operate to include the present and, second, to produce better histories of past economics.

In the discussion that follows, I attempt to motivate these conclusions by applying Andrew Pickering's view of scientific practice to the analysis of recent economics and the writing of its history. In my view, this generates a number of intriguing insights, some of which were introduced in Wade Hand's recent (1994) reexamination of Weintraub's *Stabilizing*

Dynamics. But it also creates a set of issues that derive from the fact that Pickering's thinking about scientific practice is developed almost entirely in relation to natural science. The most important of these, in my estimation, concerns the historians' participation in overlapping intellectual or interpretive communities, and what this implies regarding appraisal in the history of economics. Three sections thus follow: a rather compact summary of the principal themes and innovations in Pickering's *The Mangle of Practice*; a brief illustration of these ideas in connection with one thread of contemporary economics, Robert Lucas and New Classical macroeconomics; and a look at what would be involved in thinking about the history of economic thought from Pickering's perspective.

1. Pickering's Mangle

Pickering's *The Mangle of Practice* (1995b) offers a general analysis of scientific practice, which he calls the mangle. He charts his own development in the field of science studies as (1) beginning with the idea that science is more than a body of knowledge or collection of empirical and theoretical propositions about the world and (2) building upon documentation in the area of the sociology of scientific knowledge (SSK) on the importance of human production and use of scientific knowledge.[1] In *The Mangle* this thinking culminates in a philosophical perspective alternative and complementary to SSK—suggested previously by Ian Hacking (1983)—that emphasizes what Pickering terms the "machinic aspects" of science and their implications for understanding the day-to-day business of doing science. As compared to a history of science rooted in epistemological concerns, Pickering takes scientific *culture* as his domain—a heterogeneous multiplicity of "made things" of science, including skills, social relations, machines and instruments, facts and theories—and then makes scientific *practice*, or the work of cultural extension, his chief focus (1995b, 3).

It is important to appreciate the distinctiveness of Pickering's methodological thinking about science. He follows Richard Rorty's (1979) dismissal of the project of philosophy as mirroring nature, though without adopting the metaphor of science as conversation or suggesting that its methods are those of literary criticism. His ideas have a strong social constructivist emphasis in regarding science as a human artifact, yet he

1. See Uskali Mäki 1993 for a summary discussion of SSK.

retains a commitment to realism, albeit what he terms a pragmatic realism. In his own view, Pickering principally distinguishes his work by its commitment to a performative image of science and by its rejection of the science-as-knowledge representational idiom. Scientists operate in communities, then, though not in interpretive communities with strategies for constructing meanings from and for texts, but rather in performative or practice-oriented communities with strategies for constructing machines and instruments to manipulate nature.

Scientists, he thus emphasizes, are not disembodied intellects, but agents doing things. Moreover, they are agents doing things in a world in which the world operated upon itself possesses agency, or "fights back," as it were, when scientists attempt to control it. This latter emphasis draws out an important implication of seeing scientists as agents rather than intellects, and seems to me to be at the core of Pickering's distinctive vision. Adopting a performative image of science, he reasons, involves not just investigating human agency in science, but investigating nonhuman, material agency, or, better, investigating the dance of agency in its human and material forms. Stretching and challenging our inclination to restrict agency to human beings, and brushing aside philosophers' qualms about the dependence of agency upon intentionality (6 n.), Pickering simply argues that there is much to learn about scientific practice by supposing that objects *do* things just as people do. Here he also parts paths with many in SSK, who, he charges, do not recognize how scientists' social interests and constraints themselves get transformed and mangled in scientific work when the world does unexpected things.

But let us descend from this rather high level of abstraction and briefly consider a particular case in the history of science that Pickering uses to illustrate his approach. Any scientific culture, he begins, includes machines and instruments that may display superhuman capacities but that are also enveloped in sets of human practices associated with their employment by scientists in research and experimentation. For example, physics Nobel laureate Donald Glaser, who was the inventor of the bubble chamber—the principal tool of experimental elementary-particle research in the 1960s and 1970s—was able to revolutionize scientific practice in subatomic physics because there already existed a community of scientific practitioners in physics that could be transformed into a new form of social organization (a big-science team) competent to carry out sustained investigation with his new machine. Their expertise, Pickering explains, derived from their being able to exercise a routinized, disciplined, indeed machinelike behavior in the laboratory, and consequently collaborate with Glaser's machine in generating new particle theory results. On one level, then, what is involved in such cases is a process of tuning, whereby "just as the material contours and performativity of new machines have to be found out in the real time of practice, so too do the human skills, gestures, and practices that will envelop them" (16). But on another level, "disciplined human agency and captured material agency are . . . constitutively intertwined; they are *interactively stabilized*" (17; cf. Pickering 1989). Or, following Donna Haraway's apt metaphor (1991), Pickering characterizes "scientific culture . . . as itself a wild kind of machine built from radically heterogeneous parts, a *supercyborg*, harnessing material and disciplinary agency in material and human performances, some of which lead out into the world of representation, of facts and theories" (Pickering 1995, 145; emphasis added).

In one important respect, however, the symmetry of reciprocal effects worked by human and material agency upon each other breaks down. Scientists form intentions, aims, goals, plans; machines do not. Though machines are agents, human intentionality still lacks a counterpart in the material realm, and this implies, Pickering will ultimately go on to argue, that the modeling process in which scientists engage is an essentially open-ended process having in advance no determinate destination. How are we to reconcile this commitment to open-endedness with the idea that material agency also disciplines human agency, such that human aims and goals are bound up in and intertwined with past captures of material agency? Pickering distinguishes three stages or elements within the scientific modeling process, according to whether they reflect scientists' constraints or free discretion: *bridging*, "the construction of a bridgehead, that tentatively fixes a vector of cultural extension to be explored"; *transcription*, "the copying of established moves from the old system into the new space fixed by the bridgehead"; and *filling*, "completing the new system in the absence of any clear guidance from the base model" (116). Acts of bridging and filling are what he terms *free moves*, and they are the source of the open-endedness in scientific practice; transcriptions, by contrast, are *forced moves* that reveal how a scientific culture directs scientists' plans and intentions. This combination, Pickering argues in connection with a number of case studies, justifies our treating scientific practice as *emergent upon* scientific culture; it also tells us that human agency must have a temporal structure. The pathway scientific practice follows, then, is not predetermined, is not free of the imprint of material agency, and is located in a real-time history.

Scientific practice, Pickering thus suggests, is a dance of agency that may be described as a process of resistance and accommodation. Scientists' research goals and experimental plans, because of free moves, are emergent upon past captures of material agency. The scientist's procedure is to "tentatively construct some new machine . . . then adopt a passive role, monitoring the performance of the machine to see whatever capture of material agency it might effect" (21). Does the machine perform as planned? As the story of quark-hunter Giacomo Morpurgo illustrates, the instruments with which a research program begins—here the magnetic levitation electrometer (MLE)—invariably undergo a whole series of modifications and reconstructions, as resistance in the form of unexpected results, no results, and counterintuitive results forces both a tinkering and re-tinkering with the investigative apparatus, and a parallel transformation of the scientist's conceptualization of theoretical entities involved. The process comes to something of a resting point, not when original goals and plans are fulfilled, but when something that seems novel and substantial to the community of scientists involved in like research emerges:

> In advance we have no idea what precise collection of parts will constitute a working machine, nor do we have any idea of what its precise powers will be. . . . We just have to find out, in practice, by passing through the mangle, how the next capture of material agency is to be made and what it will look like. Captures and their properties in this sense *just happen*. (24)

The continual reconfiguration of material setups in laboratories, interspersed with episodes of observing inactivity as the material world exercises its agency, shows that scientists move forward by making accomodations to the resistance the world throws up to their efforts. It is this dimension of the dialectic of resistance and accomodation that reveals the open-endedness of a scientific practice whose destination always remains to be determined. Indeed, it is the world's resistance to our efforts, combined with space for free moves, that explains how scientific practice is open-ended.

So scientists' plans, machines, and concepts are mangled in practice. But Pickering sees the mangling that the dance of agency causes as extending beyond the "inner" social organization of the laboratory and the work of individual scientists to the wider, "outer" organization of science—namely, that network of technical-institutional-social relations that both define the tasks and place of science in society in its different forms, and which also puts the results of science to work for a variety of social purposes. One example is how the weapons laboratories in World War II influenced the postwar reorganization of academic physics. The most extended discussion of this wider ambit of the dialectic of resistance and accomodation in *The Mangle of Practice*, however, comes in an account of how numerically controlled machine tools were introduced at the General Electric Aero Engine Group plant in Lynn, Massachusetts, in the early 1960s. Lathes, milling machines, and other metalworking tools are for Pickering a prototypical capture of material agency that creates superhuman capacities. But they also require skilled operators to channel this agency; rather, they require a human-machine couple, a metalworking cyborg. And writ large, "we find sociocyborgs: arrays of lathes and milling machines in a corporate machine shop, operated by wage labor within a classic Taylorite disciplinary apparatus of specified social roles and relations—a hierarchical command structure, precise job descriptions, production targets, rewards and penalties, and so forth" (159).

At the outset, however, management at General Electric looked upon the introduction of numerically controlled machine tools into production in technological-determinist terms, supposing that "the innate properties of the new technology would themselves guarantee increased production of high-quality engine parts" (160). When production rates fell and worker protest developed, management moved to accomodate the resistance encountered by initiating a pilot program in which operators were encouraged to take over management functions, orchestrate production, assume responsibilities for quality control, monitor materials and safe functioning, and so on. Just as important, management recognized that its concept of a push-button human-machine couple on the shop floor had to be abandoned, and that it could only learn how to employ numerically controlled machine tools by letting operators learn how to operate them. The goals, theories, and social control strategies of GE management, then, were mangled and transformed in an open-ended process of accommodation to the resistance thrown up by the Aero Engine sociocyborg inseparably composed of workers and machines. Thus, while most of *The Mangle of Practice* concerns scientific practice in the narrower sense of the laboratory, Pickering clearly believes the dance of agency extends fully across science, technology, and society.

One last theme deserves attention. Though Pickering believes himself much indebted to SSK, he nonetheless distinguishes his own approach from SSK as specifically posthumanist in its treatment of human agency. SSK studies from David Bloor, Barry Barnes, Steven Shapin, and others are social constructivist in supposing scientific practice always reflects the interests of individual scientists and the social constraints on scientific practice, as if we need only understand these social causes to understand the development of science. "The tendency," Pickering comments, "is to write as if the substantive interests of actors were present and identifiable in advance of particular passages of practice, setting them in motion and structuring outcomes without being themselves at stake" (64). Yet the interests and goals of scientists "cannot be regarded as unmoved movers, as causal principles lying outside (behind, above) and explaining the extension of scientific culture" (64), since they and the social identities of scientific actors are mangled and transformed in practice just as are the concepts and machines of science. SSK, Pickering tells us, helps us understand the role of human agency in science, but it remains wedded to a humanism that is reluctant to see that human agency as "inextricably entangled with the nonhuman, no longer at the center of the action and calling the shots" (26).

A posthumanism such as this may not flatter us in our desire to see ourselves at the source of science, but, Pickering believes, it is the logical consequence of supposing that scientific practice is truly open-ended. Thus, imagine that in experimentation there are "three disparate cultural elements: a material procedure (assembling and running a piece of apparatus), an interpretive model (a theoretical understanding of how the apparatus functioned), and a phenomenal model (a theoretical understanding of the phenomenon under investigation)" (1995a, 48). These heterogeneous elements constitute for Pickering the topology of experimental practice, in that they characterize different points on the surface of scientific culture scientists must combine in the modeling process. But as they are disparate in nature, they may only be linked together through a process of association, the exact nature of which the experimenter largely chances to hit upon. Accordingly, though constraints will always play a role in defining the setting in which science operates, this part of the story fails to capture the real-time dynamic of scientific practice.

2. Lucas Mangled

To say one intends to make new economics one's subject may appear foolhardy when one considers the discipline's propensity to dispose of all but the most recently published ideas. Though I haven't attempted a systematic analysis of the matter, I suspect a study of the dates of citations in articles published in the top dozen Social Science Citation Index–ranked economics journals for any of the last few years would show dates largely concentrated over the last ten years. New economics resembles the ever-withdrawing Western frontier of the last century; as soon as the settlers seem to have reached it, it has moved on again beyond their reach. But I think one can nonetheless draw rough boundaries around our domain by distinguishing what practicing economists think (or hope) is not yet a subject for historians of economic thought. Supposing that most practicing economists hold to a Schumpeterian view of steady analytical progress in economics, new economics is the domain of breakthroughs that recasts or replaces all past ideas. Thus, though a figure such as Robert Lucas has in some respects been cast aside by later developments in macroeconomics, his contributions of the Lucas critique and development of rational expectations analysis still stand as breakthrough achievements in the eyes of even his critics.

What may we learn about Lucas from Pickering? Lucas, along with Thomas Sargent and Neil Wallace, dominated macroeconomics discussion throughout the 1970s, particularly in the United States. Though this analysis has been cast as a theoretical conceptualization of pre-Keynesian classical economic thinking, from a Pickeringian perspective it can be argued that it was rather the practical application of New Classical models, especially in the form of the Sargent-Wallace policy ineffectiveness proposition and the Lucas critique, that were the chief source of New Classicism's impact. That is, Lucas and the others in the eyes of their followers had invented a model/machine which could be used to determine which actions policy makers could and could not pursue. Strictly speaking, Pickering does not regard models as machines. But it is interesting to treat them as such to re-read the recent history of macroeconomics. Thus, while traditional Keynesians and even monetarists complained that rational expectations and continuous market clearing (e.g., Fischer, 1977) do not adequately represent the true nature of the macroeconomy, and though there was not much empirical evidence that supported Lucas's "surprise" aggregate supply view, these representationalist difficulties were of secondary importance to the followers of New Classicism, who were chiefly interested in having a model/tool, even if initially crudely crafted, that would replace the policy interventionist model/tool wielded so long by traditional Keynesians.

From a Pickeringian perspective, economic culture, like scientific culture, is a heterogeneous assemblage of "made" things: tools, concepts, posited entities, and their associated social-technical relations. Economic practice, accordingly, consists in the extension of that culture through the invention of new tools of economic analysis: new mathematical models; new econometric techniques; and new procedures for data mining, experiments, simulations, calibration exercises, and so on. The physicists Glaser and Morpurgo modified and developed existing laboratory tools to construct new machines that made possible the "discovery" of quarks and various other subatomic particles. Similarly, Lucas and the other New Classicals refined and redeveloped existing mathematical and econometric models to construct new models/machines that made possible the "discovery" of economic agents with rational expectations! Indeed, their sudden repopulation of the world with a new type of economic agent simultaneously made extinct an older type of being: the naive victim of money illusion, whose expectations adapted but gradually to changing circumstances.

That Lucas and his coinvestigators were able to redirect macroeconomics as they did, we should then suppose, was due to the successful combination of free and forced moves they adopted. The structure of their New Classical economics basically involves three principal tenets: the rational expectations hypothesis, the assumption of continuous market clearing, and Lucas's "surprise" supply function which has output deviate from its "natural" level in response to the deviation of actual prices from expected prices, generally as a result of monetary disturbances. The last element was largely taken over from Milton Friedman's natural rate of unemployment analysis, and thus can be said to have constituted transcription—a forced move. The rational expectations hypothesis might be regarded as an act of bridging, a free move, "that tentatively fixes a vector of cultural extension to be explored" because it involved imagining a new phenomenon of expectations without adjustment lags. The continuous market clearing idea, finally, might be thought an act of filling, a free move where "guidance from the base model" is lacking and where traditional, neoclassical-Keynesian models had operated with money illusion.

Thus, in modern macroeconomics human agency and material agency combine in a dialectic of free and forced moves we may distinguish to understand economic practice. Or, economists enter into a process of resistance and accommodation, where free moves emergent on past captures of material agency lead to construction of new models, whose performance is then passively monitored to see what combination of resistances and effects results. In fact, the resistances Lucas encountered to the intended use of his model were more significant than initially believed, so that by the early 1980s New Classical models had reached an important theoretical and empirical impasse. Attempts to explain business cycles in terms of money-to-output causality had turned out not to be persuasive (Sims 1980), and evidence in support of the proposition that anticipated money was neutral also did not appear robust (Barro 1993). Yet if monetary shocks were not the cause of business cycles, some reasoned, then perhaps aggregate instability could be explained in terms of models that allowed for real shocks. Real business cycle theory of Finn Kydland and Edward Prescott (1982) and John Long and Charles Plosser (1983), we might here argue, threw over the monetary disturbance impulse mechanism of New Classical models—a free move, or an act of bridging—while yet retaining the endowments-tastes-technologies propagation mechanism of those models—a forced move, or an act of transcription.

Lucas's reaction to his being supplanted as the leader of classically oriented theory shows a mangling of his original intentions. Objecting that an exclusive focus on real as opposed to monetary disturbances seemed a mistake, he allowed a hybrid model of both sorts of disturbances might be desirable. At the same time, as if to say that explaining business cyles had always been of secondary concern, he turned his attentions to analysis of the microfoundations of growth, thus minimizing the importance of fluctuations around trend growth (1987). Thus, though his model/machine did not function quite as expected, it did generate results that others could generalize upon in further modeling/machine-building, and it did create a platform for further model/machine construction on Lucas's part. As a Nobel laureate, Lucas was lauded for his contributions to economic knowledge. But economists will rather recognize his accomplishments as a sophisticated toolmaker, just as they have credited past prize winners—not with developing a better understanding of the economic world, but with advancing new models/machines with which one could operate on that world in novel ways.

Pickering, then, would have us take a second look at Lucas by going beyond the "inner" social organization of the economics profession within the academy to the "outer" organization of the science—namely, that network of social-institutional relations that both defines the ways in which the work of economics can be done and identifies the ways in which its results can be brought to bear on economic life. If we recall his account of the adoption of numerically controlled machine tools by GE management at the Lynn, Massachusetts, Aero Engine plant, we may similarly imagine how those anxious to employ New Classical economic models hoped to "manage" policy orientation in the macroeconomy by undermining traditional interventionist strategies. Indeed, the image of a self-correcting, rational expectations–laissez-faire economy offered by Lucas was an ideal sociocyborg apparatus writ large: a vast, economy-wide collection of machine-human parts, all smoothly adjusting to the discipline of the marketplace, never requiring maintenance or repair. Needless to say, Lucas's new push-button technology was almost immediately mangled by real-world individuals who were either not rational or had not heard about the "true" model, and by markets that inexplicably failed to clear instanteously. It was left to real business cycle theorists to logically conclude that real shocks must thus be pervasive!

Can we explain the history of this brief episode in recent economic thought in terms of SSK thinking? What Pickering's mangle view specifically brings to the table is an emphasis on the transformation of human agency—goals and intentions—in the interaction with material agency. Perhaps some of his language about the active powers of the latter goes a bit far, but his dialectic of resistance and accommodation is valuable for the idea that the work of the scientist/economist is imperfect and incomplete, because it gets carried out in a medium whose properties are largely unknown. This means that ongoing work must emerge in conception and results as it is pursued, and that the interests driving modeling/machine-making are relatively indeterminate at the outset. It may be a fine point to distinguish Pickering's mangle and SSK thought, but it provides a strong assist in helping one to see that pathways of investigation are relatively open. Let us thus turn to what we may understand about the history of economic thought when pursued in a Pickeringian manner.

3. Writing Recent (and Not-so-recent) History of Economics

This short sketch of Lucas and New Classical economics is meant merely as an illustration of what might be attempted from a Pickeringian perspective.[2] Its point is to show how one might begin to look at the development of economic ideas as a process of resistance and accommodation, in which models function as invented machines. But notice that having historians of economics briefly step into Pickering's shoes in this way does not actually apply Pickering's lessons to writing the history of economic thought itself, which would involve treating historians of thought as scientists, tuning and being tuned in turn by their machines of historical analysis in the same manner as Pickering's physicists. Indeed, in my sketch of Lucas, I stand outside my portrayal, offering you a new mapping grid without much comment upon how well this tool will respond to use or how it will affect the goals and intentions of historians of thought. But, for that matter, Pickering himself is not particularly good at stepping into his own shoes in this respect, since in his *Mangle of Practice* he also is almost always an outside observer of the dialectic of resistance and accommodation in which scientists are engaged. Though he does make comments on the problem of reflexivity in connection with SSK (or the stones-and-glass-houses problem), he never really asks how his own machine of analysis mangles his own intentions, professional behavior, ideas, and so on, and he even ventures rather carelessly at the end of the book that the mangle is possibly a TOE, or the holy lost grail Theory-Of-Everything.

Nonetheless, this does not prevent our reexamining the practice of the history of economic thought as one important extension of an economics culture of made things. And it may be that historians of thought can even do Pickering one better in this regard by being quicker to implicate themselves as practitioners when it comes to their relation to recent economics. That is, in regard to recent economics in particular, historians are already aware that their past practice leaves them somewhat ill prepared to develop new tools of analysis for recent thought, and that it raises questions about their goals and intentions as producers of tools of historical analysis per se. They should thus be quick to grasp the dialectic of resistance and accommodation in economics practice on the terrain of recent thought; should this result in a broad discussion of the

2. For a more systematic application of Pickering's resistance and accomodation thinking to another of the New Classicals, Neil Sargent, see Sent, forthcoming.

goals and strategies of analysis using the history of economic thought, it could also lead to changes in historians' practices in connection with past economics.

What is involved, then, in doing a Pickeringian history of recent economics? The basic idea of the mangle is that human and nonhuman agency are intertwined in cyborg-like fashion, such that human practice tunes and is tuned by the machines it builds. What sorts of models/machines would historians of recent economics construct? Other economists build models/machines which only include themselves as noneconomists—that is, as ordinary individuals to whom the models might apply—so that the dialectic of resistance and accommodation in economic practice takes place, as it were, behind their backs. Historians, however, whose subject is the development of economic ideas, build models/machines that comprehend as one unit models and their economist modelers—the economics cyborg—and, indeed, since most historians are also economists, these models also include themselves, albeit at one remove. This difference implies that historians of economics are in a position to understand economic practice, the modeler/model-building process in economics, while the practitioners/model-builders who only reflect upon their machines are predisposed to misunderstand it. Though economists act in and influence the world they study, their models occlude this central fact.

A first implication of this is that just as model-builders misunderstand economic practice, they also misunderstand the nature of their machines—their models. Indeed, though they are aware that tinkering is part of model construction, they see this rather in a Schumpeterian manner as searching for the "right" model. The idea of innocent search for the right model draws on the representationalist rather than performative idiom, and it fails to see how tools are constructed in historical contexts to do specific kinds of things. Further, these right models are thought to correspond to reality in and by themselves, and their construction is then thought a matter of developing "pure" theory, a sort of immaculate conception understanding of what economists produce that makes reference to a model's author only in the most legendary, heroic, and artificial terms. Historians of thought, it must be admitted, have tended to accept this imagery in their own treatment of the "greats." But their treatment in the last decades at the hands of their colleagues has surely disabused most historians of the idea that model-builders are dispassionate searchers for truth. Given this, it would appear to follow that a turn to the history of recent economics from a Pickeringian perspective would make a dethroning of pure theory a key item on historians' agenda.

Pure theory, we may just begin, is only one "made" thing among many extensions of economics culture: applied studies, policy analyses, proprietary business documents, economics teaching, economic journalism, surveys, think tank reports, peer reviews, statistics gathering, curriculum proposals, and so on and so on. Pure theory, it then might be argued, is hierarchically privileged over these other forms of economic practice in the eyes of its producers' on the basis of a false causal theory of the effectivity of pure theory. Formal, abstract relationships—the domain of pure theory—are thought to correspond directly to reality by outlining real world relations, or, more archaically, the eternal Platonic forms. Other, lesser, products of economics practice involve distorting admixtures of social interest, values, and irrelevant information. These more ordinary products may be seen as hybrids, if the complaintant believes "pure" theoretical relations are merely obscured (an epistemological view). Or, more neurotic theorists may hold that economic practice with social content results in bastardized products, perhaps on ancient philosophical-spirtualist grounds that human affective states are incomplete and imperfect by comparison with the fully ideational. In either case, only pure theory may capture the underlying or transcendent real world (depending on the metaphor preferred for this alienation), and only it may consequently provide knowledge of the world's causal mechanisms.

The simple reply to this false causal picture is that economic practice in all its forms plays a role in extending economics culture. How this multiplicity of extensions links together and to the "outer" science-technology-society organization in which economics culture exists is a complicated matter that requires more than unicausal thinking in social science. Historians of thought, however, because their "made" machine is the modeler/model couple itself, are in a position to pursue this richer sort of investigatation. For them, economists are not disembodied intellects, and thus do not produce pure theory. That historians have largely failed to write this multicausal history in the past seems to be because they have generally restricted their vision to past, no longer ongoing economics. On that terrain it is easy to lose sight of the mangle and think that texts capture the development of economic ideas, whereas on the terrain of recent, ongoing economics the dialectic of resistance and accommodation is there for anyone to see who merely looks. Indeed, were historians to spend some time with the historical complexity of current ideas, it is reasonable to think they would begin to find that same complexity in past ideas (as some of our more innovative colleagues have indeed begun to do).

A second implication of the difference in orientation between economists and historians concerns how we look upon the topic of appraisal. Roger Backhouse (1992a–d) and Roy Weintraub (1992a, 1992b) recently engaged in an interesting exchange on this subject, with Backhouse arguing that methodological appraisal is inseparable from history of economic thought, and Weintraub arguing that constructivist methodology makes no commitment to any particular view of truth. The exchange is especially valuable because it arose over Weintraub's *Stabilizing Dynamics* when Backhouse commented that it was but "a short and defensible step from appraising contemporary economics to appraising past economics" (1992a, 28; also see Hands 1991). That is, Backhouse (whose own history of thought text does treat recent economics) sees an intimate connection between appraising ongoing economics and historiographic methods. Weintraub, on the other hand, believes methodologically or philosophically oriented history of thought is "thin" and typically uninteresting.

I think there are merits in both of these views and that there is a way we might balance them against one another in the framework at hand. Let me first attempt to take stock. In support of Weintraub, two things may be said. First, though there are difficulties in saying what "thick" history involves, methodologically motivated histories often tend in the opposite direction, especially when they simplify away the cross-cutting complexities of the historical process to make un-nuanced judgments. Second, historians of thought do not stand outside of the economics cyborg, the economist/model couple, so they, too, are "tuned" by the model/machine upon which they work, thereby losing an element of privileging that would support appraisal. In support of Backhouse, there are also two points to make. First, even thick history is perspectival and judgment-laden, so interesting history is not necessarily unslanted. Second, though historians of thought are themselves mangled in their production, because they still have the economics cyborg as their modeling object—unlike economists who simply think about their models/machines—they achieve a vantage point that permits better judgments about the whole than their colleagues can make.

I will try to focus these points on the identity of the historian in economics. Weintraub points out that historians, methodologists, and economists belong to three, sometimes overlapping, interpretive communities which we must be careful not to conflate. Backhouse responds that the overlap between these communities is significant, and that it implies that appraisal is an inevitable part of historical work. What sort of overlap is there between these communities from Pickering's perspective? Since both historians and methodologists take the economics cyborg as their model, they possess a more comprehensive understanding of economics practice than do economists, who generally think only in terms of their models/machines. This more comprehensive perspective creates a detachment of sorts for historians and methodologists, and thus permits appraising judgments regarding economists' artificial conception of practice. But historians are also economists, and though this is generally an advantage in understanding the work of economists, it also imposes limits on historians' detachment, because it tends to restrict historians' vision to economists' narrow concerns. To this we should add that on Pickering's dialectic of resistance and accommodation, just as the goals and intentions of scientists are emergent in their work, so, too, are the goals and intentions of historians. Thus historians in their own work need to consider their judgments as provisional and subject to revision.

The upshot of this, it seems, is that historians have special opportunities for appraisal, but these opportunities are intertwined with specific episodes in the historical development of economic theory. Methodological prescriptivism as was sought in the form of ultimate criteria for theory choice must be given up for critical understanding of ongoing economics practice. This conclusion has been argued before (e.g., Caldwell 1989), but rather in light of shortfalls in the Popperian and Lakatosian frameworks. In contrast, Pickering offers a way to understand how the different communities in which historians operate structure historians' practical identities and thereby create temporary platforms for the appraisal of economics practice, which are regularly dismantled and reconstructed. On this conception, description and prescription are closely related, and a constructivist history of economics is both thick and thin at the same time.

4. Concluding Remarks

It should be noted that no attempt was made here to investigate two important issues that arise in connection with Pickering's approach. One is his understanding of pragmatic realism, which he regards as a departure from scientific realism, but which he develops all too briefly in *The Mangle of Practice*. The other is the concept of truth and how it operates in scientific practice, as understood in performative terms, where the traditional correspondence view either fails or requires significant modification in a more holistic sort of setting. A third issue was introduced—namely, Pickering's treatment of freedom in terms of the forced and free moves scientists make and, relatedly, the concept of emergence as exhibited in scientific practice. This important topic also needs more careful examination.

Finally, to return to a point made at the outset, historians' absorption in the "greats" may be related to their isolation in the economics profession. One point I made was that historians magnify the stature of past economists to diminish those of today. But this may only signal that just as Smith, Ricardo, and the others constructed models/machines, so our colleagues may compete to be "great" as well, especially when the awarding of a Nobel prize is ordinarily taken as signaling entry into the pantheon. Presented with this possibility, I would think historians would quickly get to work in dispelling the myth of greatness by explaining that ideas sometimes develop haphazardly in real historical contexts. This could indeed be done on the terrain of recent economic thought, because much of what is involved in the production of ideas is evident to us in this more familiar setting. But were this work to proceed without revision of the history of past thought, the ideology of the "greats" would persist. Thus work needs to be done on both fronts at the same time. My suspicion, nonetheless, is that new history of economic thought on recent economics will have to be done for quite some time before it will be clear that a new history of economic thought is needed for past economics.

References

Backhouse, Roger. 1992a. The Constructivist Critique of Economic Methodology. *Methodus* 4.1:65–82.

———. 1992b. How Should We Approach the History of Economic Thought, Fact, Fiction or Moral Tale? *Journal of the History of Economic Thought* 14.1:18–35.

———. 1992c. Rejoinder: Why Methodology Matters. *Methodus* 4.2:58–62.

———. 1992d. Reply: History's Many Dimensions. *Journal of the History of Economic Thought* 14.2:277–84.

Barro, Robert. 1993. *Macroeconomics*, 4th ed. New York: Wiley.

Caldwell, B. 1989. The Trend of Methodological Thinking. *Ricerche Economiche* 43.1–2:8–20.

Fischer, Stanley. 1977. Long-Term Contracts, Rational Expectations, and the Optimal Money Supply Rule. *Journal of Political Economy* 85.1:191–205.

Hacking, Ian. 1983. *Representing and Intervening*. Cambridge: Cambridge University Press.

Hands, Wade. 1991. Review of Weintraub. *Economic Journal* 102.413:953–58.

———. 1994. Restablizing Economics: Construction and Constraint in the History of Walrasian Stability Theory. *Economics and Philosophy* 10(2):243–83.

Haraway, Donna. 1991. *Simians, Cyborgs, and Women: The Reinvention of Nature*. London: Free Association Books.

Kydland, Finn, and Edward Prescott. 1982. Time to Build and Aggregate Fluctuations. *Econometrica* 50:1345–70.

Long, John, and Charles Plosser. 1983. Real Business Cycles. *Journal of Political Economy* 50.6:1345–70.

Lucas, Robert E. 1987. *Models of Business Cycles*. Oxford: Basil Blackwell.

Mäki, Uskali. 1993. Social Theories of Science. In *Rationality, Institutions, and Economic Methodology*, edited by U. Mäki, B. Gustaffsson, and C. Knudsen. London: Routledge.

Mirowski, Philip. 1995. Three Ways of Thinking about Testing in Econometrics. *Journal of Econometrics* 76:25–46.

———. 1996. Do You Know the Way to Santa Fe? In *New Directions in Political Economy: Malvern after Ten Years*, edited by S. Pressman. London: Routledge.

Pickering, Andrew. 1989. Living in the Material World: On Realism and Experimental Practice. In *The Uses of Experiment: Studies of Experimentation in the Natural Sciences*, edited by D. Gooding, T. Pinch, and S. Schaffer. Cambridge: Cambridge University Press.

———. 1995a. Beyond Constraint: The Temporality of Practice and the Historicity of Knowledge. In *Scientific Practice: Theories and Stories of Doing Physics*, edited by J. Buchwald. Chicago: University of Chicago Press.

———. 1995b. *The Mangle of Practice*. Chicago: University of Chicago Press.

Rorty, Richard. 1979. *Philosophy and the Mirror of Nature*. Princeton, N.J.: Princeton University Press.

Schabas, Margaret. 1992. Breaking Away: History of Economics as History of Science. *HOPE* 24.1:187–203.

Sent, Esther-Mirjam. Forthcoming. *Resisting Sargent*. Cambridge: Cambridge University Press.

Sims, Christopher. 1980. Comparisons of Interwar and Postwar Business Cycles: Monetarism Reconsidered. *American Economic Review* 70.2:25–57.

Weintraub, E. Roy. 1991. *Stablilizing Dynamics: Constructing Economic Knowledge*. Cambridge: Cambridge University Press.

———. 1992a. On Roger E. Backhouse's "How Should We Approach the History of Economics Thought, Fact, Fiction or Moral Tale?" *Journal of the History of Economic Thought* 14.2:271–77.

———. 1992b. Roger Backhouse's Straw Herring. *Methodus* 4.2:53–57.

Contributors

Timothy L. Alborn is associate professor of history and social studies at Harvard University. His most recent book is *Conceiving Companies: Joint-Stock Politics in Victorian England* (Routledge, 1998).

Joshua Cohen is a postdoctoral fellow at the University of Pennsylvania. His Ph.D. thesis is on the realism and measurement of utility. He recently published "Preferences, Needs, and QALYS" in the *Journal of Medical Ethics* (October 1996).

John B. Davis is in the Department of Economics at Marquette University. He is author of *Keynes's Philosophical Development* and coeditor, with Wade Hands and Uskali Maki, of the forthcoming *Handbook of Economic Methodology*.

Ross B. Emmett is associate professor of economics at Augustana University College in Canada. He continues to work on the ways Frank Knight addressed the dilemmas of modernist American social science and has recently begun research on the University of Chicago's economics department in the period from the mid-1930s to the 1960s.

Paul Harrison is an assistant professor of economics at Brandeis University. He is currently studying the history, evolving economic and popular perception, prices, volatility, regularities, and regulation of the stock market.

Daniel M. Hausman is professor of philosophy at the University of Wisconsin–Madison and is currently the Ludwig Lachmann Research Fellow at the London School of Economics. He is most recently the author, with Michael McPherson, of *Economic Analysis and Moral Philosophy* (Cambridge University Press, 1996).

S. Todd Lowry is professor of economics and administration at Washington and Lee University. His publications include *The Archaeology of Economic Ideas: The Classical Greek Tradition* (1987) and volumes 7 and 8 of *Perspectives on the History of Economic Thought* (1992).

Steven G. Medema is associate professor of economics at the University of Colorado at Denver. His research interests include law and economics and the economic role of government in the history of economic thought. His latest book, with Nicholas Mercuro, is *Economics and the Law: From Posner to Post Modernism*.

Philip Mirowski is Carl Koch Professor of Economics and the History and Philosophy of Science at the University of Notre Dame. He is the author of *More Heat than Light* and the editor of *Natural Images in Economics*. He is finishing a book on the impact of the "cyborg sciences" on late twentieth century economics, a multivolume *Collected Economics Works of William Thomas Thornton*, and a survey of the economics of scientific inquiry.

S. Abu Turab Rizvi is an associate professor in the department of economics at the University of Vermont. His research concerns microeconomics and its history. He is currently working on a book about human agency and well-being.

Esther-Mirjam Sent is assistant professor in the Department of Economics and faculty fellow in the Reilly Center for Science, Technology, and Values at the University of Notre Dame. She is the author of *Resisting Sargent: How a Representative Agent Learned about Rational Expectations Economics* (Cambridge University Press, 1998) and several articles. Her research interests include providing an internal evaluation of developments in contemporary (macro)economics by using methods of analysis developed in science studies and problematizing the use of economic metaphors in science studies.

Mary Hirschfeld is an associate professor at Occidental College. She has published in the *Journal of Economic Education*, and her research focus is on American women economists in the early twentieth century.

Philippe Mongin is a research professor at THEMA (Centre National de la Recherche Scientifique and Université de Clergy-Pontoise, France). He has written a number of articles about the mathematical theory of choice and the philosophy of economics, and he has coedited *Epistemic Logic and the Theory of Games and Decisions* (Kluwer, 1997). He is currently one the general editors of Economics and Philosophy.

Marcel Boumans lectures on philosophy and the history of economics at the University of Amsterdam. He is the author of *A Case of Limited Physics Transfer: Jan Tinbergen's Resources for Reshaping Economics* (1992). His current work involves models and measurement in economics.

Index